Also by Caroline Dodds Pennock

Bonds of Blood:
Gender, Lifecycle and Sacrifice in Aztec Culture

For James

It is called *teuatl* [sea], not that it is a god; it only means wonderful, a great marvel. And its name is *ilhuicaatl*.

It is great. It terrifies. It is that which is irresistible; a marvel; foaming, glistening, with waves; bitter – most bitter; very salty. It contains man-eating animals, life. It is that which surges. It stirs; it stretches ill-smelling, restless.

I live on the sea. I become a part of the sea. I cross over the sea. I die in the sea. I live on the sea.

Bernardino de Sahagún, and his Indigenous Nahua collaborators, *Florentine Codex*, completed c.1578

Contents

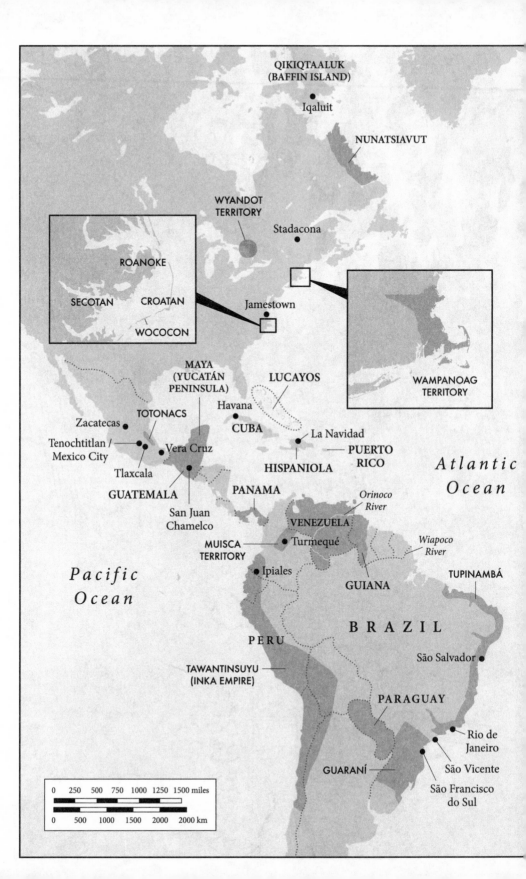

QIKIQTAALUK
(BAFFIN ISLAND)

Iqaluit

NUNATSIAVUT

WYANDOT
TERRITORY

Stadacona

ROANOKE

SECOTAN   CROATAN

WOCOCON

Jamestown

WAMPANOAG
TERRITORY

MAYA
(YUCATÁN
PENINSULA)

LUCAYOS

Havana

TOTONACS

Zacatecas

CUBA

La Navidad

Tenochtitlan /
Mexico City

Vera Cruz

PUERTO
RICO

Tlaxcala

HISPANIOLA

Atlantic
Ocean

GUATEMALA

PANAMA

Orinoco
River

San Juan
Chamelco

VENEZUELA

Wiapoco
River

MUISCA
TERRITORY

Turmequé

Ipiales

GUIANA

TUPINAMBÁ

Pacific
Ocean

B R A Z I L

PERU

São Salvador

TAWANTINSUYU
(INKA EMPIRE)

PARAGUAY

Rio de
Janeiro

São Vicente

GUARANÍ

São Francisco
do Sul

0   250   500   750   1000   1250   1500 miles

0   500   1000   1500   2000   2000 km

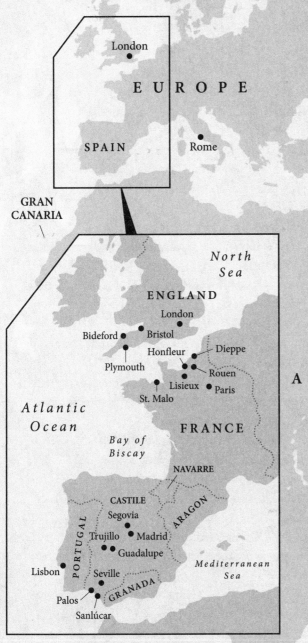

Arctic
Ocean

London
•

EUROPE

ASIA

SPAIN

Rome
•

GRAN
CANARIA

PERSIA

North
Sea

ENGLAND

London
•

Bideford •   • Bristol

Honfleur   • Dieppe

Plymouth

Lisieux • Rouen

St. Malo   • Paris

ARABIA

AFRICA

Atlantic
Ocean

FRANCE

Bay of
Biscay

NAVARRE

Indian
Ocean

CASTILE

Segovia
•

Trujillo • Madrid
•

Guadalupe

Lisbon
•

PORTUGAL

ARAGON

Seville
•

Mediterranean
Sea

Palos •

GRANADA

Sanlúcar

N

Timeline

c.950–1150	Height of Toltec influence in Mesoamerica
c.1000	Norse people temporarily settle in the lands of the Mi'kmaq and other peoples including at L'Anse aux Meadows, in present-day Canada
c.1325	Aztec-Mexica people settle at their capital of Tenochtitlan
c.1450 or earlier	Iroquoian peoples form the Haudenosaunee Confederacy and establish the Great Law of Peace, a detailed oral constitution
11 October 1492	Christopher Columbus 'discovers' America, when he sights the Caribbean island of Guanahaní (San Salvador)
November 1492	Columbus kidnaps Indigenous people from Cuba and ships them to Spain
December 1492	Spanish found La Navidad, the first permanent European settlement in the Americas, in the territory of the Taíno chief Guacanagarí
1493	Papal bull of *inter caetera* divides the 'undiscovered world' between Spain and Portugal
April 1493	Taíno people appear at Spanish court
1495	c.500 Taínos enslaved and shipped to Spain by Columbus
1497	John Cabot 'discovers' the mainland of North America
1498	Columbus sets foot on the mainland of Central America
1500	Pedro Álvares Cabral 'claims' Brazil for Portugal
1500	Vincente Yáñez Pinzón enslaves 36 people from the Amazon region; only 20 survive the crossing to Spain

1501	Portuguese expedition, led by Gaspar Corte Real, transports 57 people from what is now Maine to Portugal
1502/3	Moctezuma II becomes ruler of Tenochtitlan and leader of the Aztec-Mexica empire
1505	Içá-Mirim (Essomericq) brought to France from Brazil by Binot Paulmier de Gonneville and settles in Normandy
April 1519	Aztec-Mexica ambassadors meet Hernando Cortés at Vera Cruz, Mexico
1519	First smallpox epidemic in the Americas
September 1519	After initial fierce resistance, the Tlaxcalans ally with the Spanish invaders
October 1519	First Totonacs land in Spain
1521	Fall of the Aztec-Mexica capital of Tenochtitlan
1528	Nahua nobles and entertainers come to Spain with Cortés, who also brings his *mestizo* son Martín
1528	Guaibimpará (Catherine du Brasil) travels to France
1529	Tlaxcala is declared an independent city under the Spanish Crown
1531	Brazilian 'king' visits the court of Henry VIII in England
1532	Inka empire, riven by civil war, falls to Francisco Pizarro
1532	Portuguese establish São Vicente, their first permanent settlement in Brazil; it is known as Porto dos Escravos (Port of Slaves) and thousands of Tupi are transported to Portugal in the following decades
1534–6	Jacques Cartier claims 'New France' for the French Crown; he abducts 10 Indigenous Iroquoians from Stadacona, in present-day Quebec, to France
1542	'New Laws' outlaw enslavement of Indigenous peoples from Spanish territories
1545	Q'eqchi' Maya lords present Prince Philip of Spain with the first drinking chocolate recorded in Europe
1550	50 'Brazilians' (probably Tupinambá) appear in a replica village in Rouen at the festival entry of Henri II

1550–1	Spanish expeditions are paused to allow the Valladolid debates considering their legality
1551	Inka 'princess' Francisca Pizarro Yupanqui is exiled to Spain
1555–9	Dozens of Tupi people are sent to France by Nicolas Durand de Villegagnon during his attempts to found France Antarctique in Brazil
1576–8	Several Inuit are abducted to London by Martin Frobisher, during his failed expeditions to find a north-west passage
1584	Manteo and Wanchese are kidnapped and brought to London by Ralegh where they help to create the first Algonquian orthography
1585–90	John White, with the aid of Manteo, founds an English settlement on Roanoke that becomes the 'Lost Colony'
1594–6	English expeditions to Guiana in search of El Dorado result in the kidnap of several Indigenous 'interpreters'
1607	Foundation of Jamestown, the first permanent settlement in what we now call the USA

Why Words Matter

Names matter. What we call ourselves, how people refer to us, says something about who we are, who we were, and how others see our relationship to them. For Indigenous peoples, who have been historically oppressed, marginalised and insulted, names matter even more. This is not just a question of respect, but also an intentional push against colonial attempts to erase Indigenous identities, and to obliterate their languages and beliefs, through deliberate cultural genocide. Christian missionaries forcibly converted millions of people across the Americas from 1492 onwards. Indigenous beliefs and practices were prohibited, and Native communities uprooted and deliberately acculturated. From the late-nineteenth century, right up until the 1990s in some places, Indigenous children from across Canada and the United States were torn away from their families and put into residential schools which aimed to 'kill the Indian, and save the man'. There, the children's hair was cut, their languages were banned, and these boys and girls were subjected to appalling abuses in the service of 'civilisation'.[1] Thousands more were stolen and placed in the foster system, raised by white families, and are slowly making their way home to identity and place. As you can imagine, for survivors and descendants, and their communities, the violence of colonisation remains very real, and so they may find some of the accounts in this book difficult reading.

It is in this context that we have to understand the histories told in this book. The first crossings of the Atlantic, the fraught collision of foreign cultures, formed the roots of the intense web of global connections we find today. But this encounter was not neutral and its legacy is painful and difficult. Indigenous peoples are still marginalised and disadvantaged across the Americas by most economic and social measures, subjected to stereotypes and discrimination, and disenfranchised from their own lands. Colonisation continues.

Language can be an instrument of that colonisation. When Columbus arrived in the Americas in 1492, he promptly dubbed the inhabitants '*indios*' (Indians), because he thought he had arrived in the East Indies. This anachronistic word covered everyone from Inuit peoples in the far north, to the Tupi of Brazil, the Maya of Central America, and the Apache across the Southwest and Great Plains. Under Spanish law, 'the Republic of Indians' was indistinguishable: identities erased and distinctive pasts obliterated. For a historian, the challenge is not to add to this erasure, but rather to help reverse it. For me, the use of the word 'savage' in my title, a racial slur which crops up all too frequently in sources, is a way to invert the expectations of both conquistadors and contemporary readers. For the Indigenous travellers in my work, Europe was the 'savage shore', a land of incomprehensible inequality and poverty that defied pre-invasion values and logics, where resources were hoarded, children ruled great kingdoms, and common people were meant meekly to accept injustices without dissent. Where the slur occurs in sources, I will use it only when in quotation and as sparingly as possible.

Writing as a white, British historian – working with sources that are too often about, rather than by, Native people – I make the deliberate inversion of the imperial perspective central to my approach. I cannot, and should not, speak *for* Indigenous peoples but, wherever possible, I will centre their voices and perspectives, allowing them to tell their own stories, valuing their knowledge, and respecting the views of their descendant communities, who are – of course – far from homogeneous in their attitudes or outlooks.[2]

This book covers a kaleidoscope of Indigenous cultures, communities, peoples and individuals, each with quite specific and equally valid ideas about what they prefer to be called. None of these terms is universal. In Mexico and much of South America, people tend to use '*pueblos indígenas*' (Indigenous peoples), and the term '*indios*' (Indians) has fallen out of use because it has often been used as an insult, like calling someone a 'peasant'. But both '*indio*' and '*indígenas*' are common in Brazil, and '*indio*' is the most common term in my manuscript sources. In what is now the United States, 'Indian' and 'American Indian' are usually rejected by scholars as Eurocentric and inaccurate (after all, Columbus had *not* reached India), but these words have at times been reclaimed. The National Congress of American Indians is the oldest and largest organisation representing tribal interests in the United States, and the American Indian Movement, formed as a powerful protest group in the second half of the twentieth century, still has many chapters. There are also historical 'Indian Acts' and treaties which use the word 'Indian', giving it sociolegal and political significance. The US census counts 'American Indians and Alaska Natives', putting Indigenous Hawai'ians and other Pacific Islanders into a separate category, largely to deny them access to funding and protections.

Although many people across North America still identify themselves as 'Indian' for a variety of reasons,* it is increasingly considered to be derogatory. 'Native American' has become popular in recent decades, but is challenged by many Native peoples as centring colonial racial categories and validating the settler state by implying that the concept of 'America' existed even before the arrival of Europeans. The term can also exclude people who are not 'Americans' in the way we most often use the term: enfranchised citizens of the United States of America. In Canada, 'Aboriginal' is the official government designation for the original inhabitants of the region, who tend to prefer to call themselves 'Indigenous', 'Inuit' (who are not typically 'Indian' in legal terms), 'Métis' or, perhaps most often, 'First Nations'. The similar 'First Peoples' has also gained popularity in some quarters, removing the potentially problematic implication that 'nations' must be recognised by states. Of all these terms, only 'Indigenous' is generally seen as relatively neutral, though 'Native' has been reclaimed in recent years.[3] The former is the UN's favoured term, although even this falls foul of

---

* Or even the phonetic 'NDN', which is a playful way of reconciling older identities with newer ones.

some Canadian groups who were oppressed under the French as 'indigènes'.[4]

So, what route should be taken through this linguistic minefield? As all of these paths and preferences are valid, I think the only solution is one that defers to Indigenous peoples themselves. There are far too many uncomfortable associations for me to stride into this field and start classifying people like Columbus. It is not for me to say what people should call themselves.[5] So I will respect the preferences of particular groups, and favour their preferred terms where not limited by my sources; 'Indians' will appear only to reflect the sixteenth-century texts when they speak of 'indios'. And 'Indigenous Americans' has been used in my title as the clearest way to articulate the geographical scope of the book for readers. Much of the current generation uses 'Native' or 'Indigenous' as a collective racial or political identity, but specific affiliations are almost always preferred. Throughout, I will respect tribal, national and individual identities by calling people by the names they called themselves.*

---

* The most notable exception is my use of 'Aztec-Mexica' to refer to the people who dominated what is now Central Mexico when the Spanish conquistadors arrived. They would not have called themselves 'Aztec', but they are so well known by this name (even to many of their descendants) that, if I hope to change popular stereotypes of this often-misunderstood people, then I feel its use is unavoidable.

Introduction

In July 1519, Spanish conquistadors Francisco de Montejo and Alonso Fernández Puertocarrero set sail from Mexico to Spain with a fabulous treasure. Their ship was so overflowing with precious objects that even the ballast in the hold was gold.[1] These riches included finely worked metal, beautifully feathered shields and fans, clothes, jewels and mosaics. They were a calculated political present – Montejo and Puertocarrero were tasked with winning royal patronage for Hernando Cortés's ongoing, unsanctioned invasion of Mexico. And alongside the conquistadors, fainter in the sources but no less remarkable, was a group of Indigenous people from what is now eastern Mexico. These Totonacs were bound for strange shores with curious, savage customs. No less than the Spanish conquistadors, they too were explorers, pioneers, pathfinders for their people – and ambassadors to a foreign emperor. Indigenous peoples were part of European society from the earliest days of empire.

This book is not about Montejo and Puertocarrero and their ilk, colonisers and conquistadors, white men striding out across the globe to appropriate it. This is the story of the people who travelled the other way. For tens of thousands of Native people voyaged to Europe from the very moment of first encounter. From the 'Brazilian'* king who met Henry VIII, to the Inuit who harpooned ducks on the Avon river. From the Mexicans who mocked up human sacrifice at the court of Charles V to the Inuk (Inuit) baby who was put on show in a London pub before dying and being buried at St Olave's church, on Hart Street in the City. From the mixed heritage

---

* Brazil, like so many of the geopolitical names we recognise, was a term imposed by European invaders.

'*mestizo*' children of Spaniards who came 'home' with their fathers, to the thousands of enslaved Caribbean and Mesoamerican people who laboured in European households. This book belongs to people like them: to the earliest Indigenous people who crossed the great water between Europe and what we now call 'the Americas', and found themselves confronting strange people in unfamiliar lands.

Most people nowadays would be hard-pressed to name an Indigenous traveller to Europe apart, perhaps, from Matoaka, often incorrectly named Pocahontas, a young Powhatan woman who died in England before her twenty-second birthday and whose identity has been appropriated, fictionalised and colonised for four centuries.[2] Even academic historians – with our supposedly esoteric interests – rarely discuss Native travellers to Europe. And, when such travellers do surface, they are usually seen as oddities. They are artefacts of empire, spectacular curiosities, avatars of the riches and mysteries of far-off subjected lands. These overlooked multitudes of Indigenous travellers – nobles, diplomats, servants, translators, families, entertainers, enslaved people – overturn our understandings of early modern exploration and empire. And the vast network of global connections they inhabited – people trading, stealing, talking, marrying, coupling, fighting – sowed the seeds of our cosmopolitan modern world more than a century before the Mayflower pilgrims supposedly set foot on Plymouth Rock.

The Native peoples of the Caribbean first encountered Columbus and his men – sailing under the flag of the Catholic monarchs Ferdinand and Isabella – in 1492. Six or seven Indigenous islanders set foot on European soil for the first time the following year. By the time Columbus landed on Tierra Firma ('solid earth', the mainland) in 1498, another Italian explorer sailing under the flag of England had already reached the eastern coast of what is now Canada. Giovanni Caboto (better known to us as John Cabot) thus became credited as the 'discoverer' of North America, which must have come as something of a surprise to both the Indigenous inhabitants of the region and the Norsemen who had established settlements in Newfoundland and Greenland in the tenth century. The first

Spanish outpost in the Americas was founded on what Columbus dubbed 'La Isla Española' ('the Spanish island', Hispaniola, now split between Haiti and the Dominican Republic). At Christmas time in 1492, Taíno people helped to build the modest fort of La Navidad for the small crew of the shipwrecked vessel *Santa María*, and were doubtless shocked when more than a thousand men arrived the following year to consolidate the Spanish presence. By the time the Totonacs appeared at the Spanish court in 1519, Columbus's voracious expeditions to the Caribbean had already seen thousands of Indigenous people cross the Atlantic, mostly as subjects of enslavement or exoticism: owned and objectified.

Many of these voyagers were from the island peoples now commonly known as the Taínos and Caribs, terms that obscure a vibrant mosaic of Indigenous cultures and societies, only a few of whose names survive, due to the calamitous death toll caused by the Spanish invasion. While attempting to reflect this diversity, I will use 'Taíno' for the peoples of the Greater Antilles where no clear alternative exists, because it is the name claimed by their descendant communities. The word 'Caribs' (from which Caribbean is derived) came to have disastrous overtones for its inaccurate association by the Spanish Empire and Catholic Church with 'cannibals'. The name deliberately obscured a multiplicity of groups, including the Kalinago, many of whom now live in Dominica, but it cannot be entirely avoided in describing the peoples of the Lesser Antilles in the sixteenth century. The mobility of Native peoples in and around the Caribbean rarely forms part of our understanding of Indigenous cultures, but the forcible displacements of enslaved peoples, along with refugee populations fleeing European invasion, have resulted in Indigenous diasporas within, as well as beyond, the Americas. Today, Nona Aquan (Arima First Peoples), the Carib Queen, elected leader of the Indigenous communities in Trinidad and Tobago, is of Chinese, Carib, Indian, Spanish and African descent.[3]

While coastal peoples experienced sporadic incursions by the European invaders in the decades after 1492, they did not have to tolerate a permanent Spanish settlement on the mainland until after Cortés's invasion in 1519. When the capital of the Mexica (who we know as the Aztecs) fell after a devastating siege in 1521, Mexico City was founded on the ruins of Tenochtitlan. Countless Indigenous groups existed in the Americas at the time of the European invasion, but many were annihilated, merged or scattered. Nonetheless, their remarkable diversity is reflected in the fact that 143 languages are still spoken in Mexico today – including the Aztec-Mexica language of Nahuatl – although many are critically endangered. At the turn of the sixteenth century, Central Mexico was a region of city states where urbanisation was on the rise (though none could compete with Tenochtitlan's hundreds of thousands of inhabitants). The Maya centres of the Yucatán peninsula, by contrast, had already experienced the peak of their influence before the 'Maya collapse' brought the abandonment of cities in the ninth century.* The remains of these incredible metropolises – Palenque, Tikal, Chichen Itza et al. – stand in the jungle as cenotaphs, while millions of Maya still live across Central America today. By the time the conquistadors ventured into Maya territory, they were living largely in scattered towns and villages, although some larger states like the K'iche' and Kaqchikel had started to build empires again. The Totonac lands, many of which fell under Aztec-Mexica influence from the mid-fifteenth century, occupied the wet and humid regions of eastern Mexico; they were the world's main cultivators of vanilla until the nineteenth century. Among the first victims of Spanish kidnapping, due to their coastal location, many Totonacs also allied with the Spanish and sought to assert their imperial rights.

These Mesoamericans had sophisticated pictographic writing, law, astronomy, agriculture and medicine. In 1519, Cortés was just beginning to realise the majesty of these civilisations, and he was eager to show their riches and sophistication to the Spanish king. Montejo and Puertocarrero arrived at court as emissaries of La Muy Rica Villa de la Vera Cruz, a hastily founded settlement intended to

---

* There is no agreed explanation for the dramatic collapse of the Classic Maya centres, but environmental factors, overpopulation and persistent warfare are all possible factors.

legitimise Cortés's desire to conquer the region, in defiance of the orders of the governor of Cuba. Even the name of the town, 'The Very Rich City of the True Cross', was an unsubtle hint at the wealth and potential of this 'new' world to the Spanish king. The lavish bounty his envoys brought with them was a much more obvious allusion to the possible rewards if the king supported their fledgling expedition. The documents which Montejo and Puertocarrero carried carefully emphasised that all but one of these objects were 'gifts', given over-and-above the *quinto* tax (the 'fifth' of the value of all goods from the colonies which was due to the Crown), and appealed to the Spanish king to back the conquistadors' invasion of Mexico, and to confirm Cortés as captain and chief justice of the region.[4]

Montejo and Puertocarrero's booty must have been very attractive to a king facing challenges at home but, in truth, this glittering gift came not from the conquistador-in-chief, Cortés, but from the Aztec-Mexica ruler Moctecuhzoma Xocoyotzin, better known to us as Moctezuma.* When he heard of the arrival of invaders from the east, one of the precautions taken by the *tlatoani* (ruler) of Tenochtitlan had been to send emissaries to the Spanish with presents of huge value and beauty. Designed to awe the invaders with Moctezuma's wealth and power, this largesse was cannily appropriated by Cortés, who hoped in turn to impress Charles V†️ and win his support for the Mexican expedition.

The incredible treasures must have made a compelling argument. Most have now been lost or melted down, but they are described in staggering detail in the letter sent from Vera Cruz. Two great discs of gold and silver, as big as cartwheels, and probably representing

---

* You may know him as Montezuma, but this Anglicisation of a bastardisation of a Spanish misunderstanding of the original is just a step too far for this historian.

† Confusingly, the Spanish ruler at the time was King Charles (Carlos) I, but his election to the head of the Holy Roman Empire also made him Emperor Charles V. Even though Cortés could not have known this when he first wrote to the king, I will call him Charles V throughout for consistency.

the sun and moon, were embossed with a design of 'monsters'*
surrounded by elaborate patterns of trees and flowers. Enormous
feather headdresses, fans and harpoons, worked with gold thread,
lay alongside sumptuous turquoise mosaics. There were two spectacular necklaces of gold and stone mosaic, the largest with eight
different strings bearing nearly four hundred red and green jewels.†
Twenty-seven gold bells dangled from the border of this necklace,
and in the centre were four gold-inlaid figures, two of which had
pendants hanging from them. Four more double pendants hung
from the outside. This intricate jewellery must have been a stunning
demonstration of skill to a Spanish court used to thinking of Indigenous peoples as, at best, primitive peasants and, at worst, barbaric
cannibals. In 1521, the historian Peter Martyr d'Anghiera (Pietro
Martire in his native Italian) wrote: 'If ever artists of this kind of
work have touched genius, then surely these natives are they.' He
gives an extraordinary accounting of the treasures, marvelling not
only at their huge value, but even more the 'cleverness of the artist
and the workmanship'. His breathless account gives us a sense of the
reaction the treasures evoked – a sea of gold and precious stones.
Martyr describes the glorious Indigenous regalia in intoxicating
detail: two helmets covered with gold, sprouting gorgeous plumes,
and edged with golden bells, each crested with a green bird with
eyes, feet and beak of gold; twelve pairs of coloured-leather boots,
jingling with bells and sparkling with jade and gold; 'tiaras and
mitres', sceptres, rings and sandals sewn with golden thread.[5]

Animals and natural objects featured prominently among the
riches of Aztec-Mexica lands, as you would expect from a culture
with such a high regard for the world around them. As well as
ornamental birds, fish and jaguars, valuable animal skins were
carefully packed along with an extraordinary gold alligator head,

---

*   The face looked either like a 'devil' or like a 'fairy' depending on the author's
perspective, which doesn't give us much to go on. My guess is that they likely
resembled the famous Sun Stone uncovered in Mexico City: a mytho-historical
representation of divine power.
†   232 red jewels and 163 green jewels for those who like that kind of detail.

which came with 'two large ear ornaments of blue stone mosaic' meticulously labelled as 'for the large alligator head'. The rich Mesoamerican literary tradition was hinted at by a rather perfunctory mention of 'two books which the Indians have'. These remarkable pictographic texts were welcomed eagerly by scholars in Europe. News of the first contacts with Indigenous peoples had started to trickle across the Atlantic, and rulers and intellectuals were eager for more information.[6]

The list of gifts carried to court by Montejo and Puertocarrero is appended to a letter about Cortés's expedition, which outlines his own impressive actions (naturally), as well as the land and people he and his company had encountered, and their petitions to the Crown. But the Indigenous Totonacs who also arrived on the *Santa María de la Concepción* do not seem to have warranted a mention. The exact number of these pioneers is impenetrably tangled in the sources, but five are recorded by name, and the group included two elite men, at least two women, a young male interpreter and probably some attendants.

The Totonacs were dressed in colourfully painted linen, with cloths covering their genitals. Their legs were bare, their hair was long, and the men wore large lower-lip piercings embellished with small stones above their sparse beards. The men were of 'good stature', but the pope's representative at court, the Archbishop of Cosenza, Giovanni Ruffo di Forli, was not at all impressed with the women, whom he found to be 'small and of ugly expression'; we can only imagine what they thought of him.[7]

This is a serious problem for a scholar studying Indigenous travellers: the sources we have are almost always written by Europeans who either observed, accompanied, kidnapped or enslaved the Native people in question. It's tempting to say that the voices of Indigenous travellers have been 'lost', but in reality they were rarely recorded (at least in alphabetic writing) in the first place. As a result, these travellers have tended to be seen as objects: of curiosity, of desire, of greed, of prejudice, of ambition. They have become ciphers for European ideas and aspirations, rather than actors at the centre of their own story. The sources are partly to blame for this: it is much easier to find historical documents about European attitudes to Indigenous peoples than about Indigenous attitudes to Europeans. But unless we admit that weakness, and attempt to overcome it, we will never recognise the importance of Indigenous peoples in European and global history. The omission of the Totonacs from the Vera Cruz letter is not an accident. It represents the wider and sometimes purposeful exclusion of Native peoples from the history of early modern Europe.

The erasure and exclusion of Indigenous peoples is a fundamental part of national narratives across the world. The 'Doctrine of Discovery', a legal fiction that granted Europeans and their descendants the right to 'discovered' territories, has its roots in the fifteenth-century papal bulls that divided the world between Spain and Portugal, making Indigenous peoples 'politically non-existent'.[8] This doctrine has a powerful legacy in United States law, and patriotic myths are often framed around the 'absence' of Native Americans: discovery, the wilderness, the untamed frontier, the 'opening' of the West – these are compelling fantasies that deliberately erase Indigenous presence and set the scene for the settlement of empty lands by industrious 'pioneers'. The violent displacement of Native peoples from their lands is obscured, and even their presence is blurred so that they become merely a distorted caricature in the origin story of the nation.[9] In Latin America, erasure is often coupled with assimilation. In twentieth-century Mexico, in a deliberate attempt to confect an ideal '*mestizo* (mixed) nation', the *indigenismo* movement appropriated the 'good' parts of Indigenous heritage while leaving living communities marginalised.[10] Across South America, Indigenous peoples are fighting for recognition and political rights. In Rio de Janeiro, where many of Brazil's most remarkable monuments were built by enslaved Native labour, 'people have become naturalized not to see Indigenous peoples', according to the historian Ana Paula da Silva, who is among the scholars and activists struggling to have Brazil's rich Indigenous histories recognised.[11] Meanwhile, the popular image of early modern Europe remains an extraordinarily white, ruffed and cod-pieced Tudor and Golden Age fantasy, where Indigenous Americans, Africans and Asians existed only as 'curiosities' from distant lands. Scholars pointing out the ubiquity of people of colour in the European past are routinely denounced as politically correct historical revisionists, shaping the past to fit an idealised multicultural present. Even pseudo-historical fantasy universes replicate and reproduce this cultural homogeneity, which has become not just an issue of ignorance but also of politics. 'Historical whiteness' has become a battleground.

But most people, I believe, assume the European past is incontestably all-white simply because that is the impression they have been given. Migration may be a topical issue now, but there has been an ebb and flow of peoples into and across Europe for millennia – a tangle of travellers, voluntary and involuntary, invaders and refugees, traders and explorers, exiled and enslaved. And there is a growing recognition that the European past may have been a more diverse place than it is sometimes painted, driven by groundbreaking scholars and communicators like Onyeka Nubia, Imtiaz Habib, Olivette Otele, Johny Pitts and David Olusoga. But Native peoples often remain neglected in this story. It's not as if the existence of Indigenous travellers has entirely gone unnoticed – my footnotes are a testament to the toil of historians who have gone before – but this work, and its subjects, have not had the impact on our collective understanding of the past that they should. This book aims to change that.

The ship carrying the Totonacs from Mexico arrived in Sanlúcar de Barrameda in southern Spain in October 1519. Lying at the mouth of the Guadalquivir river, Sanlúcar was unavoidable for ships on their way to Seville, and was notorious for 'the dreadful sandbar which has thrown so many bars of silver into the depths'.[12] A hub for travel to the Americas, this busy port was well used to adventurers and opportunists seeking the wealth of foreign lands. Twenty years before, Columbus had set sail from this harbour on his third voyage to the Indies, which verified for Europeans for the first time the existence of an entirely new continent to the west. Only a month before the Totonacs' arrival, Magellan's five ships had departed mainland Europe from Sanlúcar, on his attempt to find a westward route to Asia which would end in the first circumnavigation of the globe.* By 1519, fleets from the Indies regularly anchored there, so the arrival of two officials from the Americas probably caused little surprise. Given that Columbus had sent thousands of enslaved people to Europe from the Caribbean by 1519, the Totonacs were certainly not the first Indigenous people to set foot on the Sanlúcar docks.

It is possible that, like many colonial opportunists, Montejo and Puertocarrero took advantage of the pause at Sanlúcar to remove some gold (avoiding the eyes of customs officials some fifty miles up the river in Seville). But they didn't stop long, moving quickly up the Guadalquivir and docking in Seville by 5 November, where their precious cargo – along with some 4000 pesos brought for their own expenses – was promptly confiscated by Juan López de Recalde, the accountant of the Casa de Contratación (House of Trade) which controlled all commerce and travel to the Indies. It seems that the governor of Cuba had managed to get word of Cortés's rebellion to his allies in Spain. Fortunately for Montejo and Puertocarrero, they were able to get a message to the king ahead of their enemies, and to impress him sufficiently with an account of their cargo so that, before long, they had a letter from the king ordering them to come to court, bringing the treasure and their Totonac companions with them.[13]

Charles V was clearly intrigued by the Indigenous visitors and seems to have shown an unusual degree of personal concern for the details of their well-being. His letter commands that they be brought to meet him and be treated as well as possible. Realising the Totonacs would be poorly dressed for the chilly Spanish weather, the king made detailed provision for them to be supplied with elegant clothes. The Crown would pay for velvet tunics, which he insisted should be 'of some good colour', capes of fine cloth, satin doublets and gold stockings, as well as all their other needs, including transport to carry them to court. Officials followed the

---

*   Only one of the five ships, the *Victoria*, survived the voyage. Magellan did not.

king's orders to the letter, acquiring a range of luxurious fabrics, including blue and green velvet and white cotton from Rouen. Two prominent tailors and a stocking maker – Juan de Alcalá, Martín de Irure and Juan de Murga – were hired to outfit the Totonacs with all manner of Spanish garments. The visitors were thoroughly provided for, with caps, shirts, cloaks, shoes, hats, hoods and jerkins, as well as the basics ordered by the king. Five pairs of gloves are scrupulously recorded in the accounts, along with the services of a jeweller, Beatriz Franca, so it seems that the party would have been warmly and richly dressed by the time they finally departed Seville for the royal court.

Showing the care taken for the Totonacs' well-being, a nephew of the treasurer of the Casa de Contratación, Domingo de Ochandiano, was tasked with accompanying the group to court, and on 7 February 1520 they set out – well mounted on mules – and accompanied by three muleteers, and three other servants. But, in an era of roving authority, finding the king was easier said than done. Wielding newly acquired authority as Holy Roman Emperor after an aggressive election campaign, Charles was busily travelling his kingdom, trying, largely unsuccessfully, to placate a groundswell of discontent in Castile. There is some confusion in the records about exactly where and when the Totonacs eventually caught up with the court, but it must have been an exhausting journey. They chased the king around Castile for several weeks, fitting in detours to Córdoba to buy more hats and shoes, and to Tordesillas to be forcibly baptised, before finally arriving at court. Even the king noticed that hurrying after the court in the cold winter must have been 'contrary to their health' and ordered that the Totonacs should be treated very well and carefully. His fears seem to have been justified, as one man – Jorge – was taken ill in Córdoba and had to return to Seville.[14]

As a historian, following in the footsteps of this hurried journey, I find myself buried in sources which are almost impossibly dense. Sixteenth-century officials write in a style designed for speed, the ink darkly looping and curling, scrawling across the page, omitting letters, abbreviating and improvising. The printed sources – though much easier to read for this historian trained with Mexican codices – may be more comprehensible but are often even less informative. Striving to make Indigenous people subjects, rather than objects, of the newly cosmopolitan world in which they found themselves, involves poring over European accounts searching for snippets, reading them against the grain, trying to tease out insights from documents which were never intended to be used in this way. Most of the time, the best we can do is to recover outsider perspectives on Indigenous people's experiences: to say what happened to them, to show why that mattered, and to tentatively suggest how they may have thought or felt about it, given their background. Such readings must always be speculative, but can be enriched by an understanding of the vibrant diversity of Indigenous people's world views and cultural knowledge. Sometimes we can trace Native reactions, or detect their possible motivations. Occasionally, we are even afforded a small but direct window onto the Indigenous view of their transatlantic experience, as with the *cantares* songs that come from oral tradition.

Royal decrees and account books hint at the material aspects of Indigenous lives: we have bills for clothing, food, transport, medical care, lodging, and even, occasionally, burial expenses. These seemingly dry records can give a sense of Native people's itineraries, their names, and their lifestyles. The tiny details that they yield may seem mundane. But they allow us to imagine ourselves in the shoes of these travellers, to picture their experiences, and to restore them into our image of the sixteenth century. Occasionally richer, but more subjective, voices, appear. These must be treated with great care, as they sometimes say more about the authors than the people they are writing about.

Two typical documents are accounts by men who saw the Totonacs at the Spanish court: a letter from Archbishop Ruffo di Forli to his master Pope Leo X; and the work of Peter Martyr, commissioned by the Spanish king Charles to write his great chronicle on the 'New World'. Both described the Indigenous travellers in detail, but even the reality that these sources describe was sometimes manufactured. We have seen that the Totonacs were well supplied with European-style clothing during their journey, but when they appeared at court it was as Indigenous nobles, in rich painted linen, feather and fur cloaks. The papal legate describes meeting them attired in traditional style, with a breechcloth and cloak. Did the king order them to demonstrate their Indigenous dress at court? Or had they decided to return to their own clothing for such an important formal occasion? We will never know.

So who *were* these Totonacs, and why did they travel to the Spanish court? Archbishop Ruffo (though he was not keen on their appearance) saw them as powerful figures. Not sure if they were official 'ambassadors', Ruffo claimed they were 'sent by a *cacique* (chief) who wanted friendship and peace with Christians'. It seems they may have been envoys, ordered to report what they found in Spanish lands.[15] The Totonacs were no naive barbarians – they were seen by their contemporaries as one of the more sophisticated peoples of Mexico; their Nahua (Nahuatl-speaking) neighbours reportedly admired their 'humane, civilized life'. The region was a major cotton producer, and the Totonacs were famous for their magnificent clothing, expert embroidery, rich jade and feather adornments, and elegant appearance: 'the men and women were beautiful, fair, tall, slender, firm'.[16] Now perhaps most famous for their 'flying' *voladores*, a fertility ritual which has been named as an intangible cultural heritage by UNESCO, the Totonacs are often overlooked in narratives of the conquest but – keen to reassert their authority in the region – they were to prove important allies to Cortés in the coming years.

It is tempting to suggest that the reason the Totonacs don't appear in the Vera Cruz letter is that they had *chosen* to travel, rather than being sent as 'curiosities' by Cortés, but this is probably an imaginative step too far. Nonetheless Peter Martyr saw the Totonacs as 'great leaders'. For him, the two women were just servants 'assigned for their service' 'according to the national usage'.[17] But women in Indigenous Mexican culture were highly respected and, if they were indeed of noble birth, the female Totonacs could easily have been expected to play a diplomatic role in their own right.

Diplomacy in such situations was tricky because there was a significant language barrier, especially in these early years. Fortunately, there was a young man in the Totonac group who 'had learned some of the Castilian language'.[18] This is a particularly interesting fragment, as we are usually left to guess at the intricacies of Indigenous–European communication. The sources tend to claim that the invaders held detailed negotiations with Native people (usually ending in the latter cheerfully agreeing to be vassals of whichever crown the newcomers represented), but this is obviously, at best, wishful thinking. More likely, it was a simple way of legitimating invasion.* The concern of colonisers to make their actions appear 'legal' may seem strange to us, coming from a perspective where invasion and colonisation themselves are now recognised as, at the very least, ethically dubious. Yet – surprising as it may seem – Europeans in this period spent a lot of time worrying about the legality of their actions, or at least worrying about whether their actions *appeared* lawful.

This desire to cast a veneer of legality over events often obscures our sources, and it is visible in other accounts of the Totonac group. While the witnesses at court saw them as high-status emissaries, the conquistador Bernal Díaz del Castillo – who wrote a famously vivid account of the invasion of Mexico – claimed that the Totonacs were captives who had been saved from human sacrifice in Cempoala. According to Díaz, they had been 'kept in wooden cages to fatten, so that when they were fat they might be sacrificed and eaten'. Francisco López de Gómara, Cortés's chaplain and chronicler, who could always be relied upon to make his master look good, also claimed Cortés had heroically freed the four men along with two women who were 'willing', despite staunch opposition from

---

* Cortés's letters regularly claim that Mexican rulers agreed to become 'vassals' of Charles V, a term which – even if the Spaniards bothered to translate it – would have had little meaning in the Nahua world. For the Spanish, though, it conveniently justified violence against the Mexicans because any vassal who fought against their master instantly became a 'rebel' who might legitimately be suppressed.

Indigenous people worried they might anger the gods.*[19]

So were the Totonacs noble ambassadors, or liberated captives? It's possible that they were both. They could, theoretically, have been noblemen who were held as prisoners and then, once released, become ambassadors for their own people – but that's a bit of a stretch. More likely, this backstory was window dressing designed to justify the conquistadors' actions in Mexico. The idea of 'white saviours' – heroic Europeans delivering unfortunates from their own barbarism – is common throughout imperial history.† On top of that, *rescate* ('rescuing' someone from a worse fate) was a pretext for slavery in Spanish law, and so was often used to justify the 'taking' of Indigenous people. The story of the 'rescued' Totonacs fits suspiciously neatly with Spanish expectations.‡[20]

If the travellers *were* originally sacrificial captives, they must have undergone a significant makeover during the voyage because, by the time they arrived at court, they were clearly positioned as noble visitors who should be treated as representatives of their people. If they *were* rescued from sacrifice, why didn't Cortés's emissaries – Montejo and Puertocarrero – mention that at the time? It would have made for a great story. It seems more likely that Cortés either took, or asked for, some Indigenous representatives to travel to the court. But whether these people were kidnapped or curious, we will never be able to say.

What we do know is that the Totonacs were sharp enough to realise how best to turn the situation to their own advantage. Speaking through their young interpreter at court, the men responded

---

* It's interesting that López de Gómara says Cortés 'took' (*tomó*) the men – a word which suggests rather more compulsion than one would expect from a 'willing' (*dispuestos*) person.

† It was even the, quite explicit, framing of Mel Gibson's 2006 film *Apocalypto*, which opened with Will Durant's quote 'A great civilisation is not conquered from without until it has destroyed itself from within.' In other words, it was the fault of the Maya people that the Europeans conquered them.

‡ The idea of 'fattening up' should also make us immediately suspicious of Díaz's account. It plays into European images of the Indigenous peoples as animalistic, and there's no evidence it really happened.

to questions about whether the king 'ordered' their baptism with judicious (possibly forced) politeness: 'they were happy being Christians'. Fascinatingly, Ruffo thought that the great treasures sent by Cortés to impress the king had actually been 'brought' by the Totonacs, as part of their diplomatic mission. If the court believed this, it must have bought them real political capital, but I would be surprised if Montejo and Puertocarrero allowed such a rumour to last for long. Nonetheless, the Dominican friar Bartolomé de Las Casas, who claimed to have seen the treasures on the same day they reached the emperor, recognised them as gifts 'sent by Moctezuma' in a futile attempt to persuade the Spaniards to leave his lands.[21]

We have no idea whether Charles ever read Cortés's carefully crafted letters but, judging by the admiration the treasure attracted, it made a much bigger impression than the Totonacs who accompanied it. Martyr claimed to have admired 'a thousand figures which it is impossible to describe'. For all his experience, he had 'never seen anything, which for beauty could more delight the human eye'.[22]

When Charles returned to the Low Countries to be crowned Holy Roman Emperor in 1520, he took the Aztec-Mexica artefacts with him. Having spent more than two years in Spain – a country largely unfamiliar to the Flemish-born monarch – Charles would have been keen to demonstrate his majesty and prestige ahead of his coronation at Aachen. He put the treasures on display at the town hall in Brussels, where he was holding court. There, in the late summer of 1520, the artist Albrecht Dürer saw 'the things which have been brought to the King from the new land of gold'. Recording his impressions in his notebook, Dürer remarked on the golden sun and silver moon, but was also overwhelmed with the variety of human nature revealed in these extraordinary objects. He saw 'two rooms full of the armour of the people there, and all manner of wondrous weapons of theirs, very strange clothing, beds, and all kinds of wonderful objects of human use . . . valued at 100,000 florins'. Reflecting on the treasure with an artist's eye, Dürer wrote: 'in all the days of my life I have seen nothing that rejoiced my heart so much as these things, for I saw among them wonderful works of art, and I marvelled at the subtle ingenuity of men in foreign lands'.[23] This famous quote is often trotted out to illustrate the cultural encounter between Europe and the Americas, but the human encounter that is so evident in Dürer's writing is usually overlooked. The artist did not see merely treasure, but also the human hand behind it.

When we realise that there were thousands of Indigenous people in Europe from as early as the 1490s, it becomes impossible to dismiss them as insignificant oddities. Across Spain and Portugal, France, Italy, England and the Low Countries, Europeans were meeting Indigenous people, as diplomats, performers, translators, sailors, servants, family members and enslaved people. A majority were involuntary migrants – kidnapped or coerced from their homes – but there were also a significant number of free people, travelling individually or in small groups. Most went to Spain and Portugal rather than England, the Tudors being busy with their domestic issues and giving little time to overseas exploration until Elizabeth I's disastrous Roanoke venture in the 1580s. But even England had several high-profile Native visitors, including Manteo and Wanchese, the Coastal Algonquin men who – as we'll see – became a critical part of early imperial enterprises, translating for Walter Ralegh and helping to compose an orthography for the Ossomocomuck Algonquian language in London.[24] These men's explicit role as go-betweens, helping to translate the novelties of the 'New World' and inform European views of the Americas, is obvious, but a similar role was being played by Indigenous people at every level of European society, from the enslaved to the nobility.

One of the most 'modern' things about what we call the 'early modern' period* in European history is the beginning of globalisation: the mesh of networks, connections and exchanges which link together every person and every part of the world. As the Spanish were striking out across the Atlantic, the Portuguese were looking to the east and south, establishing the first tenuous links, leading

---

* The exact period is a subject of tremendous contention among historians, but from about 1492 to 1800.

to regular networks of exchange that spanned the world. Not long after, English, French and Dutch ships too began to plough the oceans and plant the seeds of imperial domination. This was the moment when the global connections of our entangled world were inexorably, and often violently, forged in a cosmopolitan, complex and reciprocal confluence of ideas and influences. This book is a project of recovery – of filling a gap in our knowledge – but it is more than that: each Native traveller in whose footprints we follow enriches our understanding, challenges our preconceptions, and transforms our impression of history. Their lives, so often ignored or erased, are woven into the foundations of the world we live in today.

Indigenous people in Europe were vital conduits in the so-called 'Columbian Exchange', which flooded Europe with new tastes and sensations, as people, plants, animals, microbes, resources, commodities and ideas flowed across the Atlantic after 1492.[25] Yet although the transatlantic exchange, the invasion and colonisation of America, and the 'Special Relationship', are pretty well known, Native American influences rarely seem to feature as part of our understanding of European identity. Somewhere in the back of our national imaginations is a vague sense of Walter Ralegh's association with potatoes and tobacco, but their Indigenous nature has been lost.*

Products like tobacco, cacao, tomatoes, potatoes, chillies, and corn have been divorced from their Native context and appropriated by European narratives, losing their distinctively Indigenous character and significance. Tomatoes are seen as Italian rather than Mexican; potatoes are Irish, not Andean. Many things we think of as an intrinsic part of our everyday lives and culture were originally American. It's hard to imagine a world without things like chocolate, sweet and spicy peppers, chips (whether fries or

---

* In the UK, potatoes have become part of our collective personality – as British as a Sunday roast – yet they were not widely eaten in this country until about 250 years ago. (The turkey for our Christmas dinner is also an American immigrant.)

crisps), peanuts and vanilla, the 'Three Sisters' of beans, corn and squash, or (alas) tobacco. The recent flourishing of microhistories of a single object – biographies of commodities such as the potato or tomato – has added a little global colour to this Eurocentric story, but Indigenous travellers and traders still rarely feature as part of popular understandings of Atlantic exchange.[26] Native people were vital to production, trade and commerce. So why do we hear so little about them? Quite simply, because most people seem to have forgotten that Europeans and their descendants weren't the only ones moving in this period.

There is a European monopoly on Atlantic exchange in people's minds. Sometimes Native Americans are seen as skilful traders, playing on the greed or desperation of white colonists. Sometimes they are the guileless innocents who swapped gold for trinkets, and 'sold' Manhattan for $24. But either way, they are portrayed as static recipients of transatlantic encounter, never reaching out across the ocean, influencing the Atlantic trade only in their local interactions with Europeans. And so we end up with a world in which exchange and encounter – in both directions – are mediated by Europeans. Where Indigenous influences and ideas *do* defy the dominant current and flow east towards the metropole, they are believed to be carried by others. And so, despite thousands of earlier Indigenous travellers to Europe (many of whom smoked, and brought tobacco with them), and despite never going to a part of the Americas which cultivated the potato, Sir Walter Ralegh, with his tobacco and potatoes, stands as the discoverer and pioneer of American products in popular culture. Only by recognising the mobility of Native peoples, and their presence at the heart of empire, can we loosen the crushing grip of Europeans on transatlantic exchange and recognise the direct influence of Indigenous peoples, not only on that exchange, but on European culture itself.

Native travellers challenge our historical preconceptions about early modern Europe, as well as the origins of our contemporary, cosmopolitan world. And whether the Totonacs were former prisoners or official ambassadors, they made one man at least think hard about his own prejudices. Peter Martyr, after staring in horrified fascination at the hefty plugs worn in the men's lower lips, wrote:

> I cannot remember that I have seen anything more hideous; but they think that nothing more elegant exists under the lunar circle. This example proves the blindness and foolishness of the human race; it likewise proves how we deceive ourselves. The Ethiopian thinks that black is a more beautiful colour than white, while the white man thinks the opposite. A bald man thinks himself more handsome than a hairy one, and a man with a beard laughs at him who is without one. We are influenced by passions rather than guided by reason, and the human race accepts these foolish notions, each country following its own fancy. In deference to another's opinion, we prefer foolish things, while we reject solid and certain ones.[27]

The Totonac travellers made Martyr stop and reflect on his own certainties about the world, and the lives of the earliest Indigenous travellers can help us to do the same. As diplomats, curiosities, entertainers, traders, servants, spouses, children, tourists, and sadly, most often, when enslaved, Indigenous people were integrated into, and influenced, European culture, as well as carrying it home to the Americas, long before the landing at Plymouth Rock marked a start to the Anglophone Atlantic world.

This is not to idealise the encounter between Europe and the Americas. We must not forget the tragedy which hangs over these isolated emissaries to a foreign land. Agency is meaningless if it is divorced from understandings of oppression. And Indigenous peoples were exploited, enslaved and oppressed from the very moment of first encounter. At the same time as the cultural and material wealth of Mesoamerica was being displayed at court, their civilisations were being destroyed by greed, disease and violence.

Only a month after Dürer marvelled at the Indigenous treasures in Brussels, a devastating outbreak of smallpox spread by conquistadors hit the Aztec-Mexica capital, Tenochtitlan, wiping out tens of thousands of people. The epidemic swept through the region, often moving ahead of the Europeans, causing a death toll which has been put as high as eight million people. Already weakened by European violence and displacement, and unable to care for the sick and dying while ill themselves, Indigenous people saw their communities annihilated by previously unknown waves of plagues.

The following August, Tenochtitlan fell. The remarkable island city was in ruins, its people ravaged by the war and the brutal reprisals exacted by Cortés's allies on their old foes. Fernando de Alva Ixtlilxochitl, a direct descendant of the rulers of both Tenochtitlan and Texcoco (a former ally of Moctezuma, forcibly persuaded to defect to the Spanish in 1520), described the carnage: 'On this day some of the cruelest things ever to occur in these lands were inflicted upon the unfortunate Mexica. The wailing of the women and children was such that it broke the men's hearts. The Tlaxcalteca and other nations that were not on good terms with the Mexica cruelly took revenge on them for past deeds and plundered everything they had.'[28] This rivalry among Indigenous peoples is often blurred out in narratives of the conquest, but there were hundreds of independent polities in Mexico, all struggling to maintain themselves in the precarious world created by the European invasion. For the Aztec-Mexica, this moment, five hundred years ago, shattered their world, but history has many faces, and many paths. The one we see most often reflects European influence, but look a little harder and we see other perspectives, other possibilities. We often talk about 'the Spanish conquest of the Aztecs', but we might equally call this the Tlaxcalan* conquest of the Tenochca. Ending a century-long rivalry, the confederacy of Tlaxcala had triumphed over their old enemies in a famous victory which they told and retold in their own histories, carried across the Atlantic and used as currency in the colonial world.

In the years following the fall of Tenochtitlan, Indigenous peoples across the Americas found themselves grappling with

---

* The people would have called themselves 'Tlaxcalteca', but I have retained the Europeanised form (except in quotation) for clarity.

European invaders who sought to establish their authority through negotiation, intimidation, and outright violence. While Charles V (as Holy Roman Emperor, in possession of the greatest number of realms ever then to have been united under a single ruler) claimed as his motto '*plus ultra*' – his power stretching 'further beyond' the known world and encircling ocean – Indigenous peoples were also stretching their wings in this expanding global space. Despite the decimation of populations through violence, slavery, disease and the forcible dismantling of their communities, Native people remained in the majority throughout most of the Americas in the following centuries. Even in the capital, the flagship of 'New Spain', the population was overwhelmingly Indigenous, with only about 5 per cent white and a similar number of African-descended people by 1570, a figure which barely doubled in the next hundred years. Although our perception of the past is dominated by Europeans, the Americas remained a predominantly Indigenous space until well into the eighteenth century.[29]

But even if white people were firmly in the minority, European influence reached inexorably across the ocean, drawing Indigenous people – especially those in urban centres – into a transatlantic network of colonial bureaucracy and structure. For many, even though the ocean was beyond the far horizon, they still found themselves dealing with the Atlantic world on their doorstep. Some groups and families naturally retreated where they could, attempting to preserve their traditional way of life. Some reluctantly accommodated the Europeans, or fought them ferociously. But many Indigenous people saw the opportunity, or necessity, to throw themselves into this new world.

And so, in 1528, when Hernando Cortés returned to Spain for the first time since the invasion, a large group of Nahua nobles, including three sons of Moctezuma and one of the rulers of their exultant Tlaxcalan adversaries – 'don Lorenzo of Tlascala' – travelled with him. These men held powerful claims as the *señores naturales* (natural lords) of the land, and were recognised as official envoys by a Spanish Crown keen to legitimate its American empire. Unlike the Totonacs, these were clearly men of royal blood and high rank, typical of the Indigenous diplomats we will meet later. They sought to shore up their claims, and 'to give obedience to the Emperor', realising the importance of tangible connections in this tenuously linked transatlantic network of power. Personal fealty to the king was central to political success – petitioners constantly reminded the monarch in their letters that they were the very men 'who had kissed the hands of Your Majesty'.[30]

Lorenzo died in Spain, along with at least five of his companions, but his embassy secured a commitment protecting the 'the Tlaxcalans, their Indians and the Indians of their city' from ever being granted as an *encomienda*,* liberating the city from the whims of the local authorities and making them free vassals governed directly by the Crown to whom they would pay only a nominal tribute. Most of the surviving travellers returned to New Spain, at the Crown's expense, in 1529, but at least some of the noblemen remained at court receiving grants and posts in the royal household. Such men would be drawn back to the heart of empire again and again, bent on securing their status and privileges and gaining greater rewards.[31]

Cortés, struggling to assert his authority in New Spain, was also profoundly aware of the need to impress the emperor and so, as well as his small *mestizo* son (who we will meet again later), the conquistador was accompanied by an eye-catching entourage intended to dazzle the emperor with the wealth and glamour of his newly acquired realms. Along with entertainers, tumblers, conjurers, 'dwarves' and other 'curiosities', he brought glittering treasures and curious creatures never before seen in Spain such as an armadillo, a possum, pelicans, and jaguars. Among the group were jugglers who tossed logs into the air with their feet, dancers, and musicians, along with about a dozen Tlaxcalans who played *ullamaliztli*, the traditional Mesoamerican ball game, astounding the court with their dexterity and strength. Not only the players, but

---

* An *encomienda* was a grant giving the holder the right to demand tribute and labour from Indigenous communities, theoretically in exchange for evangelising and protecting them. It was a bad bargain.

also the ball itself were quite a spectacle for the Europeans. More than two centuries before the French geographer Charles Marie de La Condamine is credited with becoming the first European to encounter rubber, the Spanish colonist and writer Gonzalo Fernández de Oviedo y Valdés described 'the heavy ball which is made from the sap of certain trees and other mixtures, which made the ball bounce greatly'. Cortés's sensational return attracted a lot of attention and he was very well received. Charles was understandably enthusiastic. All the wonders of the Americas were laid out for the emperor at his feet: the luminous treasures, remarkable animals, and unique entertainers. Charles V was apparently so delighted with the entertainers that he sent them on to Rome to amaze Pope Clement VII.[32]

It is an arresting image: these expert Native men mesmerising the Europeans with their skill and power, spinning large logs with their feet, deflecting dangerous rubber balls, and performing with great precision and harmony. And, thanks to an Augsburg medallist named Christoph Weiditz, we are able to take a peek at these men and witness their marvels. Having travelled to Spain in 1529 to seek a royal licence, Weiditz produced an unpublished 'costume book' showing the personalities and peoples he encountered at court. And among the throng are thirteen pages showing the 'Indian people whom Ferdinand Cortez brought with him from India, and they have played in front of his Imperial Majesty with wood and ball'. Weiditz has captured the men juggling the logs, bouncing a ball between their hips, and crouched on the grass playing a gambling game with pebbles (probably *patolli*). A 'warrior' holds a jagged metal spear and feathered shield, while 'nobles' bear parrots, feather standards and luxuriant feather cloaks. These men all have brown skin, facial piercings and adornments, and short, straight, dark hair. Finally, Weiditz depicts an Indigenous woman, a striped sash tied around her head, with an extravagant, matching feather robe in red, white and green. This is a rare record of a female traveller (although in largely invented regalia), and the text reads: 'In this manner go Indian women, not more than one has come out.'[33]

These pictures were certainly inspired by the Indigenous

travellers at the Spanish court, but the facial jewels are more typical of Brazilian practice than Nahua, and it seems the gloriously feathered 'noble' figures are exoticised stereotypes, rather than the real Native people in Cortés's company.[34] Nonetheless, in Weiditz's pictures, we can see the athleticism and grace that fascinated Charles V, as well as glimpse these men at leisure. Perhaps they are figments, composites of imagination and observation. But they remind us of the impact the Nahuas made. They remind us that they were there, and that people saw them, talked and wrote about them, painted them, even spoke with them. A small thing, but so often forgotten.

So what became of the Totonacs at court? Their story, with all its lacunae, is pretty typical of such accounts. Once they drop out of the limelight of court, the details become sparse, and sometimes contradictory, though they were much better treated than the vast majority of Indigenous people brought to Europe in this period. After the Totonacs had formed part of the king's entourage for a short time, Charles realised that the men were suffering from following the swiftly moving court in the cold, and ordered them to be accompanied back to Seville and treated with great care.[35] He was right to be concerned about their health for, only a couple of weeks later, the Crown paid a bill for the travellers – named for the first time as Tamayo, Carlos and Jorge – that included 'a maid that served them in the cooking of food and curing and for the ailments that they had and washing the clothes and for medicine and physic and surgeons'. Poignantly, the same document records the expenses for the burial of Systan, an *indio* (male Indian),* in Seville on 24 March 1520.

We have no way of knowing which of Seville's many health hazards struck him down. With waste in the streets, foul water and poor sanitation, the city was a dangerous enough place for its regular inhabitants, but Indigenous travellers were also vulnerable

---

* *Indio* (male) and *india* (female) are the Spanish terms used for Indigenous people in this period. *Indios* could mean an all-male or mixed-sex group.

to the germs that would attack their contemporaries across the Atlantic. Diseases such as measles, typhus, influenza, plague, dysentery and smallpox were all endemic and lethal to Native people, who lacked much immunity from previous exposure.

Systan does not seem to have been one of the high-status Totonacs because he is referred to as 'another Indian that came with' them. But the Crown paid to bury him honourably, covering the cost of a wax candle weighing half a pound and three men to carry his corpse to the church – as well as the 'rent of the bed on which they carried him'. The bill also included a decent shroud, costing 119 *maravedís*, priests' fees of 150 *maravedís*, and the cost of a sexton: one *real*. At the end of March 1521, the Crown paid for the other Totonacs to sail for Cuba, where they disappear from the records, and from our sight. We know they were entrusted to the dubious care of the governor – Cortés's rival, Diego Velázquez – and that their ship arrived safely, but of these first 'Mexicans' to set foot on European soil we know no more.[36]

The men (and possibly women) who travelled with Cortés in 1528 are often seen as remarkable. Better known than most Indigenous travellers, they have been sprinkled throughout popular accounts for hundreds of years as a colourful anecdote in the early history of empire, a curio to be scrutinised and marvelled at, but which is rarely seen as at the heart of the story. But these were men with a clear mission, who travelled with intent, and the most remarkable thing about them is how unremarkable they were. The entertainers and athletes were wondrous in their dexterity and musicality – and unsurprisingly an object of curiosity at first – but the noblemen were quickly recognised as ambassadors representing titled families who had the right to deploy influence and make demands on their emperor and, as we will see, such visitors soon became regular petitioners at court. Indigenous elites were vital allies to a Spanish Crown seeking to legitimise and stabilise its fledgling empire, and – experienced in their own sophisticated legal systems – the Nahua and their neighbours rapidly learned to deploy the rhetoric and tactics of Spanish law to their own advantage.

But in the people enslaved by Columbus, the avarice of the con-quistadors, and the relentless toll of death among the travellers, we see a darker side to this exchange. While the sons of Tenochtitlan and their enemies in Tlaxcala were reimagining their world as a transatlantic realm, the city of Tenochtitlan lay in ruins, its inhab-itants ravaged by disease and violence. By the time the Nahua men sent their embassies to Spain in 1528 with a huge retinue, the age of the Aztec-Mexica was past, its last ruler murdered out of avarice and suspicion. How difficult must it be to display the glories of a world which you know is gone forever?

For all their fascination, persistence, and colourful curiosity, the Nahua visitors to Europe were remnants of a world that was fast being remade. The exhibitions at the Spanish court might almost be seen as an epitaph to the Tenochca way of life, a moving reminder of all that had been washed away by the Spanish arrival. The chroniclers at court were naturally oblivious to this tragic sub-text, but I wonder how the Nahua themselves must have felt, dancing for the Holy Roman Emperor when they knew they would never again dance for their own. Indigenous elites adapted fast, clinging onto their historic rights and fighting to preserve their personal and familial power in the shifting sands of colonial rule, but these early travellers were also caught between worlds, trying to fit their actions and expectations to the demands of a foreign culture, while performing the traditions of their past* for the benefit of a curious public. Did Indigenous peoples see the Spaniards as merely a new player in regional disputes, or did they recognise them as savage men who threw fire and demanded submission to a new god, changing their world forever?

Individually and collectively, Native peoples responded force-fully, learning to apply their considerable administrative, rhetorical and legal skills to the challenge of European politics, deploying their historic claims and rivalries in the new climate of interna-tional diplomacy. But in their style and speech (and, doubtless, in

---

* Or what Europeans imagined to be their past. It's not at all clear how far the Indigenous travellers were 'dressed up' for their appearances at court.

their memories) they constantly evoked the conventions of their own 'Old World', a world of beauty and brutality, of compassion, education, and strength.

We rarely are able to hear Indigenous voices in this world. But through the *Cantares Mexicanos*, the surviving products of the Nahuas' ancient tradition of lyrical composition, we can glean the Indigenous view of this transatlantic landscape. Dialogue and performance were highly respected skills in the Indigenous world, and the Nahua naturally used this long-established form of expression to grapple with the new experiences and images that confronted them, engaging with current affairs as well as preserving their histories and cultures.[37]

One *atequilizcuicatl*, or 'Water-Pouring Song', recorded in the mid-sixteenth century, and preserved in the National Library in Mexico City, blends memories of an Indigenous journey to Spain with Christian and Nahua ideas about afterlife and paradise. This long and eloquent poem describes the meeting between Cortés and Moctezuma, and the shattering defeat of Tenochtitlan. At last, after a dangerous ocean crossing, beyond the 'jade waters', the speakers find themselves at the Spanish court (presumably that of Charles V). The song melds Indigenous and Christian forms to give a resonant account of transatlantic travel. Glowing images of flowers and pouring water dominate much of the *canto* – these are metaphors for the warrior captives of the Aztec-Mexica world, and for the nourishing of the earth with blood. The first line is given in the original Nahuatl to give a taste of the flowing verse, translated by David Bowles:

> *Çan moquetza in ehecatl cocomocan tetecuicaya yc poçonia yn*
> *ilhuicaatl huiya nanatzcatihuaya yn acallia, ohuaya ohuaya*

> The wind now rises, howling and moaning. Thus does the
>   ocean seethe and the ship creaks its way along.
> Verily the wonders of God wash over us. We behold massive
>   waves.
> Flowers rain gently down, and the ship creaks its way along.[38]

O, friends! Marvel here in the midst of the water! You're
  slicing through it, Don Martín! The ocean crashes in waves
  against us . . .
We are already wanted here. Long is the house of the
  Emperor; let its waters flow [lit. appear]!
He is respected. Thus does God already see him.
Let us call out to the Only God. Perhaps in that way – for a
  single day
by his side, in his presence – we [will be] his vassals.
We go there to the sea to admire things, just we Mexicah.
  There the Emperor says goodbye, telling us, 'Go see the
  Holy Father.'
ohuaya ohuaya [ecstatic vocables, which appear at the end of
  sections]
He has already said, 'Perhaps what I need is gold. May all bow
  down. Verily
cry out [plural] to the celestial one, God.'
For the same reason, he sends us off to Rome. He told us that:
'Go see the Holy Father.'
Our hearts fully willing, he sends us off to Rome. He told us
  that:
'Go see the Holy Father'
In the Pope's long house, where stands the multi-hued crypt,
scripture writ with gold brings us dawning light.[39]
Conches make things stir. God's word is guarded there where
  it stands. The trogon.
Arrayed. Closed.[40] It brings us dawning light.
Harken unto it, you princes. It rests here beside us in this very
  place, this place like the House of God in Rome where the
  Pope keeps watch over all.[41]

It is rarely a good idea to take poetry too literally, but here we
have actual experiences of transatlantic travel overlaid with
spiritual metaphors and Indigenous understandings of heaven.
The narrators, finding themselves in the 'house of the Emperor',
'call out to the Only God' (an Indigenous way of understanding

the monotheistic Christian deity). The phrasing here blurs the distinction between the emperor and God himself – it is in calling to God that the 'vassals' are able to spend 'a single day by his side, in his presence'. Is this God's presence? Or the emperor? Religious and imperial power are inextricably entwined. The singers are then sent to Rome, to 'see the Holy Father', with the striking (possibly sarcastic) suggestion that 'gold' is linked to the glory of God. In the pope's 'multi-hued crypt',* a wonderful image of the old basilica where mosaics sprinkled the walls with glowing colour, the 'scripture writ with gold brings us dawning light'. This evocative line conjures up at once both the splendour of Christianity and the fabulously illuminated books that enclosed it. There, in the House of God, the pope keeps watch, surrounded by Indigenous symbols of power: heralded by conch trumpets, and guarded by the 'trogon' – the colourful quetzal, a sacred bird whose precious feathers carried religious significance for the Nahua. Religious and imperial ideologies are fascinatingly intertwined in this song. The emperor is explicitly linked not only with power and religion, but also with gold. His authority is unambiguously related to Rome, and the house of the pope is fused with heaven itself. In the earlier verses, we also hear that the 'tree of sustenance' – the suckling tree from which the spirits of all Aztec-Mexica babies dangled, nursing on its branches before they were born – was to be found beyond the 'seething ocean'. Here we see memories of real transatlantic experiences merging with Mesoamerican ideologies and missionary teachings, as the Indigenous people blended Nahua ideas of birth and the afterlife with Christian conceptions of heaven, and fused imperial, papal, and heavenly authority into a claimed source of shared power.

In this song, we see the news of the transatlantic travellers and their discoveries becoming part of the Nahua world. They were being celebrated, remembered, and sung about in the streets. Several groups of Nahua nobles had been to Rome by the time this was

---

* 'Crypt' or 'cavern', *oztotl*, has sacred overtones in Nahua culture, with links to origins, the womb, and the afterlife.

composed, but the mention of being sent to Europe by the emperor ties it to the 1528 delegation. That said, by the time the song was recorded, many Indigenous voyagers had made the round trip to Europe, and the Martín being remembered here by the anonymous composer could be one of at least three travellers we know about: Moctezuma's son, who reaped the rewards of petitioning the Crown; the *mestizo* son of Cortés and his Indigenous translator Malintzin; or Martín Ecatzin, a nobleman who, according to the Annals of Tlatelolco, spent five years in Spain in the 1520s. Given the link to Rome, and the fact that the song is of Mexica origin, the reference is most likely to Martín Cortés Nezahualtecolotl, who crossed the Atlantic repeatedly, and – as one of the last surviving sons of Moctezuma – was entangled in Nahua histories and politics.[42] But whether the *canto* references a specific transatlantic journey, an imagined bundle of associations, or both, it is clear that the Atlantic was a vivid and topical sphere in the Indigenous world view.

For the Aztec-Mexica, the *uei atl* – 'great water' – of the ocean held powerful meaning. Before the arrival of the Spanish, they believed the world was surrounded by the sea. The world itself was *cemanahuac* (the place surrounded by water), and the land rested on a great disc or crocodile named Cipactli, which floated on primordial liquid. *Teuatl* (sea) can also mean 'divine liquid' or blood, that most primal of life-giving fluids, which fuelled the Aztec-Mexica realm. The Indigenous informants who spoke with the Franciscan friar, Bernardino de Sahagún, told him that the *ilhuicaatl* (the ocean, literally 'sky water' or 'heaven water') 'stood resting in every direction . . . It was as if the water walls were joined to it. And hence they called it "water which reaches the heavens".' Thus the people of *cemanahuac* lived within a glittering orb of water, a boundary of their existence which was both terrifying and wondrous:

> It is great. It terrifies, it frightens one. It is that which is irresist-
> ible; a great marvel; foaming, glistening, with waves; bitter – very
> bitter, most bitter; very salty. It has man-eating animals, life. It
> is that which surges. It stirs; it stretches ill-smelling, restless.[43]

The 'Water-Pouring Song' shows that the Atlantic remained a vibrant realm in the Indigenous imagination, a place of mystery and danger, but one that had been transformed from a metaphysical boundary into a theatre of activity: a place of possibility. It was only later that the unequal nature of the ocean's promise would become obvious.

The earliest 'Mexican' travellers to Europe are typical of many of the people we will encounter in this book. Their lives become visible to us for a short time – stepping into the foreground as our sources allow us to see them – before dropping out of view again. But there are thousands of them. And by layering their stories, gathering them, piece by piece, into a mosaic of glimmering fragments, we can construct a narrative. It is not always pleasant to contemplate. It shows humans in all their frailty and cruelty, endurance and compassion. But it is a story of humanity, of connection, of cosmopolitanism. It is a story of empire, of slavery, of racism, and of globalisation. It is the story of how the Americas, and their original inhabitants, made our world.

1

Slavery

From the earliest encounters, Native peoples were seen by Europeans as a commodity to be exploited. On 11 October 1492, Columbus's crew 'discovered America', or more accurately, they first sighted the Taíno island of Guanahaní,* which they 'took possession of . . . in the names of the King and Queen', undeterred by the fact the island was quite obviously 'possessed' already. That day, Columbus concluded his diary: '[The people] ought to make good slaves for they are of quick intelligence since I notice that they are quick to repeat what is said to them, and I believe that they could very easily become Christians, for it seemed to me that they had no religion of their own. God willing, when I come to leave I will bring six of them to Your Highnesses so that they may learn to speak.'[1] And take them he did.

Exactly a month after Columbus's crew first spied land, five young Indigenous men who had paddled a canoe out to his flagship, the *Santa María*, found themselves 'detained'. Seven women and three children were also abducted from a nearby house and carried on board. According to Columbus's letters, these people – not even the first to be stolen from the islands – were taken 'by force' in order to 'learn our language, so that we would know what there is in this land and so that on their return they could act as interpreters'. Based on his experience of African enslavement, Columbus was

---

* Columbus called this island 'San Salvador' (Holy Saviour). The exact location is unknown, but it is widely believed to be Watling Island in the Bahamas, named after the seventeenth-century English pirate who used it as his hideout.

convinced that 'the men would behave themselves better in Spain with their own women than without them' because 'if they have their women, they will be more willing to provide the cooperation expected of them'. Fascinatingly, Columbus also seemed to think that it was the women who would 'do much to teach our men the language', disturbingly foreshadowing the later trafficking of Native women, ostensibly as intermediaries, but often also into sexual slavery. The following night, a man of about forty-five years old rowed out to the ship and begged to be allowed to accompany his wife, son and two daughters, who were among the prisoners. The man was allowed aboard, becoming perhaps the first Indigenous American to 'voluntarily' travel to Europe, albeit under extreme duress. Tragically, we do not know whether he or his family ever made the trip, as only six or seven of the islanders survived to be presented to the Catholic monarchs, Ferdinand and Isabella, in April 1493.[2]

These Indigenous people may not have intended, or wanted, to be explorers, but they were still the first of their people to set foot in the 'new world' of Europe. These were Lucayan Taíno people, their name deriving from the Arawak words 'Lukkunu Kaíri' (good island people). They were the main inhabitants of the larger islands, and their lifestyle seemed in some ways to conform to European expectations of 'primitive' people: they frequently went naked and lived in communal houses built of wood, straw and palms. But they had sophisticated polities and kinship networks which the Spanish (and, for many years, scholars) failed to recognise. Despite the decorous protocol and complex etiquette which typified his early exchanges with Taíno chiefs, Columbus nonetheless behaved as if their people were objects, grabbing Native men, women and children as he journeyed along what is now the Bahamian archipelago. In November 1492, the Admiral kidnapped around two dozen people from Cuba,* and shipped them to Spain as 'curiosities' and potential translators. The careless objectification of the Taíno

---

* The name 'Cuba' comes from the Taíno language, but its exact origin is obscure – it may have been the name of the capital city.

is typical of European attitudes to Indigenous peoples; they were valued and treated according to what would make them of most use. But the Spaniards were also aware that these were humans, and potential Christians, a fact which proved of considerable importance in the years to come.

It must have been overwhelming for the Taíno travellers. Ripped away from their homes, they spent several months trapped on a strange ship, facing the terrors of the ocean, and watching their companions die one by one. No strangers to waterborne commerce and transport, these island men would have been well acquainted with travel in large canoes, and with the vicissitudes of being on the water. But a long ocean crossing on an enclosed vessel was an entirely different proposition. We have few records of the minutiae of life at sea in this period, but the Spanish judge Eugenio de Salazar left a fabulously evocative record of his transatlantic passage when he was posted to Santo Domingo in 1573. Although written close to a century after the Taínos' voyage, Salazar's account gives a rare insight into life aboard an ageing caravel similar to the smaller ships used by Columbus. The crowded conditions and cramped quarters he describes are almost unimaginable. As a senior official, he was granted the 'great privilege' of 'a tiny cabin, about two feet by three', in which he was crammed with his wife and daughter while suffering relentless seasickness in almost complete darkness. The less fortunate were crowded together in 'dwellings [that] are so closed in, dark, and evil-smelling that they seem to be more like burial vaults or charnelhouses [where skeletons were stored]'. Complaining of the stinking water, the corrupt and draconian crew, 'flights of cockroaches', 'rats so fierce that when they are cornered they turn on the hunters like wild boars', he abhorred the communal life, people of all ranks crowded cheek by jowl, eating, cooking, belching, vomiting and emptying their bowels without restraint. 'At sea there is no hope that the road, or the host, or the lodging will improve; everything grows steadily worse; the ship labors more and more and the food gets scantier and nastier every day', he wrote. It is hard not to reflect on the experiences of enslaved Black and Native people who were crammed into the holds of the European

ships which ploughed the same route. If the accommodations of
free people were like 'the caves of Hell', 'dark by day and pitch-black
by night', what horrors were inflicted on those forced to endure
sickness and excrement without relief?[3]

When the Taínos disembarked in Palos, Columbus left two or
three 'that were sick' behind and took the 'six that were healthy' on
the journey to court. We know that two of the survivors were men,
but no children are mentioned as arriving in Seville, so we are left
wondering whether they were simply invisible to the chroniclers,
or if they perished on the voyage and their bodies were tossed carelessly into the roiling ocean. The few Taínos that survived arrived
in Seville, before travelling to Barcelona, where they were presented
to the king and queen, along with beautiful green parrots, worked
gold objects, small pearls, ornate belts, and other curiosities which
'no one had seen or heard of in Spain before'. The Indigenous people
must have been a subject of incredible curiosity, for Columbus was
at pains to trumpet his discovery, and people crowded the streets
to look at them. We know about their arrival because Columbus's
triumph is described in slightly cynical detail by Bartolomé de Las
Casas – an author and friar who spent his later life campaigning for
better treatment of the Indigenous peoples, who he saw as childlike
innocents, in need of salvation – in his unfairly neglected and
never-translated-into-English *History of the Indies*. Ever modest,
when the newly confirmed 'Admiral' arrived at court he gave a
stirring speech intended to shore up his position and secure future
investments, conjuring up a picture of a land where coarse grains of
gold were to be found just lying around, ready for melting. Mindful
of the reputation of the 'Catholic monarchs', he also described
another 'precious treasure': the multitudes of people, who were
simple, meek and naked, perfectly suited to being brought to the
Christian faith. At this point, Columbus ushered forward the Taíno,
and Ferdinand and Isabella – inspired to help and convert these
poor innocents – threw themselves on their knees, crying pious
tears. The royal choir – apparently primed for this moment – then
burst into song, and it seemed at that ecstatic climax that they were
'communicating with celestial deities'.[4]

We can only imagine the Taínos' reaction to this elaborately choreographed spectacle. Ritualised weeping was not unusual among Indigenous cultures,* and they were not complete strangers to the oddities of Europeans by this point, but were surely baffled by the rulers' fervent response to their arrival. Given the significant imbalance of power, it must have been quite disorientating to have the rulers kneel at their feet. The Taínos' sense of the encounter may also have been interlaced with the objects on display. Among the marvels around them were *guaízas*, small sculptures of faces, often made of shell. These 'faces of the living' were a symbol of kinship in Taíno culture, an embodiment of a person's spirit, often given by *caciques* as a way of cementing relationships. *Zemís* – objects connected to the life force of ancestors with complex ceremonial purposes – were also probably among the objects brought to court by Columbus. The gold figures, parrots, jewelled belts, and *guaízas* were gifts from Caribbean *caciques*, Indigenous chiefs who likely saw these symbolic exchanges as gaining some control by sacrificing part of themselves.[5] How must the Taínos have felt, presented as objects to a foreign ruler, but surrounded by tokens of their own power? It's hard not to think these few survivors would have been despairing and overwhelmed, but what possibilities might they have seen reflected in the *guaízas* and other treasures, echoing the Taínos' spirits back from their surroundings?

Unlike the later Totonacs, these first travellers did not have a translator, but we know that they had quickly learned to communicate with the Spaniards 'by speech or by signs' and had been 'of much service'. According to Peter Martyr, it is due to some of these travellers that we have what may be the first Indigenous American dictionary in a Latin alphabet, for 'thanks to [them] all the words of their language have been written down with Latin characters'. Columbus himself wrote admiringly of the Taínos' swift ability to adapt, calling them 'men of very subtle wit' and, according

---

*   The Taíno chief Guacanagarí and his men wept ostentatiously when Columbus's ship, the *Santa María*, struck a reef in December 1493.

to Oviedo,* the Taíno were astute enough to go along with the situation they found themselves in. 'Of their own will and counsel, [they] asked to be baptised', a favour which was graciously granted by the Catholic monarchs who, with their eldest son John, agreed to be the godparents. Most of the Taínos were given unknown names picked by their new sponsors, but the most important men were honoured (and colonised) by being baptised 'Fernando de Aragon' (Ferdinand of Aragon) after the king and 'Juan de Castillo' (John of Castile) after his son.† These two 'principal Indians' were apparently relatives of the *cacique* Guacanagarí, ruler of Marién on what became Hispaniola, who allowed Columbus to establish the short-lived settlement of La Navidad, the first European colony in the Americas, on his lands. The emergence of a *cacique*'s relatives among the captives complicates our understanding of these events, as it seems less likely they were kidnapped, and they must also have joined Columbus's company after he seized the Taíno in Cuba. Were they official representatives of Guacanagarí? An eighteenth-century account, the first to be written by a Hispaniolan, says that two of Guacanagarí's sons, along with eight other *indios* 'of their own will wanted to go to Castile'. It is possible that the agency and engagement of the Taínos was later written into their history to create a more coherent Christian history of Hispaniola, but we also know that Guacanagarí had a strategic (if incompletely informed) attitude to his encounter with Columbus – it is not hard to imagine that he might have sent his sons as emissaries. We know that Guacanagarí himself gifted a belt and a *guaíza* mask to Columbus when he arrived on Hispaniola.[6] Assuming that these objects were among those presented to the king and queen, Fernando's role becomes almost a diplomatic one: cementing the friendship secured by this exchange.

---

* Oviedo is famous for his *General and Natural History of the Indies*, which was most Europeans' introduction to pineapples, tobacco, barbecues and hammocks.
† To try and avoid confusion, I have stuck with the well-known, Anglicised names for the monarchs, but kept the original Spanish for their Taíno godchildren. I would, of course, prefer to use their Indigenous names but – as they are unknown – at least this way they are individuals, not just part of an anonymous mass.

Along with these two nobles, a young Taíno – who will reappear in the next chapter – was baptised 'Diego Colón' after Columbus's son,* marking the beginning of a long association with the Admiral which would lead him to cross and recross the ocean. Such familial naming is a pattern which will confusingly recur in our tale; it is a form of arrogant symbolic – and sometimes literal – possession, and also shows the way in which godparentage and patronage shaped social networks and opportunities.[7]

These forcible baptisms marked the start of five centuries of ostensibly benevolent violence against Indigenous Americans, highlighting the problematic role of Christianity in the colonial world. While friars such as Las Casas were undoubtedly involved in campaigning for legal and practical protections for Native peoples, they were also irretrievably entangled with the 'civilising mission' that led to the extermination of Indigenous cultures and beliefs, stood complicit in the 'legal' trafficking of Native peoples, and held an unwavering conviction in their own 'sacred' mission that often led them to take brutal measures in their attempts to 'save' what they saw as Christian souls heading for damnation. Columbus's 'adoption' of Diego powerfully evokes the theft of Indigenous children across the centuries: from children torn from the arms of their enslaved mothers to the 'residential schools' where Native children were ripped away from their communities and cultures, with a view to 'civilising' and 'Christianising' them. The devastating legacy of these 'schools' in the United States and Canada – revealed in excoriating detail by the 2015 report of the Truth and Reconciliation Commission of Canada – has recently come to international attention, as the efforts of tribal groups to recover their ancestors have led to the discovery of the remains of thousands of Indigenous children in unmarked graves at Canadian sites alone, including Kamloops Indian Residential School, on the unceded lands of the Tk'emlúps te Secwépemc First Nation.[8]

*

---

* Colón was the Spanish for Columbus.

We know that the newly baptised Fernando, along with most of the other Taínos, set sail with Columbus on his second voyage. We have no way of being sure if Guacanagarí's representatives arrived home safely – the secretary to the Venetian ambassador suggests that 'only three survived; the others died because of the change of air' – but the 'alliance' tentatively established by their gift-giving certainly had not lasted. When Columbus returned to Hispaniola he found the settlement of La Navidad razed to the ground and the crew he had abandoned there dead due to infighting and Indigenous resistance. During this period, we find plenty of what Anna Brickhouse has called 'unsettlement' – the active thwarting of European colonisation – which is often overlooked in our tendency to focus on more 'successful' settlements.[9]

The recently baptised Juan remained in Spain as part of the royal household, for it seems that his namesake Prince John 'wanted him for himself'. Oviedo assures us that Juan was treated extremely well, taught in the ways of the faith, and given 'much love' by his royal patron. By the time Oviedo met him, Juan could speak Spanish fluently and was living as if he were the son of a leading Spanish gentleman. Two years later, he died.[10] In common with many Indigenous voyagers, Juan's life is obscure except for these few snippets. He appears as a bit-part character in Oviedo's account of Columbus's triumphal return, and becomes an object of Spanish paternalism and curiosity, before abruptly exiting the stage. We have no way of knowing how he died, but it was probably not of old age, as an elderly person was unlikely to have been selected to adorn the royal house as a courtier and curiosity. Juan's feelings about his fate also remain obscure – he was fortunate by the standards of some of his contemporaries, but he still perished far from his home and family. Nonetheless, like many Indigenous people, it seems Juan made the best of his situation, integrating into his adopted surroundings as best he could. This deft cultural adaptation, here only obliquely glimpsed, is something we will see in the lives of many Native people as they tried to navigate the turbulent waters of early encounter.

These first Indigenous voyagers were intended largely to satisfy

European curiosity and as involuntary interpreters – Columbus admits they were taken 'by force' – and Queen Isabella's immediate demand that they be freed suggests that this fact was recognised at the time. The boundary between enslavement, kidnapping, coercion, and persuasion was a porous one, and is often quite difficult for us to detect at this distance. And in one sense it is unimportant whether a person's forcible transportation was seen as slavery or some other kind of service. When you lose your will and liberty, does it matter whether you are technically a slave? There are many categories of dependence and coercion that overlap in this period, formal and informal, and though their definitions vary across time and space, they often made little difference to people's lived experience of oppression. But actually, for Indigenous people, as for everyone in the early modern world, legal status could be vital in shaping their lives and so – although the book will discuss many forms of coercion and violence that were suffered by Indigenous people as individuals and communities – this chapter will focus on people who were 'enslaved' through the system of chattel slavery, which treated people as the legal property of another person, deprived of all their personal and private rights.

Strange as it may seem to us, the legality of the slave trade itself was not in question. Enslaved people were part of life in the fifteenth century and Muslims, eastern Europeans, Africans and Canary Islanders were all among the people regularly sold in slave markets across Spain, Portugal and Italy. Even the 'Defender of the Indians', Bartolomé de Las Casas, originally advocated licensing the introduction of slaves from the African coast to ease the lot of the Indigenous islanders. This was a decision he was later to bitterly repent, and which has marred his legacy ever since. Las Casas was born and grew up in Seville in the early 1500s, where as many as one in ten of the population were enslaved people, mostly of African descent, who lived and worked in household and industrial roles as part of the local economy and society. This early domestic bondage had its own horrors, but the relatively small-scale trade within Europe was a pale foreshadowing of the monstrosity of the

Middle Passage. Immodestly writing of himself in the third person, Las Casas later wrote: 'the cleric, many years later, regretted the advice he gave the king on this matter – when he saw it proven that the enslavement of blacks was every bit as unjust as that of the Indians'. Once he realised the brutality of the transatlantic trade, the way it devastated families and destroyed communities, 'he would not have proposed it for all the world' because 'Africans were enslaved unjustly, tyrannically, right from the start, exactly as the Indians had been'. Las Casas was a man whose views feel sympathetic from our modern point of view, who believed in the equal value of all men before God (if not on earth), and came in his later life to the profound realisation that the Atlantic slave trade was 'brutality, theft, tyranny – nothing more'. But he was also a man of his time, and so even he did not denounce the condition of slavery itself, just the merciless transatlantic slave trade.[11]

So when Columbus arrived in the Americas, it was perhaps not surprising that one of the resources which caught his attention was the people themselves. Apparently inspired by the infamous Portuguese slaving fortress, São Jorge da Mina – which he had visited a decade earlier – Columbus viewed the Caribbean islands rapaciously. Of his first voyage, Columbus wrote to one of the investors that he could bring 'slaves as many as they shall order to be shipped'. In 1494, during his second voyage across the Atlantic, Columbus wrote to Spain for more ships and provisions, suggesting: 'We could pay for all that with slaves from among these cannibals, a people very savage and suitable for the purpose, and well made, and of very good intelligence.' A year later, he proposed to Ferdinand and Isabella that he should 'send all the slaves needed that they could sell'. Columbus had aggressive plans for expanding the transatlantic trade in stolen lives: 'if the information that I possess is correct, we could sell four thousand slaves who will be worth at the very least twenty *cuentos*'. This was a huge sum of money, which would have covered the cost of Columbus's first voyage ten times over, but Ferdinand and Isabella wavered.[12]

In the spring of 1495, Columbus sent to Spain around five hundred enslaved Taínos, captured after ferocious resistance from the Indigenous inhabitants of Hispaniola.* Their leader Caonabó – the 'highly esteemed' *cacique* of Maguana – had been transported himself, but died on the voyage, his body consigned to the Atlantic, with so many others. When the captive Taínos arrived, the monarchs were initially inclined to allow their sale. But, only four days later, they ordered the process to be suspended 'until we know whether we can sell them or not'. It is tempting to suggest that Ferdinand originally approved the sale, before being challenged by his wife, who persistently opposed the enslavement of her new vassals.† In 1499, infuriated by the constant stream of new 'slaves' arriving from the Caribbean, Isabella finally lost her temper with the Admiral: 'Who is this Columbus who dares to give out my vassals as slaves?' In 1500, perhaps prompted by the waves of enslaved people arriving from the Caribbean and the coast of Tierra Firme (the mainland), Isabella finally ended her legal vacillations, declaring the Indigenous peoples of the 'new lands' to be free subjects of the Spanish Crown.[13]

While we may see this as empty rhetoric, the fact that Indigenous people were seen as 'vassals' by Isabella is an important clue to the way they were viewed and treated in the early colonial world. One of the first things that Ferdinand and Isabella did, after hearing of Columbus's 'discoveries' was to ask Pope Alexander VI to confirm their rights to the 'new lands'. In response, Alexander – a Borgia pope born in Aragon, and widely suspected of being sympathetic to the Spanish – issued the bull of *inter caetera*. This wide-ranging declaration granted to the 'true Catholic kings' the rights to all the 'islands and mainlands found and to be found, discovered and to

---

* This is often called a 'rebellion', but that assumes legitimate Spanish authority on the islands, and rather obscures the fact that the Taínos were resisting Spanish invasion and mistreatment.

† The eventual fate of these Taínos, who fought the Spanish invaders and were seized and transported, is obscure, but it seems that they filtered into the wider community, despite the Crown's initial opposition. Fifty were sold as galley slaves, and one – (re)named Francisco – was sold to a widow in Seville two years later at a cost of 3000 *maravedís*. You have to wonder how Francisco came to be possessed by the two Genoese mariners who traded him.

be discovered' west of a north-to-south line drawn one hundred leagues west of the Azores and Cape Verde.[14] The condition of this astonishing grant, which entirely ignored the authority of Indigenous rulers unless they happened to be Christian, was that they should evangelise the population.* This set the stage for the intricate dance conducted by Spain in the following years, as the Crown and its agents attempted to balance the extraction of profit with their obligation to convert the inhabitants of the Americas to Christianity. Isabella's exclamation acknowledges that these people are not merely people to be exploited, but 'vassals': subjects, whom the Crown bore a responsibility to teach and protect. But how were these people to be brought to knowledge of the Faith, and how far did the Crown's authority extend over them? What kind of people were these? Were they fully human? And, if so, by what rights did the Spanish impose their authority?

These were the sort of questions that exercised the Crown, the Church and the colonisers as they confronted the Americas. The legal status of Indigenous peoples was a matter of incessant debate in Spain during the early years of empire, as scholars, theologians, lawyers and politicians tried to decide whether it was legal to go to war to impose Christianity. Law and practice varied constantly throughout this period until, in 1550–1, Charles V suspended all further expeditions and ordered a council of legal and theological experts to gather at Valladolid and hear expert testimony for and against spreading Christianity in the Americas through force. It is actually remarkable that a European power in this period might pause to consider whether their actions overseas were legal and just, but that is exactly what Charles V did. While these questions may seem esoteric to us now – theoretical debates intended to cast

---

*   The Portuguese had received a similar bull (*Romanus Pontifex*) in 1455, granting them a monopoly on African trade and exploration. They felt *Inter Caetera* potentially infringed on their rights to the east and so, in 1494, Spain and Portugal signed the Treaty of Tordesillas, which nudged the line of demarcation to the west. Spain were convinced the treaty was to their advantage until they realised that they had inadvertently chopped off a large, wealthy, curve of the continent: Brazil.

a veneer of legitimacy over the brutal invasion and suppression of Mesoamerican and Caribbean cultures – they actually possessed powerful significance, not only in principle, but also in reality.

As 'vassals' of the Crown,* Indigenous people were theoretically protected from arbitrary enslavement, just as any Spanish citizen would be, but there were three important exceptions to the royal prohibition on slavery in the early years of colonisation. Indigenous people could be enslaved if they were 'cannibals'; had been captured in a 'just war';† or, as mentioned earlier, if they were subject to *rescate* ('ransom' from a worse fate, like human sacrifice, or being enslaved to a non-Christian). Significantly, also, only those from Spanish territories were protected by their 'vassal' status, meaning that anyone from beyond their borders (or whom the slaver claimed was from elsewhere) could be enslaved. These loopholes in the law meant that the debate over the subjection of Indigenous peoples was mainly focused not on whether slavery was wrong, but in what circumstances people had been, or could be, legally enslaved.

It is important to challenge a general preconception that Indigenous peoples were unaffected and unaware of these discussions about their lives. In fact – as we shall see – thousands of Native people, enslaved through both 'just' and 'unjust' causes, were keen to exploit these debates and recover their freedom when the opportunity presented itself. So we see Indigenous people in court, pleading for their release from illegal bondage: 'I am a free man of my nation and a rational son of free men', insisted the Mexican,‡ Martín, in 1537, when he petitioned the Crown to regain his

---

* Remember this is the Spanish legal perspective. Many Indigenous rulers would have had something to say about the idea that their authority had been usurped by a distant emperor.

† But what made a war 'just'? This is obviously the critical question, and one which exercised many of the best minds of the day. For them, it was an intellectual, legal and theological exercise. For Indigenous peoples, it was the difference between freedom and bondage.

‡ I will use modern regional identifiers such as 'Mexican' only for clarity, or when I have been unable to find out the specific identities of the travellers in question.

freedom.[15] Nahua people had long traditions of litigation and record keeping, and Indigenous people quickly adapted their experience to Spanish formulas, often with the assistance of religious men and lawyers, who were able to help them navigate the demands of the legal system. In theory, Indigenous people were offered many potential protections under Spanish law; it was just a question of how and if they could access them.

A court record from 12 June 1543 shows the lawyer Gregorio López securing the freedom of three Mexicans in Seville, who were to be allowed to return to New Spain 'on the first fleet'. Andrés and Magdalena were married and had somehow miraculously been able to stay together and keep their three-year-old daughter Juanica with them. The third adult complainant, Alvaro, was not so lucky: his wife Teresa had died on the voyage, leaving him widowed. Alvaro's experience is sadly typical. Deaths were frequent in the early years, enslaved people suffering not only from the usual issues of over-crowding and poor nutrition, but also from lack of immunity to European diseases. Suicide was common, and many Native people, separated from families and homelands, cast themselves overboard in despair rather than give up their liberty and face enslavement in a strange land. A report of 1544 describes mothers throwing themselves into the sea in anguish at being separated from their small children.[16] The agonies of enslavement speak across the centuries.

Andrés Reséndez has estimated that between 2.4 million and 4.9 million Native Americans were enslaved between 1492 and 1900. Most of these enslaved people were traded within the Americas and Caribbean, rather than shipped overseas, but tens of thousands – maybe hundreds of thousands – of 'indios' were also sold, legally and illegally, in the slave markets of Europe during the sixteenth century. Yet, with the exception of Andrés Reséndez's groundbreaking book *The Other Slavery*, the idea of Indigenous Americans as enslaved people barely seems to have touched the popular imagination.* Important new scholarship has started to

---

* Reséndez's title brilliantly, and deliberately, evokes the idea that this was both

reveal the extent of Indigenous enslavement, but it still rarely features as part of wider histories of Europe and the Americas, and studies of global slavery revolve almost exclusively around African and African-descended victims. The claim that America was built on stolen Black bodies and Native land is ubiquitous. And while this neat model is literally true, it effaces the many Native people whose lives and labour were also stolen by Europeans and the shared experiences of Indigenous and African peoples in the early colonial world.

Reséndez's painstaking research suggests that between one and two million Native people were enslaved prior to 1600, during the period of Iberian Atlantic dominance, many of whom found themselves transported to Europe.[17] The historian Nancy van Deusen, whose work has shed light on the hidden lives of enslaved *indios* in sixteenth-century Spain, conservatively estimates that 650,000 Indigenous people were forcibly transported to foreign lands during this period.[18] About 300,000 Africans crossed the Atlantic in the same period, around 2 per cent of the estimated twelve million victims of the infamous Triangle Trade which took place between 1492 and c.1838.[19] These figures fail to capture the harrowing reality of enslavement, but they do allow us to imagine the sixteenth century a little differently. The same ships that ploughed westwards, crammed with abducted Africans, very likely also plied their miserable trade east: forcibly displanting Indigenous people to Europe, where most would join the thousands of enslaved people of African descent already working and living in the Iberian Peninsula. The legacy of Indigenous enslavement is not visible to us in the same way as the global Black diaspora and its many vibrant cultures, the progeny of the millions of Africans and people of African descent who were forcibly scattered across the world. Many Europeans may be descended from distant Indigenous ancestors,* especially

---

'other' than African slavery and also another type of slavery, one encompassing many types of forced labour, similar to present-day forms of coercion: the 'new slavery'.

* Though an ancestry test will tell you absolutely nothing useful about it.

in Spain and Portugal, but their legacy – as we will see – is more intangible, more inextricable, and too often rendered silent. The devastation of Indigenous communities by disease and violence, combined with prohibitions on travel and forced labour, gradually drove down Native enslavement (or at least drove it out of the records) and Indigenous people disappeared into the mixed Iberian community of Mediterranean peoples, North African Muslims, and other peoples from across the Holy Roman Empire. They were there. We just have to look harder to find them.

Less than a decade after Europeans first laid claim to Indigenous soil, and despite royal decrees against Native slavery and exploitation, a stream of kidnapped Indigenous Americans was crossing the Atlantic to serve as enslaved people and servants, as well as in other pernicious forms of forced labour such as *encomienda*: bondage by another name, against which the subject had very little recourse.[20]

Columbus himself seized and forcibly transported between 3000 and 6000 Caribbean men, women and children to Europe, becoming one of the largest single traders of enslaved Native Americans, and the surviving sources paint a picture of shipments of Indigenous people arriving in Europe in most years, many of whom were destined for domestic service. Unlike the African trade, most Indigenous people transported across the Atlantic into slavery were women and children, chosen for their greater adaptability, vulnerability and sexual availability. These household servants became a part of Spanish society, and baptismal records show *indios* appearing as a significant minority in sixteenth-century Spain, particularly in regions closely linked to Atlantic networks, especially Seville, but also Extremadura and the west of Andalucía.[21]

Sending dozens of Caribbean people to Spain in 1494, Columbus wrote that they could 'take many of the males every year and an infinite number of women'. In his appraisal, each Native person was 'worth more than three black slaves from Guinea in strength and ingenuity', and Columbus's enterprise quickly grew. Only a year later, in February 1495, according to Michele da Cuneo, a Genoese volunteer on the second voyage, Columbus captured around 1600

Macorix-speaking people from eastern Hispaniola, selecting 550 of 'the best males and females' to send to the slave markets of southern Spain. Afflicted by the harsh conditions of the winter Atlantic, and crushed into four small caravels with inadequate sustenance, the Taínos were seriously weakened, and around two hundred of the islanders died 'because they were not used to the cold weather' (and presumably were not provided with adequate shelter or warmth). 'We cast their bodies into the sea', wrote Cuneo without a shred of compassion.[22]

Columbus's actions set an awful precedent for numerous explorers, opportunists and raiders in the following years. Two of his companions on the early voyages quickly followed their admiral's example and led their own expeditions. In 1499, Alonso de Ojeda – a man famed for being tiny but brutal – was commissioned to lead a voyage to what he named 'Venezuela', meaning 'Little Venice', in reference to the houses he saw perched on stilts.* The expedition proved a financial disappointment, so Ojeda set about recouping his investors' costs through kidnapping the locals. From Lake Maracaibo, he 'obtained some Indian women of notable beauty and disposition', according to the letters of the navigator and self-publicist Amerigo Vespucci.† Returning home via the Bahamas, where they 'violently seized 222 persons for slaves', Ojeda's crew landed in Cádiz in June 1500, and 'sold many of the 200 slaves that arrived, the rest having died on the voyage'. With only about one in six of his original crew still alive, the enterprise was a flop: his crew could have made more money working in Spain.[23] This was presumably little comfort to the Indigenous Lucayans who found themselves forced into a life of servitude in a strange land.

That same year Vincente Yáñez Pinzón, who captained the *Niña* on Columbus's first voyage, returned to Spain with thirty-six inhabitants of the Amazon region, seized during another unprofitable

---

* Although one of his crew later claimed that the name actually came from an Indigenous group called the 'Veneciuela'.

† You may have noticed that the word 'obtained' is doing a lot of work here. Were the women given to him? Abducted from their homes? Seized in battle?

trip. Only twenty survived the crossing. The members of Columbus's crew were striking out on their own, and Indigenous people were vital to their enterprise. In 1501, an intriguing snippet in the archives reveals Pinzón fighting (successfully) for the return of an Indigenous 'slave' who was 'very necessary' because he spoke good Spanish. It seems that Pinzón had at some point promised to give the mayor of Palos an '*indio* slave' – perhaps to pay a debt, as his financial problems were notorious – but objected when the mayor took a fancy to his valuable translator.[24]

In the decades after first contact in particular, Native people were vulnerable to abduction and enslavement by Europeans, and economic concerns were in tension with humanitarian ones. From 1503, a series of decrees allowed the enslavement of the so-called *indios caribes* ('man-eating Indians'), which put the inhabitants of much of the eastern Caribbean under threat.[25] In 1504, Ojeda's pilot, Juan de la Cosa,* mercilessly enslaved 600 supposedly 'cannibal' men, women and children from the island of Codego, near what is now Cartagena. Despite these early excesses, Isabella's restraining influence became most obvious after her death in 1504, as her husband Ferdinand swiftly expanded the trade in Indigenous lives. He authorised the enslavement of people from what were termed 'useless islands', such as the Lucayas, widening the scope of supposedly 'Carib' lands. In 1511, most of what we know as the Lesser Antilles were arbitrarily declared as Carib, and therefore 'cannibal'.[26] Those who wish to diminish the brutality of colonisation frequently point to legislation which theoretically prohibited enslavement of Indigenous peoples, but the reality was far removed from the ideal as legal definitions were stretched to breaking point by rapacious traffickers.

Even our limited records show that Indigenous people quickly became ubiquitous among the enslaved people of all backgrounds

---

* Juan de la Cosa is usually remembered as a navigator and cartographer: the first man to make a European map showing the Americas. Like many of his contemporaries, his biography should also read 'enslaver'.

who were to be found throughout the Iberian peninsula, from a sweep of nations from North Africa to Eastern Europe. The Portuguese Crown, much less reticent than the Spanish, jumped on the opportunity to expand on their African enterprise and began to grant contracts to enslavers from almost the moment they arrived on the coast of what swiftly became known as 'the Land of Brazil' after the dense, russet wood that formed its principal export. Indigenous people from the region first appear in the records of transatlantic slavery in 1502, when the Crown granted Fernâo de Noronha and other 'new Christians' (converted Jews) a contract to ship brazilwood, with the trade in human lives appearing as merely a subclause. Four ships returned crammed with both in 1504. Since the profit margin on brazilwood (what is called in the Tupi language *ibirapitanga*, 'red wood') was not large, the ability to kidnap local people was an attractive bonus for avaricious captains. This was no *ad hoc* arrangement. It was happening regularly and with official consent.[27]

Damiáo de Góis, the official chronicler of King Manuel of Portugal, records a visit to court in 1513 by Brazilian men, brought by the merchant Jorge Lopes Bixorda. 'They came dressed in feathers, with their faces, lips, noses and ears full of thick pendants', and the king asked them some questions through a Portuguese interpreter. Each carried a bow and reed arrows made with colourful parrot feathers, tipped with wood and fishbone, 'so strong that they pierced a plank'. The men demonstrated their remarkable skill by shooting small chunks of cork bobbing past in the river, never missing a shot and amazing the court. 'I was there when this happened!', boasted de Góis.[28]

So entwined was slavery with the Portuguese project that São Vicente, their first stable settlement, quickly became known as Porto dos Escravos (Port of Slaves). In 1515, a pamphlet publicising an expedition to Brazil boasted that the ship had returned with the hold full of brazilwood and the deck covered with 'the boys and girls we bought. They cost the Portuguese little, for the most part they were given willingly, because the people there think that their children are going to the Promised Land'. Whether this is tragically

true, or ruthless dishonesty, Guaraní children were being shipped
to Portugal from their relatively peaceful, farming communities in
the forested coasts of southern Brazil and present-day Paraguay,
their bodies traded as property, or treated as 'curiosities'. In 1526, the
Spanish captain Diego García complained that Sebastian Cabot (son
of John) had ruined the productive and peaceful conditions among
these 'good Indians'. This interloper had repaid kind treatment by
the locals, when his crew were starving to death, by kidnapping four
sons of the local lords and carrying them off to Spain, where three
of them went to a senior official, probably to serve in his household
as objects of curiosity.[29]

To the north of the Guaraní lived the Tupinambá, who gained
a ferocious reputation as 'cannibals', thanks to the German Hans
Staden, who wrote a sensational account of his time as a captive
among them. Unlike the urban civilisations of Central America,
or the small settlements of the Caribbean, the mobile Tupi peoples
lived through skilled hunting and slash-and-burn agriculture. Num-
bering maybe a million people before disease and violence shattered
their lives, they were united by their language, but lived in hundreds
of independent communities. These courageous warriors and expert
archers effectively resisted European incursions in many places at
first. Indigenous people shipped into bondage by the Portuguese
were often 'ransomed' (*resgate*) rather than seized under 'just war'
claims in the early years. Prisoners of war were swapped for European commodities like axes and scissors. Sometimes this may have
literally 'rescued' captives from sacrifice and cannibalism,* only to
plunge them into the horrors of transportation and brutal bondage
far away from everything familiar.

From the mid 1530s, the Portuguese Crown authorised the
transportation of around 200 Tupi each year, meaning that more
than 3000 people were shipped to Europe via this route alone over
the next fifteen years. Until 1570, when the Crown began to regulate

---

* Given the religious and social significance of ritual execution in Tupi culture,
this would not necessarily have been welcomed by either captor or captive, who
both gave up significant prestige in avoiding sacrifice.

the trade in Indigenous people, every letter granting royal authority to a captain for his expedition came with permission to bring at least twenty-four enslaved people into Portugal annually; in 1524 Pero Lopes de Souza was allowed to import thirty-nine Indigenous Brazilians tax free. In 1526, the Portuguese governor of Brazil, Pero Capico, was permitted to retire from his post, and bring home with him 'all the pieces of slaves and *fazendas* [plantations, presumably their profits] that he had'. The value of these enslaved people and estates was expected to be so great that he was ordered to march directly to the Casa da Índia to pay the relevant taxes as soon as he returned.[30]

In 1511, the surviving records show that the Portuguese ship the *Bertoa* returned to Lisbon with 125 tons of logs, plus parrots and other novelties, including thirty-five Tamoio people, almost as many as the crew of thirty-six which manned the bulging *náo*. More than half of the people enslaved were children, the vast majority of whom (sixteen in all) were girls, and their distribution among the crew after landing gives us a depressing insight into the preferences of Portuguese enslavers, with all the senior men electing to take children, especially girls, as their share. The exploitation of girls and women is a pernicious, and often concealed, aspect of colonial encounter, where the issue of consent was frequently elided with the use of terms such as 'wives'.[31]

Columbus's second voyage is notorious for the detailed account of the rape on an Indigenous Caribbean woman by his friend, the Genoese Michele da Cuneo. His shocking report leaves nothing to the imagination and shows all too clearly the dispassionate entitlement with which Indigenous peoples were viewed by Europeans:

> While I was in the boat I laid my hands on a gorgeous Cannibal woman whom the lord admiral granted me; when I had her in my quarters, naked, as is their custom, I felt a craving to sport with her. When I tried to satisfy my craving, she, wanting none of it, gave me such a treatment with her nails that at that point I wished I had never started. At this, to tell you how it all ended,

I got hold of a rope and thrashed her so thoroughly that she raised unheard-of cries that you would never believe. Finally we were of such accord that, in the act, I can tell you, she seemed to have been trained in a school of harlots.[32]

The monstrosity of enslavement, of taking another's body and treating it as your possession, is laid bare in Cuneo's letter. It is hard to imagine the response of the Carib woman to such violence, but her defiance is clear: she fought him for the right to her body.

Children were sadly easier to seize and control, appealing for their youth, attractiveness and vulnerability – a fashionable 'curiosity' that bestowed an exotic air on those who claimed to own them. Enslaved people who served in homes tended to be better fed and clothed than those who laboured in fields, but their expensive vestments would have been no protection from the violence and sexual predations of their owners. A child alone, in a strange country with a foreign language, would have been at the mercy of those they encountered. If they were fortunate, they might be kept together with a compatriot, or fall in with a kind ally in the household. If not, they could easily have been persecuted by other servants, let alone the family. Perhaps some young people found it easier to accept their new lives than those who were ripped away from spouses and children, but the loneliness for all must have been acute.

We do not know whether the crew of the *Bertoa* took the Tupi home or sold them for a profit, but each would have been first inspected and registered by an official from the Casa dos Escravos de Lisboa (Lisbon Slave House) and assigned a value to determine the appropriate import taxes. (A similar system applied in Seville, where any import or purchase of enslaved people had to be registered to ensure the appropriate customs and sales taxes were paid.)[33] Boys and girls, men and women, were reduced to property, their humanity stripped away and their worth determined by age, sex, health and appearance. Thousands of Native people passed through this brutal system, shackled alongside the mass of West Africans who were dragged to Lisbon each year, before being flung across Europe and the Atlantic. Lisbon was already a hub for the grim trade in human lives, and – as the Spanish tightened their restrictions on Native bondage – so the Portuguese tightened their grip on the trade in Indigenous enslaved people, becoming a conduit for the booming illegal traffic in enslaved people from Mesoamerica and the Caribbean.

At the turn of the sixteenth century, Lisbon was a thriving port and it is all but certain that Tupi people were among the diverse throng living and working in the city. Several of the *Bertoa*'s crew lived in Alfama, a maze of streets on the slope above the king's new waterfront palace, and they may have chosen to keep some of the Tamoio people on as labourers, attendants, or translators. Its Islamic origins resonant in the name (from the Arabic *Al-hammah*, the 'hot springs' in the area), Alfama is now an atmospheric labyrinth of alleys and steps which attracts tourists who want to experience 'old Lisbon'. It was home to North Africans and converted Jews – forced to abandon their religion in 1497 – as well as hundreds of Black Africans, enslaved from many different nations, who made up about 10 per cent of the city's population at that time.

The vibrant neighbourhood is captured in an anonymous Flemish painting from the mid-1500s, crammed with people of all colours hauling, selling, serving, labouring, drinking, kissing, strolling, dancing, and being dragged away. To this dynamic portrait, which shows Black Africans interwoven in Portuguese society, as elite horsemen, performers, servants and tradespeople, we should mentally add the Indigenous Tupi and Guaraní who we know frequented this square, which lay on the waterfront below the Alfama. The 'King's Fountain' at the heart of the painting was Lisbon's main water source, and so Native people would have been among those collecting the water, renowned for its purity and freshness. In 1517 the fountain in the picture was covered with an attractive shady porch, and from 1551 the press of water-sellers, servants and thirsty poor were controlled by restrictions on who could use each of the curving bronze spouts. Native people, both free and enslaved, were common enough in the city that they were assigned to share two spouts with Black and '*mulatta*'* women.[34]

We cannot say with certainty how many Indigenous people were trafficked through Lisbon, likely a few hundred each year, judging by the ships' licences and the regularity with which Indigenous claimants in Spain argued that they had been illegally traded into slavery through Lisbon and should be freed. In Brazil, the relentless European demand for labour thrust tens of thousands of Indigenous people into slavery and forced labour, relatively few of whom made their way across the Atlantic. But among the estimated two thousand captives who trudged to the auction blocks of the Casa dos Escravos in Lisbon each year were undoubtedly a number of Indigenous people, from as early as 1501, when the Portuguese navigator Gaspar Corte Real kidnapped and transported fifty-seven men, women and children, probably from the coast of what is now Maine.[35]

The French and British were also major intercolonial traders in enslaved Native peoples in later years, but their numbers were small in the sixteenth century.[36] The Iberian peninsula, on the other hand, quickly saw an influx of enslaved Indigenous people, compelled to labour in homes and businesses across the region. Fragments of their lives become increasingly visible to us after the first frenzy of largely unbridled violence and arbitrary enslavement subsided and enslaved people realised their ability to challenge their oppressors through the courts.

This resistance – a refusal to accept the loss of liberty and identity – becomes increasingly evident in our sources as the fight for Indigenous rights and recognition gained traction in religious, intellectual and royal circles. 'Those with whom Americo [Amerigo] went had neither just cause nor right to make war on the natives of those islands and carry them off as slaves, without having received any injury from them, nor the slightest offence', wrote Bartolomé de Las Casas of Amerigo Vespucci's (possibly invented) first voyage to the Americas. In 1542, partly as a result of Las Casas's tireless

---

* Now a racial slur, '*mulatto*' at this time referred to someone of mixed African and white ancestry.

campaigning, the 'New Laws . . . for the good treatment and preservation of the *indios*' were issued. These closed the existing loopholes and made it theoretically illegal to enslave Indigenous people under any circumstances, as well as heavily restricting their use as workers. It is common to claim that all this had no tangible impact on the lives of Indigenous people; that they remained oppressed and enslaved; and that these debates were simply the philosophical writhings of a society concerned to legitimate oppression. And it is true that decrees such as the New Laws did not ensure Native rights, nor transform Indigenous people's circumstances. Just war remained a pretext for enslavement, and the outcry from Spanish colonists severely weakened the application of the laws in the Americas,* but their mere existence (albeit in watered-down form) gave enslaved people the ammunition to fight for their liberty. They were wrestling an unfair, unreasonable system, but fight they did, and it is in those struggles that Indigenous people often appear most clearly to us.

After 1542, hundreds of Indigenous people from across Spain appear in the archives appealing for their freedom. Perhaps surprisingly to us, the Spanish Crown was proactive in trying to make sure that fledgling Christians were not held in bondage, instructing that people holding Indigenous 'slaves' should be inspected, and circulating decrees of freedom when they became aware of enslaved *indios*. Many of the complainants were supported by Gregorio López, a jurist and royal official who was paid by the Crown to conduct an 'inspection' of enslaved *indios* in Seville in 1543, with a view to ensuring that none were held illegally. The records of such appeals offer us a window onto the complex, diverse, and often horrifying experiences of Indigenous people who were enslaved. They provide a rare chance to glimpse their lives and to hear their voices, though at times muffled by legal formulas.[37] Through these

---

* The conquistador Gonzalo Pizarro – brother of the famous 'conqueror of the Inkas', Francisco – decapitated the Viceroy of Peru and carried his head around as a trophy. The colonists were really quite piqued at losing their rights to exploit Indigenous peoples.

documents, we can see Indigenous people in Europe struggling to cope with their dislocation and retain emotional bonds with their homelands, all while trying to find a place within European culture.

After the New Laws were issued, a young Guatemalan couple living in Ciudad Rodrigo in western Spain – Francisco and Juana – pleaded for their freedom on the grounds that they had been illegally enslaved as children. In 1545, following a royal order, Francisco had been declared free by the local *corregidor* (magistrate), but his enslaver Cristóbal de Cueto was refusing to accept the situation. According to a decree of 1534, only boys over fourteen years old could be seized as prisoners in a 'just war'. Like many children, Francisco had been enslaved and branded as an enemy combatant. Only around eighteen or twenty at the time of the court case, Francisco 'came to this land when he was ten or eleven years old' and 'very young and small', according to his witnesses. Barely an adolescent when he was taken captive, the young man bore the signs of the royal brand on his face. But although owners frequently argued that a brand was conclusive proof of legal ownership, in this case it proved the opposite, argued his lawyer Lope de Valderrama – the boy had been much too young for the Crown to have allowed his enslavement at the time he was brought to Spain. Juana too was only a young girl, so should clearly be a free woman under the law. Francisco and Juana, with the help of their scrupulous advocate, managed to elude the various legal snares thrown out by their captor, and were declared free on 13 May 1549. Wasting no time, they appealed to the Crown to pay their passage home, and that summer Francisco, his wife Juana, and their daughter, took ship at the Crown's expense, and vanish from the historical record.[38] Assuming they survived the journey, it must have been quite a shock for the little family to return 'home', to a place they had known only as children. During their time away, the great *cocoliztli**

---

* A Nahuatl word usually translated as 'pestilence', but which actually suggests pustules. It may have been smallpox, or perhaps a form of typhoid-like enteric fever.

epidemic had swept the region, killing millions of people. This was one of the most catastrophic plagues in history, wiping out maybe half of the remaining population, so – even if they made their way back home – Francisco and Juana would have found their families and communities desolated.

Disease was compounded by the violence of colonialism as Indigenous peoples, often displaced and herded into smaller settlements to ease the 'civilising' process, found themselves suffering famine and isolation from traditional networks of support. In some regions, including the densely populated Mesoamerican lowlands, the death rate may have been as high as 90 per cent by 1600. The devastation was unimaginable. Nahua testimonies, recorded by the Franciscan friar Bernardino de Sahagún in the mid 1500s, paint a graphic picture of the suffering:

Before the Spaniards appeared to us, first an epidemic broke out, a sickness of pustules. It began in Tepeilhuitl. Large bumps spread on people; some were entirely covered. They spread everywhere, on the face, the head, the chest, etc. [The disease] brought great desolation; a great many died of it. They could no longer walk about, but lay in their dwellings and sleeping places, no longer able to move or stir. They were unable to change position, to stretch out on their sides or face down, or raise their heads. And when they made a motion, they called out loudly. The pustules that covered people caused great desolation; very many people died of them, and many just starved to death; starvation reigned, and no one took care of others any longer.

The stories of our Indigenous travellers must be imagined against this backdrop: of separation, suffering and death. All would have seen horrors and sadness, and even survivors would often have borne the physical scars of these ordeals. It is impossible to understand Indigenous histories without recognising the calamitous repercussions of the epidemics, which – along with violence, enslavement, famine, forced labour, displacement, and the utter devastation of communities – led to a population collapse so precipitous that it is widely regarded by living Indigenous peoples as a genocide.[39]

For families like Juana and Francisco, freed along with their small daughter, liberation from enslavement on foreign shores meant a return to a homeland that had become equally alien. Was there a joyful reunion with their families, an oasis in this desert of grief? We will never know. But we do know that many enslaved Indigenous people chose to take up the Crown's standing offer to pay for their voyage home, without knowing what they might find. Other freed people made a different choice, and responses to enslavement naturally varied according to circumstances, personality and possibilities. Some people fought against their captivity, struggling to regain their freedom and return to the Americas. Others, kidnapped and often branded as children, had little memory of their families and homelands. For them, Europe had become home, and many formerly enslaved people chose to continue as paid workers for their masters even after being freed.[40]

We might wonder what it was like for Francisco, returning to life as a free man in Guatemala, but bearing the scars of enslavement on his cheek. Would he have burned with embarrassment at his disfigurement? How often would he have been asked to prove his free status, with the mark of ownership stamped upon his face? Or were brands and other scars – from diseases like smallpox and measles, or from the everyday violence of colonialism – so common that his scars were simply mundane? Thousands of Indigenous people bore the stains of bondage on their bodies, their skin seared with glowing metal to mark their 'legal' enslavement, and the usurpation of their liberty.

Exactly what the brands looked like, and where they were placed, could immediately tell a lot about the journey of an enslaved person. Royal officials, and those who wanted to claim royal authority, often used a 'G' for *guerra* (war), meaning the victim was enslaved in a 'just war'. 'R' indicated *rescate* (rescue or ransom) for people who were already captives or enslaved. Initials were also frequently burned into the skin, etching the name of the enslaver onto his or her property. In July 1511, King Ferdinand had declared that enslaved people imported to Hispaniola from other Caribbean islands such as the Lucayas should be branded on the legs to distinguish them from the supposedly 'free' Taíno people. Branding was so appallingly common that there are even records of people asking to be marked with the sign of their current 'owner' because they were afraid of being kidnapped and sold on.[41]

So accepted was branding that, much like the debate over slavery, what we see in the courts are not disputes about whether a person should have been horrifyingly maimed or not, but over whether it was done legally. Branding *indios* in Castile was illegal and subject to heavy fines, but it seems that, even when their bodies were their own, Indigenous people were not entitled to expect their skin to be unscathed. Barbola – the daughter of Felipa, an Indigenous woman of debated ancestry whose case has been sensitively disentangled by Nancy van Deusen – told a court how her 'master' had ordered her branded by a barber. Showing her cheeks, disfigured with the words 'slave of the Jurado Diego López of Seville', Barbola named the perpetrator of this sickening crime as 'the son of Castroverde who lives in Alfalfa' and asked 'the judges to order them to be apprehended, jailed and punished for the branding and because I am a free woman'. López tried to defend the act by claiming it was the norm, and that it really didn't matter because Barbola had been branded before, but fortunately the judges disagreed. Barbola was declared a free woman and awarded 10,000 *maravedís* compensation (about enough to meagrely supply a household for a year) from the 30,000-*maravedí* fine imposed on her former enslaver.[42]

The scars of enslavement also played an obtrusive part in the life of a young Mexican (likely Nahua) known as Martín, whose appeal for freedom in 1536 offers us a harrowing insight into the precarious nature of life in the early colonial world. Martín testified that he was a boy of only around nine or ten when a royal *factor* (a sort of treasury official) called Gonzalo de Salazar came to his village of Tenayucan, near Mexico City, asking if there were any young men who would like to become a page. Martín and his witnesses emphasised that at this time he was 'free by birth', not branded in any way, and that his people were 'free of all service and were not slaves'.[43] Salazar is a notorious figure in the history of New Spain, a rival of Cortés who usurped government in the mid 1520s and ruled tyrannically and voraciously, but this likely seemed a respectable opportunity for Martín, and so his family and the elders of the village agreed that he should enter Salazar's service.

Events then took a shocking turn when the ruthless Salazar ordered the young man to be branded on the face. Body modification was quite common among Nahua people. Most people had elaborate ear piercings, and boys were given lip plugs that became part of their warrior adornment as they got older. Scars on the chest and hip were used to mark out boys for priesthood, and adults' bodies would have been littered with small scars from bloodletting ceremonies. During Izcalli, the last month of the Aztec-Mexica ritual calendar, men made small burns on the wrist in honour of the Fire Drill constellation and Xiuhtecuhtli, the fire god, their bodies becoming a site for the kindling of fire and rebirth.[44] For Martín's people, scarification indicated maturity and religious conviction. The forcible branding, marking him as a commodity, was an extreme violation of his person and spirit, and would have been entirely alien to his view of the world (although it's possible he may have witnessed such assaults on other Indigenous people enslaved after the fall of Tenochtitlan).

For a time, the young Nahua served as a translator in Cortés's household, but when his tyrannical master was exiled to Spain (at least temporarily), Martín found himself dragged across the Atlantic, likely as one of the thousands of *criados*, unnamed 'dependants', who were licensed to accompany prominent Spaniards to the peninsula. (These could be anyone from family members to enslaved people.) Martín spent five or six years labouring in various households in the southern Spanish cities of Segovia, Seville and Granada, before lodging a plea for his freedom in 1536. For three years or so, Martín worked in the home of Pedro de Villate, a canon of the cathedral in Granada, which was under construction in the shadow of the famous Alhambra palace, where Columbus had been granted royal permission for his 1492 expedition. Martín would not have been particularly noticeable among the mixed community treading the steep, labyrinthine streets of Granada, a city with a large population of *moriscos* (converted Muslims). Like most Indigenous workers and enslaved people in the peninsula, Martín was a domestic servant, forming part of a diverse household, and not obviously discriminated against any more than the rest of Spain's toiling masses. When the canon died, Martín was entrusted to his brother, Diego de Villate, who lived in Segovia, around three hundred miles to the north, showing both his tremendous mobility, and how dependent it was on the vagaries of circumstance.

We know very little about Martín's life in Segovia, except that he had been sent there along with some of Salazar's other dependants, possibly fellow Mexicans. Here, Martín lived and worked alongside many other people 'as a free person' and it seems he was reasonably content in his lot. But the instability of life for such Indigenous dependants was thrown into sharp relief when his new master also died. A few months later, the tyrannical Salazar returned and 'took me to his house and tried to make me serve as a slave', even though, as Martín pleaded, he had done nothing to merit the loss of his liberty. His case reveals the porous boundaries between different types of coercion and how people experienced them. Although Martín was treated as enslaved for much of his life, it was only when the brutal Salazar attempted to wrench him back into service that the young man sought to assert his status in the courts: 'I want to be free', he declared. Perhaps Martín had learned more about his rights from other Native people in Segovia, or been encouraged to appeal by the community he found there. Or perhaps he found the prospect of returning to Salazar's household simply too horrifying to contemplate; he would certainly have had good reason. Salazar was furious when Martín lodged his appeal for freedom with the royal courts, lashing out with threats and violence. 'He hit me and hit my head into a wall and if it wasn't for some men and women who took me away he would have killed me . . . I ask and supplicate Your Highness to take me away from his power and put me in a safe place where he cannot hurt me, while the case is decided', begged Martín. In this case, his request was granted.

Salazar, while agreeing outwardly to comply with the demands of the court, fought furiously to retain the person he regarded as his property. He claimed that Martín was legally enslaved through the process of *rescate* (rescue), which is why he was branded on the face with a 'V' for 'Vaca', the name of the man who had 'rescued' Martín. (In reality, it seems Vaca was simply the thug who branded him.) Martín was lucky really, claimed Salazar, as he had treated Martín well, buying him 'good clothes like a free person' and only expecting him to do personal services. Much of Salazar's case rested on two things: Martín's brand, and the fact that Salazar had been able to 'dispose' of him as he liked, which speaks to how much servants were at the whim of their masters, especially in a foreign country. Whether enslaved or not, stability was hard to come by. Despite legal provisions intended to protect them, Indigenous people often struggled to escape the power of unscrupulous masters and mistresses.

Martín, having managed to escape Salazar's grasp, was determined to cling onto the few assets he had managed to acquire during his service, and complained bitterly that the *factor* had appropriated his clothes. Salazar, furious at being asked to forgo items he believed were his property, nonetheless handed them over to the courts and on 4 September 1536, we have a detailed list of the garments received by the lawyer: a plain black wool cape and tunic, two pairs of white corduroy hose (one short, and one long), and an old doublet lined in white linen. For Salazar these were likely of only token value, but for Martín these few warm clothes represented his independence and right to liberty.

With the temporary details of Martín's property and safety resolved, the case proceeded to the substance of his legal status. Although both sides presented witnesses, the bulk of the testimony was from Martín's supporters, affirming his free status and the cruelty of his master. 'He always served as a free person, not a slave', declared the lawyer Iñigo López. 'If sometimes he was forced to serve him, it was against his will and without cause or just title. Martín *indio* is not a slave and I will keep saying he was always free by birth . . . he has the presumption of right in his favour'. It was not the custom to enslave the peoples of New Spain from birth, he continued – correctly citing the law – and if Martín was branded 'it was as a child', and was a 'malicious fraud' which should 'incur serious penalties'. López gave a detailed account of Martín's transition from a free child in Mexico to a servant in Spain, 'branded by force' on the orders of Salazar. The scar on Martín's right cheek was clearly 'not the brand of His Majesty', he insisted. López, well rehearsed in Spanish legal expectations, pointed out that Martín deserved to be compensated for all his years of service: '3,000 *maravedís* and more'.

Another Indigenous person then appeared, testifying on Martín's behalf: Francisco Martín, from Santiago, near Mexico City, had known Martín for ten years, since they were boys in Tenayucan. Such personal connections criss-crossed the Atlantic world, as Indigenous people clung to reminders of their homeland, but they are often very faint and hard to trace in our records. Francisco's testimony is relatively brief, but again focuses on the fact that the 'letters that he has on his cheek are not the brand of His Majesty', a twisted scribble which sadly he had 'seen many times'. A hint of the extreme pressures that Indigenous communities were under creeps into Francisco's testimony when he says that the leaders of Tenayucan – Tacatecloc and Tezacoatl – granted Martín to Salazar as a page because 'they were afraid of him, and he was strong'. The young man may not have been technically enslaved, but neither was he an entirely willing servant, and, as the testimony in his case piled up, we get a hint at his daily hardships.

Salazar presented as a witness a priest from Seville called Antonio Gómez, who claimed that – as well as the 'V' on his right cheek – Martín had originally also borne the king's brand on his left cheek, but 'had used herbs' to get rid of the mark. Now, he was left with a scar which Martín said had been caused when he was kicked in the face by a frightened mule. Whichever was true, the young man in front of the court – brown skinned, likely slightly smaller than the Spanish average and strong from physical work in Spanish homes and fields, probably wearing plain woollen clothes like those he claimed from Salazar – was marked on both sides of his face. A clear 'V' scored on his right cheek, and a vague dark brown mark smeared on the left – inscriptions of the everyday violence against Indigenous people in the colonial world.

Salazar tried to claim that Martín had been branded according to colonial custom and practice,* and a procession of his supporters swore that the mark appeared just like those on enslaved people in New Spain. Another witness, Lope de Saavedra, even declared that Martín must be a slave because 'a man of good life' could not possibly have those letters on his face. The court, concerned more with legality than morality, disagreed. In 1537, Martín was declared a free man.

Making a mockery of Lope de Saavedra's claims, many innocent men, women and children 'of good life' were branded at this time. Witnesses on both sides made the horrors of burning flesh sound utterly banal. But, although branding was frequently treated as a commonplace by sixteenth-century people, its inherent violence is clear in the way it was used as retribution against enslaved people who sought their freedom. Those who claimed ownership often branded 'their' *indios* hastily, and illegally, after workers asked the courts for their liberty. In one typical case, Diego, from Pánuco in Mexico, appealed to the Casa de Contratación in 1534 because his mistress had branded him on the face and made him wear 'an iron ring around his neck engraved with some lettering that says "Slave of Inés Carillo, resident of Seville in La Cestería"'. La Cestería district – nicknamed for the basket-weavers' guild that was based there – was in the area now known as El Arenal, a busy neighbourhood alongside the Guadalquivir river, full of people supplying the ships that were helping to fuel the booming city.

Diego was from another riverine region: the Pánuco river basin on the Gulf Coast, in the north of what is now Veracruz. Before the arrival of the Spanish, the Huastec people held sway, but a multiplicity of languages and cultures thrived in the region. Diego, who was born before the European incursion, is most likely to have spoken either Huastec or Nahua, but could also have been Pame, Guachichile, Olive, Alaquín, Magoaco, Meco or Maixita. These

---

* This was very likely, but it didn't make it legal.

northern Huastec territories, encompassing more than 100,000 people, were plundered by Cortés and his Indigenous allies shortly after the fall of Tenochtitlan; 'within a few days they destroyed everything and killed vast numbers of Indians', according to the chronicler Fernando de Alva Ixtlilxochitl.* The invaders swiftly set about illegally trafficking in Indigenous captives from the region. It was 'expedient to send slaves to the islands in exchange for horses, mares and other profits', an official report baldly stated in 1529.[45]

Diego survived these initial predations, only to be enticed onto a ship by an unscrupulous Spaniard. One afternoon in Pánuco, he encountered Christoval Sánchez, who trapped him on board a vessel and brought him to Castile. Diego had served Christoval and his wife, Inés Carillo, ever since – at their table, and at their side – until one day he asked for his freedom. So Inés ordered that he be branded on the face. The vulnerability of an enslaved person if they spoke out is all too clear. When Diego asked for his freedom, 'they branded me and treated me as badly as a slave, which I am not'. Despite this horrendous and illegal treatment, on 18 August 1534, the judges ordered that Diego be returned to Inés on bail, a decision he appealed immediately. How could they justify this, he argued, when Inés had 'violently possessed me for seven or eight years' and had failed repeatedly to show title of possession for his enslavement. 'I did not submit nor consent to submit to the said Ines Carrillo', Diego implored. 'It is clear that she has hatred and serious enmity towards me and that she has in her house a Portuguese who treats me very badly and even once cast a noose around my neck to hang me from a mulberry tree.' But despite all these 'scandalous crimes and wrongs' against him, and Diego's fears that the anonymous 'Portuguese' may 'injure or kill me', he was nonetheless returned to Inés's house. Looking back, it seems

---

* Although a *castizo* (¾ white), Ixtlilxochitl was a direct descendant of the noble families of both Texcoco and Tenochtitlan, and played up the importance of his ancestors in his writing, making a powerful case for the role of Indigenous people in the fall of Tenochtitlan and the following 'pacification' of New Spain.

an extraordinary decision. Inés's witnesses thus far had testified only that Diego was from Pánuco, and that he must therefore be enslaved, as they had seen such *indios* arriving on ships to be sold, an assumption which hints at the magnitude of the illegal trade in Indigenous lives. We have no way to know why the judges handed Diego back to his enslavers, but at this point Diego prudently asked Juan de Aranda, the *factor* of the Casa de Contratación, for help with his case. This was a smart choice. Aranda, an experienced administrator, and a bit-part player in Magellan's expedition to circumnavigate the globe, was likely responsible for the crowd of witnesses speaking on Diego's behalf, as well as for the appearance of Juan de Cárdenas – inspector of the vessels which arrived in Seville from the Americas – as Diego's advocate.*

On 16 April 1535, almost a year after Diego had first launched his bid for freedom, Juan de Cárdenas spoke to the court, pleading with them to take Diego out of Inés's house while the case was decided: 'The aforementioned Ines Carrillo and a Portuguese that she has in her house have treated and treat him [Diego] very badly and they have hit him and they have cast him out and brought him [here] naked and dead from hunger.' It is a powerful image, of a man brought to his knees by cruelty, but still facing his enslavers and demanding freedom. The 'Portuguese' reappears as Diego's principal tormentor in the statement of another witness, Antón García Espartero, whose account was confirmed by his servant, Juan:

> One day, Diego *yndio* brought a cart loaded with wood to the Puerta de Triana, in front of his house. I witnessed a Portuguese that was in the house of Ines Carrillo. Because he said that Diego *yndio* was not unloading the aforementioned cart of wood quickly enough, he lashed out at the aforementioned Diego *yndio* and hit him with a cattle prod until he fell on the ground and then certain men came there and they took it away,

---

* One wonders if this is the same Juan de Cárdenas who was granted a licence to take two caravels to the Caribbean to 'rescue' gold, jewels, pearls and 'slaves' in 1520.

it seeming so bad to them . . . and the *yndio*, after they had stopped it, took his cattle prod and went with the cart.

With this compelling testimony, and his distressing appearance, Diego finally managed to escape the clutches of Inés Carillo for a short time, for she next appears before the judges on 12 May, complaining that her 'slave' is missing. Given that he seems to have been hiding out at the Casa de Contratación, it is likely that the judges were at last persuaded that he should be taken into some kind of protective custody. Inés promptly demanded Diego's return, but the judges – whose trust in her seems finally to have been exhausted – asked Inés to prove her good conduct, with witnesses. In reality, her procession of supporters instead largely emphasised Diego's disobedience, and what a lazy, 'shameless and ungrateful' '*yndio esclavo*' (enslaved *indio*) he was, deserving of the punishments she meted out to him. The emphasis in the testimony is once again that he was treated 'as other slaves', fed, clothed and given the necessities, and not treated badly 'without cause'.* Thankfully for Diego, after various agonising appeals and counter-appeals, the case somehow made its way to the attention of the queen† and, on 15 October 1535, she issued a royal charter declaring him free. As an *indio*, Diego could not legally be *esclavo* (enslaved). On 4 November, this decision was confirmed by the judges, and on 23 December 1535, the Council of the Indies issued a final sentence: after a decade of enslavement, and close to two years of legal struggle, Diego was a free man.[46]

The records give us an unusual amount of detail about Diego's situation, but we can only imagine the experiences of the mass of

---

* A careful observer will notice that this leaves plenty of scope for ill-treatment for, as Inés claimed, 'moderate punishment' of those enslaved by law was permitted.

† Or at least her representatives, for Queen Juana (commonly known as Juana or Joanna the Mad) had been imprisoned, ostensibly on the grounds of her mental health, since 1516.

people who found themselves torn away from their homes and forced to make the best of their submission to strangers in an odd land. For many Indigenous people, accustomed to slavery in the Mesoamerican world largely as a form of unpaid servitude, the utter deprivation of the right to their person would have been a distressing shock. The available sources give us very little sense of the trauma of enslavement, or the sheer scope of enslaved experiences. Since the enslavement of Indigenous peoples was, for the most part, illegal in the Spanish empire, its victims are often effaced from the records – hidden from both society and history – and its magnitude is almost impossible to detect. Andrés Reséndez also points out that 'since it had no legal basis, it was never formally abolished like African slavery', further ensnaring its victims in legal complication.[47] The failure to clearly liberate Indigenous Americans had extraordinary ramifications, and many of them remained in forms of forced labour into the nineteenth and even twentieth centuries.

Prohibitions on Indigenous trafficking and travel led sixteenth-century enslavers to lie, obfuscate and omit their activities from the official records. Words like '*loro*' (intermediate/brown), *blanco* (light), and *loro casi negro* (brown almost black) are often used in place of *indio* (Indian).[48] Enslaved Indigenous labour is concealed by euphemisms such as *encomienda* (entrusting), *repartimiento* (distribution), or simply *esclavo* (slave) – terms obscuring the vassal rights of *indios*. It is important to be aware of the distinctions between these different forms of forced labour, which carried different rights and obligations, but any person who is forced to carry out work, and is not free to leave, is effectively enslaved. Many thousands of Indigenous victims of this 'other' slavery existed in a shadowy space, hidden from public view, both intentionally and by the nature of the sources available to us.

The deliberate attempt to obscure Indigenous enslaved people is compounded by frequent legal machinations. So in 1561 when Cristóbal, a cook from New Spain, appealed for his freedom from doña Isabel de Finolete, she claimed that he was from India, rather than the Indies, and therefore ineligible for protection under the laws on the freedom of *indios*. This sort of defence was quite common in the sixteenth century. We regularly see Spaniards claiming that their victims were 'legally' acquired from Portuguese colonies in Brazil or the Maluku islands (the Moluccas, which used to be colourfully called 'the Spice Islands'). To prove his case, Cristóbal, aided by Francisco Hernández de Liebana – a hugely influential and charismatic lawyer who was then prosecutor of the Council of the Indies – produced a parade of supporters to testify to his Mexican origin. You could tell he was a 'native of the province of New Spain . . . by the physiognomy of his face, hair and head', said the witnesses. Because Cristóbal looked like an *indio*, he was an *indio*. Despite Finolete's witnesses arguing that the cook had been enslaved in Portuguese territory and therefore fell outside Spanish guardianship, the court (doubtless encouraged by his powerful advocate) supported Cristóbal, and he was freed.[49]

Identities mattered. They mattered so much that enslavers wanted them erased from the record. One Pedro de Hermosilla – a sword maker from the famous steel-working centre of Toledo – demanded that the court stop using the word '*indio*' to refer to his 'slave' Gerónimo. It was unfair, he argued, that the court records called Gerónimo '*indio*', when the entire case hinged on the question of whether he had the right to that title or not. This defiant man claimed he was from New Spain, and therefore 'cannot be captive', but Hermosilla alleged that he was a '*mulatto*', the child of a Spaniard and an enslaved African, born in the famous sherry city of Jerez de la Frontera and raised in Málaga. This fascinating case shows the networks of communication which sprang up between enslaved people. Gerónimo was only appealing for his freedom because 'he had heard that they gave freedom to other *indios* that are natives of there and not because he was in truth that himself', accused Hermosilla. Indigenous people were becoming aware of their right to freedom; gossip about official inspections was spreading across the country, news of masters being beaten by the law; freed people were walking the streets, boasting of their new liberty. In 1558, when a Mexican woman named Beatríz finally sought liberty for herself and her six children after two decades of enslavement, the courts wanted to know why she had not gone to the House of Trade to petition for freedom after the New Laws of 1542. Surely she must have known that she had the right? Beatríz's response, and that of her witnesses, was that she had known she was free all along, and was content in her situation until her enslaver attempted to sell her son. After two decades of servitude, she felt driven to assert her free status under the law.*[50]

Whatever the truth of his own case, Gerónimo was clearly not a man to wait around. In May 1560, the Crown lawyer Cristóbal de San Martín visited Hermosilla's house and found Gerónimo shackled uncomfortably by his feet 'like a cricket', with knees akimbo; this was to stop his track record of thieving, according to Hermosilla. When Cristóbal ordered that the chains be removed so that the plaintiff could appear in court, Gerónimo promptly disappeared, taking 'certain things' from the house. From Toledo, Gerónimo fled towards the French border. Less than a fortnight later, he was apprehended in Hita, a small, fortified town on a hill. According to the mayor of Hita, who ordered his arrest, Gerónimo was stopped for being 'unruly'. As a stranger in a small town, with his unfamiliar 'boiled quince' skin colour and the brand scarring his cheek, Gerónimo was challenged to prove his free status, and admitted he was a 'dependant of Pedro de Hermosillo', who lived in the Calle Concha (Shell Street). Some soldiers also testified that they had met Gerónimo near Guadalajara on his way to Hita, and he had asked them how he could get to safety in France. Clearly Gerónimo, whatever his origins, did not trust the courts to grant him liberty and had decided to seize it for himself. We do not know whether he ever got his wish.

Gerónimo's case shows how knowledge of Indigenous rights permeated the networks of enslaved people, showing a glint of light to those able or opportunist enough to exploit them. It also tragically illuminates the ways in which Native identities could be

---

*   Nancy Van Deusen suggests that this may have been the deciding moment. Beatríz sadly lost her case for freedom, but was posthumously declared free, for her daughter Catalina continued the family's legal struggle.

erased. One ostensibly matter-of-fact phrase in the manuscript of Gerónimo's lawsuit actually holds a poignant clue: 'In the name of Pedro de Hermosilla, swordmaker, in the lawsuit that deals with your [the Crown's] lawyer about the freedom of Ger[oni]mo ~~yndio~~ his slave . . .'[51] Gerónimo's claimed Indigenous identity has literally been scored from the record. The court rulings show that, if an enslaved person argued for freedom on the grounds of their Indigenous heritage and lost their case, then they would no longer be recorded as *indio/india*, but become merely *esclavo/esclava* (enslaved). Their identity was erased, and along with it their rights.

2

Go-Betweens

It is easy to forget the language barrier, when reading accounts which report direct and detailed conversations between Indigenous people and invaders. European sources confidently recount eloquent speeches and complex negotiations, never mentioning the fact that the two parties would have had little or no sense of what the other was saying. Some of this startling confidence can, of course, be put down to literary convention. The grand orations supposedly exchanged by Cortés and Moctezuma evoke classical traditions, positioning the opponents as stately protagonists; they are a reflection of writing conventions and readers' expectations, rather than reality. The language barrier could also be an advantage to colonisers: if your opponent doesn't really understand what you're saying, then it's easy to claim that they agreed to all kinds of things. The accounts of colonisation are frequently invented as much as they are observed. As Stephen Greenblatt wrote: 'The Europeans and the interpreters themselves translated such fragments as they understood or thought they understood into a coherent story, and they came to believe quite easily that the story was what they had actually heard.'[1]

But many of these discussions were not as unintelligible as we might think. From as early as 1493, exchanges were often facilitated by go-betweens: people (usually Indigenous, but occasionally European) who stood between worlds, as channels of communication, and also of cultural exchange. Go-betweens become obvious by their absence if you scrutinise any account of an event where people spoke different languages and ask yourself: how could these people understand each other? Standing right in the middle of events, but totally invisible, must be another person: essential to the interaction, yet ignored by those who recorded it. The few stories we will follow in this chapter are emblematic of a mass of Indigenous people who inhabited this in-between space: between European and Indigenous, between languages and cultures, between seen and unseen. They are always in the background, interjecting.

Such mediation is often ignored in the sources, but it was invaluable to both sides. Unsurprisingly though, it was the Europeans who – desperate for local knowledge to promote their imperial enterprise – began to kidnap Indigenous people with the explicit aim of training them as translators. One of Columbus's first thoughts after arriving in the Caribbean was to bring some of the Native people to Spain 'so that they may learn to speak'. He claimed that the first people he 'took by force' from the Caribbean were quick to learn Spanish, managing to communicate effectively through words and gestures within only a few months.[2] The abduction of Indigenous intermediaries is a ubiquitous part of European descriptions of encounter, explorers and colonisers carelessly describing the casual violence with which they acquired 'helpers' for their missions. We have few records that would allow us to understand how Indigenous peoples felt about such kidnappings, but an Indigenous oral tradition, recorded in 1807, describes the aggressive arrival of an English ship in Wampanoag territory in modern-day Massachusetts.

> As to traditions, there is, though but in a few mouths, an Indian tradition, which purports that some ages past, a number of white men arrived in the river, in a bird; that the white men took Indians into the bird, as hostages; that they took fresh water for their consumption at a neighbouring spring; that the Indians fell upon and slaughtered the white men at the spring; that, during the affray, thunder and lightning issued from the bird; that the hostages escaped from the bird; and that a spring, now called White Spring, and from which there runs a brook, called White Man's Brook, has its name from this event.[3]

Unlike many Indigenous captives, these 'Indians' managed to escape before being stolen away from their homeland, but this evocative image of an immense bird – a prominent character in Eastern Woodlands cultural belief, which sometimes carried away humans – gives us a glimpse at the ways in which the invaders' actions may have been understood.

Among the Taínos kidnapped by Columbus was a young man who we know only by his Spanish baptismal name: Diego Colón. Diego was just a boy when he met Columbus and seems to have developed a close bond with the Admiral, becoming a *guatiao* of his son (also called Diego).[4] Taíno people used '*guatiao*' (friendship or brotherhood) rituals to form ties of kinship and alliance. An exchange of names bonded people in *guatiao*, making them 'perpetual friends and brothers in arms', and this ceremony was central to Indigenous understandings of early Caribbean encounter. In 1503, after days of vicious battle, a *guatiao* ritual was used to affirm a ceasefire between the Spanish and the Taíno on Hispaniola. Native people were not passive recipients of European expectations – they too shaped the relationship – but even in the enactment of Indigenous rituals we see Spanish influence. Unlike in the Taíno world, the adoption of names became a hierarchical practice: Indigenous people took Spanish names, but we have no evidence of this happening the other way round.[5] We might argue that Spaniards used the *guatiao* ritual to draw people into their networks, or we could say that Native people employed the *guatiao* ritual to promote their influence with these powerful new invaders. It's all about perspective. From a Spanish point of view, this was certainly a paternalistic act: Indigenous people were 'adopted' into their families. But this also mirrors some pre-contact Indigenous kinship and adoption practices, and perhaps there is no record of Spaniards adopting Taíno names simply because all of the records are Spanish.* For Diego Colón, his *guatiao* with Columbus's son

---

* There are occasional cases elsewhere. The friar Toribio de Benavente embraced the name he was given by the local Indigenous people: Motolinía, Nahuatl for 'poor one', in recognition of his unassuming Franciscan robes.

effectively tied his fortunes to the Admiral and would shape the course of his life.

One of the first Indigenous islanders to set foot on European soil, Diego was also one of the few to survive the trip, and remain healthy, as most of his compatriots fell prey to the devastating diseases that ripped through vulnerable Indigenous populations; lacking immunity and weakened by European invasions, Native people were cut down in their millions. Diego for some reason resisted the germs that assailed his compatriots, and became close to his *guatiao* father and brother, being 'brought up with his [Columbus's] own children' and becoming his regular interpreter, according to the historian Peter Martyr, who knew the court circle well. On 26 February 1495, Columbus, writing to the king of his most recent exploits, mentioned 'this *indio* that I bring, one of those who came to Castile, he already knows how to speak our language very well'. By this point, Diego was an experienced explorer, having risked the arduous journey across the Atlantic four times and assisted Columbus in his (utterly disingenuous) attempts to persuade the Taínos that he meant them no harm.

Martyr probably exaggerates to say that Diego was brought up by Columbus 'from his infancy', but he certainly became part of his extended family. After returning to the Caribbean for the third time, Diego deployed his *guatiao* in reverse, consolidating his position amongst Indigenous islanders by marrying the daughter of a *cacique* called Guarionex who wanted 'a more intimate friendship with the Admiral'.[6] Sadly, we don't know anything more about Diego's wife; perhaps she was part of the reason he decided to stay on Hispaniola when Columbus returned to Spain from his second voyage in 1493. A decade later, it seems Diego was ready to risk the transatlantic voyage again, for we have a record of three *caciques* travelling to Spain, along with one of their sons, a boy named Diego Colón. We cannot be certain that this was Columbus's adopted Taíno 'son' and interpreter Diego, travelling with his own child, but it seems extremely likely, especially as when the elder Diego returned to Hispaniola in 1505 (his two companions again having succumbed to the fate of so many and died in Spain) the boy remained at court, being educated, clothed and supported by the Crown. Accounts show that the chaplain Luis de Castillo was paid a moderate annual salary of 8000 *maravedís* to feed and teach 'Diego el *Yndio*, son of the *cacique* that . . . the governor sent to the officials to be taught the things of our holy faith'. They also paid him around half this sum for clothing – a significant expense, suggesting luxurious garments – which included shoes, hats and shirts, all in the European style.

Like his father, the younger Diego had become acculturated to Spain. This was a power play by Indigenous nobles, but also a deliberate colonising tactic by European authorities, who were determined to show that Native peoples could be 'civilised' through Christianity. A decree from the House of the Trade shows that they were very aware of the potential of these young nobles as go-betweens for their faith. In August 1505, the Crown ordered that the '*indio* son of the *cacique* that has been made Christian' continue to be very well treated with care for both his spiritual and temporal needs. Thus, they imagined, when 'at God's pleasure he will return to Hispaniola leaving here very content . . . the *indios* will have knowledge of how they are treated here and the things of the faith will thus be caused to be more lightly brought to them'.[7]

Unfortunately, the younger Diego fell ill in Spain, and never lived to fulfil the Crown's (and very likely also his father's) aspirations for him. He survived the first serious complaint – likely some kind of throat goitre – in 1505, but, perhaps weakened by his earlier illness, he died in Seville in August 1506, in the house of one García Sánchez de la Plaza, who had been paid to look after him during the two months of his illness. How long did it take his father and mother to learn of this tragedy? Was the news delivered by the next fleet to arrive in the Caribbean? Did Columbus's family visit Diego during his illness? Did he die alone, with only the most perfunctory care, or did *guatiao* extend to nursing him during his last days?

The elder Diego survived his son by a decade or so, and was even granted land and some Indigenous 'charges' to work it because he was considered so Hispanised.[8] Yet even this stalwart translator, with his evidently strong immune system, died in his thirties, very likely succumbing to one of the waves of European diseases which battered Indigenous communities in the sixteenth century. In 1518, the first documented outbreak of smallpox in the Americas erupted in the Caribbean.[9] When this pathogen reached the mainland, it would precipitate one of the most destructive epidemics in history. What the Nahua called *cocoliztli* ravaged Mesoamerica, causing one of the highest death rates ever recorded.[10] Although genetics is beginning to transform our understanding of historic populations and epidemics, statistics can only ever be estimates, but it is clear that the loss of life was devastating. This was the first-known plague to strike the Americas and many more would follow – flu, measles, cholera, typhus, fevers – which would ultimately wipe out as much as half of the entire Indigenous population of the Americas by the early 1600s, in what the Wampanoag call 'the Great Dying'.[11]

The unprecedented impact of introducing virulent diseases to a 'virgin population', lacking any natural or acquired immunity to foreign viruses, is a central thread in most histories of the Americas, but this is not only an American story. The vast majority of Indigenous people who crossed the Atlantic would have witnessed, or experienced, these shattering plagues in their homelands, and Native men, women and children living in Europe also suffered and died in great numbers. This was a transatlantic scourge, something which happened on Europeans' doorstep, not just to strangers far away.* All but one of the ten people abducted by the French explorer Jacques Cartier from Stadacona, an Iroquoian settlement near present-day Quebec City, perished in Brittany within a few years of their arrival in 1536, except for 'one little girle about tenne yeeres old'.[12]

For the Indigenous people (typically men) that survived, it was possible to flourish in, and even to profit from, the turbulence of

---

* In fairness, Europeans were also pretty plague-ridden in this period. Epidemics were common, and people frequently suffered from incurable illnesses, but the mortality rates in the Americas – and the hereditary impact when combined with the excesses of colonialism – were unparalleled.

this early modern Atlantic. In the cracks and gaps between the cultures – what the Nahua call *nepantla*, the 'in-between space' – there were prospects for those nimble and healthy enough to exploit them. We think of colonisation as a violent, oppressive enterprise (and it was), but what we would now call 'soft power' was also central to European tactics, and helped to create a flow of transatlantic travellers, mostly younger elite men, like the two Diegos. European rulers not only brought Indigenous nobles into their orbit and into their debt through grants and posts, but also deliberately transported Native people – often children – across the Atlantic to be indoctrinated, with the intention that they would lead by example, spreading Christianity and 'civility' on their return. As early as 1512, Columbus's son Diego, by then Governor of the Indies (like his father before him), suggested sending Indigenous people to Spain with the intention that they should take religious orders before returning to the Indies as 'much more fruitful' people. These plans, and many later aspirations, were foiled by the exclusion of *indios* from religious office, but the principle remained appealing and a surprising number of Native people were entrusted to monasteries in Spain in the early part of the sixteenth century.

The French too saw Native go-betweens as part of their strategy from the earliest days of colonisation. Cartier systematically kidnapped Indigenous Stadaconans to serve as intermediaries. In 1534, he kidnapped two sons of the local *agouhanna* (leader), Donnacona. The young men, named Taignoagny and Domagaya, spent just over eight months in France, learning some of the language, and witnessing enough of French life to understand the custom of baptism and to gain a clear sense of the accurate value of European goods (much to the irritation of Cartier). These two reluctant travellers were tricked into travelling to France a second time in 1536, along with eight others, including their father Donnacona, who was baptised in France, supposedly at his 'owne desire'. In 1540, King Francis I of France recognised the importance of these go-betweens when he commissioned Cartier to found a colony in Canada, 'from which country we brought various men that we have long supported in our Kingdom, being instructed in the love and fear of God, and the Holy Faith and Christian doctrine, with the intention of taking them back to the aforementioned country in the company of a good number of our subjects of good will, in order to more easily induce the other people of that country to believe in our Holy Faith.[13]

In July 1516, Charles V ordered that six women and four men (of unknown origin) should be instructed in the essentials of Catholicism in Spain. This early experiment is unusual for including women, and because their education was to be under the direct orders of the Archbishop of Seville, Diego de la Deza, a Dominican known for his efforts 'converting' Jews and Muslims as Grand Inquisitor. The archbishop barely had an opportunity to speak with these neophytes before the summer epidemics eroded their number. By October, only one man and four women remained, living at the Convent of San Leandro. Tourists now flock to this unobtrusive convent to buy luscious *yemas* – candied egg yolks, made to a four-hundred-year-old recipe – from the cloistered Augustinian nuns, who remain hidden behind their traditional hatch throughout. It's unlikely the *indios* would have been permitted these treats, but we know that the Crown ensured they were well provided for, paying generously for clothing, food, lodgings and medical care.[14]

Such bills for maintenance are typical of the few traces we have of Native novices in the archives, along with formulaic orders to 'teach them the things of the Holy Catholic Faith'. The influx of Indigenous novices intensified after 1526, when Charles V ordered that twenty *indios* of the best 'ability and understanding' (and of elite birth if possible) should be brought to Spain to be taught the faith 'on the first ships', so that they would be able to 'return to their lands and instruct their natives'.[15] We can only imagine how a young boy, taken away from his family across the terrifying sea, would have felt about adopting and promoting the beliefs of his captors. His parents would presumably also have felt constrained by such an arrangement. From their perspective, this was not so much an educational trip as a hostage-taking – another reason why noble children were so popular in these schemes. Nonetheless, the Catholic zeal for evangelisation should not be underestimated and continually shaped their treatment of Native peoples in sincere, albeit often profoundly violent, ways.

Careful digging in the Crown records reveals Indigenous people – variously listed as 'children', 'youths' and just '*indios*' – residing in at least five monasteries in the years either side of 1530. Most lived in Seville – the port hub of the Indies' trade – and Indigenous people pop up all over the city: at the Convento de Santo Domingo, the Monasterio de Santa María de Duenas, the Monasterio de Las Cuevas, and the Convento de San Francisco* – the Franciscan motherhouse – which housed two men from Hispaniola.[16] These two men (likely Taínos) lived with the Franciscans for at least four years, with the Crown paying their maintenance throughout, so – assuming they survived – they may have been keen to spread the news of salvation. Having lived every day smothered by the friars' unceasing piety, these Indigenous emissaries for the Faith could easily have been indoctrinated. Or perhaps they claimed as much in order to be allowed to return home. Some may have returned to the Americas as missionaries; three *indios* – probably young men who had learned the 'things' of the Catholic faith – accompanied seven Franciscan friars who took ship for New Spain in 1532, on a carrack appropriately named the *Santa Cruz* (Holy Cross). In the 1580s, we hear of 'an *indio* Ambrosio Pires, who had been to Lisbon with father Rodrigo de Freitas' playing the part of an *anhangá* (a Tupi forest deity which often took the shape of a deer) during the festivities to mark the arrival of a senior Jesuit delegation in Brazil.[17] Was this man, returned from Portugal, a convert? Or a go-between?

The epitome of such evangelical mediation was the remarkable missionary and scholar Diego Valadés, who spoke three Indigenous languages (Nahuatl, Tarascan and Otomí). The first known *mestizo* to join the Franciscan Order in Mexico, Valadés travelled via Spain and France to take up a senior post at the Vatican in 1570. There he completed his *Rhetorica christiana*, a truly transatlantic work

---

*   Confusingly for an English speaker, 'convent' and 'monastery' here have nothing to do with monks and nuns, but instead refer to mendicant (travelling and begging) and cloistered orders of monks.

of scholarship that was intended to aid evangelisation in Mexico. Superbly illustrated and highly intellectual, the *Rhetorica* was published in a small, accessible format, and would have attracted a wide readership. More controversial was the *mestizo* Jesuit Blas Valera, a courageous advocate for Indigenous civilisation and for a distinctively Andean form of Christianity. The son of a conquistador and a Quechua-speaking Native mother, Valera – physically broken and severely ill – was exiled to Spain after six years of imprisonment and abuse for his beliefs. Arriving in 1596, he was permitted to teach humanities in Cádiz, as well as visiting the Jesuit house in Naples. But tragically, just as his voice was beginning to be heard in European circles, he was fatally injured and much of his work was burned when English and Dutch forces sacked the city of Cádiz. But the creation of an Indigenous Christianity in Europe continued.[18]

One hundred and fifty miles to the north of Seville, ten or more Indigenous people lived with the austere friars who guarded the shrine of Our Lady of Guadalupe, nestled on the edge of the Sierra de las Villuercas mountains in Extremadura. Here, in the Royal Monastery of Santa María de Guadalupe, Jeronymites lived a life of contemplation, singing the Divine Office for between eight and fourteen hours a day. Did the Indigenous people join them, becoming like novices to the order? Or were they guests in the hospice next door, a haven for pilgrims and royalty alike, and now converted to a gorgeous four-star *parador* (a state-run 'hostel'), where you can stay alongside the monastery, as travellers have done for more than five hundred years. Now a World Heritage site, the monastic church was (and remains for many) a place of transcendent devotion and fervent belief. The cedar-wood statue of Mary at the shrine, supposedly carved by Saint Luke the Evangelist, is quite a diminutive figure – painted in colours that have muted over the centuries – but is made majestic by richly embroidered and adorned vestments. She is an image of hope and salvation – believed to have saved Rome from the plague in the sixth century – and, most poignantly, she has dark skin. A decade after the first great Mexican smallpox outbreak, with much of the Caribbean in ruins, Indigenous people were being urged to worship an icon with a familiar face, a woman who offered salvation from the epidemics that had demolished their communities.

Four children entrusted to the friars for 'education' in 1530 must have missed their families desperately, perhaps tried to cling onto some small token or fragment of memory which felt like home, but – trained from infanthood to obedience and industry – they likely assimilated quite quickly, probably attending the recently built Colegio de Infantes that still forms part of the *parador* building. As children, they may have picked up Spanish with relative ease, and absorbed the 'truths' shared with them by the friars. But for the adult Taínos and others sent to live in the monastery, the essence of this dark-faced Madonna would have been more tangled. Adorned in dazzling embroidery and gold, her power would have been obvious. As a mother, primal and nurturing, baby tucked into her arm, she might even have evoked Indigenous earth goddesses such as Atabey, the Taíno Mother Earth, or the Nahua fertility goddess Tonantzin – the 'Sacred Mother' who is closely associated with the Virgin by many Mexican Catholics. We know that blending of belief – syncretism – happened across the Americas after the European invasions, but we do not typically think of it as happening at the very hearth of Catholic conviction. Yet here, in the foothills of Extremadura, home to so many conquistadors, 'truths' were being questioned and faith remade.[19]

The town of Guadalupe prides itself on its transatlantic significance. Columbus, Cortés and Pizarro all went on pilgrimage to this shrine, and Cortés credited the Virgin Mary with protecting him on his brutal campaigns, carrying Our Lady's banner into battle and erecting her image in Indigenous temples. Here Isabella and Ferdinand met Columbus, and the Admiral came to praise God and Mary for his safe return. Above the Madonna, a small, gilded image shows Mary astride the Atlantic, her light radiating across the world. To the west, in Mexico, there is a tiny sketch of the 'other' Mary of Guadalupe, whose image on an Indigenous *tilmatli* (mantle or cloak) is now venerated as a symbol of Mexican identity. Her basilica in the north of Mexico City is one of the world's most visited sacred sites.* Juan Diego, the pious Chichimeca who saw apparitions of the Virgin on this spot, became the first Indigenous saint in 2002, when he was canonised by Pope John Paul II.† The Virgin Mary – carried by conquistadors into battle – has been converted into an emblem of both Indigenous faith and Mexican culture.

Tourists who have trailed (or been bussed) up the hill to Guadalupe's imposing monastery are told that the ancient font, now in the Plaza de Santa María at the foot of the steps, is where the 'first Indians brought by Columbus from his second journey to America were baptised'.[20] We already know that this is a bit of local puffery, but it may be built on a snippet of truth. In the archives of the monastery, a record from 29 July 1496 registers the baptism of two *criados* (dependants) of Admiral Columbus called Cristóbal and Pedro, most likely *indios* brought from his second voyage. Both archives, and our readings of them, are structured by European perspectives, working to distort and repress Indigenous voices and prevent Native people from appearing, except within the expectations set for them. But if we look outward, beyond the rugged walls of the monastery, we can see Indigenous voyagers in this early period already slipping into ostensibly 'European' realms, and transforming them.

To be a go-between was to balance precariously between two worlds, often belonging to neither.[21] These *nepantleras* (people in the in-between) were not always Indigenous. Claudia Rogers, inspired by the work of the Chicana activist and author Gloría E. Anzaldúa and the anthropologist Greg Dening, identified two kinds of go-between in the first encounters: *nepantleras* (Indigenous people 'caught between the different sides of early

---

* So popular is the Basilica that pilgrims and tourists have to view Our Lady from a travellator.

† Juan Diego was mysteriously forgotten when the seventeenth-century Mohawk woman Kateri Tekakwitha was canonised as the 'first Native American saint' by Benedict XVI in 2012.

encounters') and 'beachcombers' (Europeans who came to live in Indigenous communities, often as a result of shipwrecks or capture).[22] One famous 'beachcomber' was Gonzalo Guerrero, who we will meet again shortly. A Spaniard shipwrecked on the Yucatán coast, Guerrero integrated with the Maya people, marrying a local woman and becoming a successful warrior – a rare example of a European choosing to fully assimilate into Indigenous culture in this early period.

Native people aligning themselves with European values and expectations, on the other hand, was very common. Intermediaries were a familiar sight at the Spanish court from as early as the 1490s, and the frequent passing mentions of them hint at the ways in which Indigenous people were deliberately brought across the ocean and into Christian circles and ways of living. A few of these go-betweens are highly visible in the sources, and so have also become highly visible in the stories we tell about this period. Famous figures like Matoaka (Pocahontas) and Tisquantum (Squanto, who was at the 'first Thanksgiving') have been mythologised in popular history as 'good Indians', who saved the lives of starving colonists and joined hands with the invaders.[23] But perhaps the most fascinating thing about these historical celebrities was how common they were. There were a few interpreters who were particularly skilled, lucky, or successful, but a mass of others aided almost every early interaction. Mentions of the need for interpreters are persistent in the sixteenth-century sources. The demand naturally came earlier in Spain and France than England, but we can see the same patterns popping up across Europe as the century progresses, hinting at the ubiquity of Indigenous intermediaries. In 1587, Jacques Noël, a nephew of the French explorer Jacques Cartier, along with his business partner Etienne Chaton de La Jannaye, applied for a monopoly of the Canadian fur trade. In trumpeting Noël's experience, they mentioned in passing that he had previously brought several Indigenous people to France to learn how to be interpreters.[24] How many more went unmentioned in the records?

The lives of even the most famous interpreters are hard to discern in the surviving sources. Ironically, given the translators' prominent role as speakers and negotiators, the sources often remain silent on their own thoughts and views and so we find ourselves trying to infer their attitudes from actions, piecing together their stories from the fragments of personal history which lie in the cracks between their clients' interests and interactions. These ambiguities are exemplified by the case of Madalena, a Tocobaga woman from what became Spanish Florida, who was seized in 1539 and acted as Hernando de Soto's translator when he became the first European to cross the Mississippi.* Madalena was enslaved in the home of de Soto's wife, Isabella de Bobadilla, in present-day Cuba, then carried to Seville as part of her household in 1542. She was technically freed by Prince Philip a year later, only to be declared Crown property due to her value as an interpreter. Somehow returning to Havana after a decade abroad, Madalena became vital to a missionary expedition among her own community, not only teaching the Dominican friar Luis Cáncer her language but also leading religious rituals in her own right, before the killing of Cáncer and his fellow priests by local people ended their doomed mission.

We do not know what happened to Madalena after this – perhaps she just went home – but her life has been painstakingly pieced together in an article by the historian Scott Cave. Yet even he admits that 'the Madalena of this piece may in fact be several women, each going through similar experiences, though I believe this not to be the case'.²⁵ This is typical of the jigsaw of our sources. Was there one Madalena, or many? Was there one Diego Colón, or many? In some ways, what matters most is to recognise that there *were* many go-betweens, *nepantleras* – translators, decipherers, people who stood in the in-between. We try our best to follow their paths, but when they fork, we have to pick a road; when they vanish, we have to sketch a trail. But in this mire of uncertainty, some traces nonetheless remain.

*

---

* The first *important* European. Someone else in de Soto's company may well have got their feet wet first, but he was in charge, so he gets the credit.

There are gaps in every story between what happened, what the records say happened, and what people say happened. Through these gaps, we often fall implicitly into the European point of view. Columbus tells us his Taíno informants were an essential source of local information, but he also claims they were convinced that the Europeans were 'from heaven'. Here, we see the different histories in tension, as expectations clash with observation and become tangled in retrospective explanations for what happened.

The idea of the Europeans as 'white gods' is a famous story, but it tends to appear only in retrospective sources looking back on events. It is a fabulously elaborated myth, which may well have been created by Indigenous people trying to understand their devastating losses (who could stand up against a divine invasion?) and it also suited the Europeans' superiority complex quite beautifully, so I am deeply suspicious of claims that Columbus's interpreters ran from house to house in every community crying 'Come, and see the people from heaven!'[26] Of course, they may have done so – perhaps they wanted to please their captors, or perhaps Columbus misunderstood the meaning of their words – but that doesn't necessarily mean they believed the Europeans were divine. Even if such a belief existed in those first confusing days, it could not have lasted. It's hard to imagine the Taínos could believe the Europeans to be anything other than men, after several months spent with them, sharing the indignities of shipboard life. And yet the 'white gods myth' pops up constantly in accounts of colonial encounter.

Wide-eyed Native peoples fall at the feet of the sophisticated white people, astonished by pale faces, strange clothes, and their power to wield thunder and lightning (at least, when damp didn't hamper their firearms, as happened very frequently). In Peru, late-sixteenth-century chroniclers claimed that the conquistador Pizarro was believed to be the reincarnation of 'Viracocha who had come, just as he had promised them when he went away'. Captain James Cook was allegedly identified with an incarnation of the god Lono on his arrival in the Pacific. White colonisers across the world have infamously claimed they were 'seen as gods' by the supposedly naïve peoples they met.[27]

One of the most famous examples of this reputed deification in the Americas is the claim that Cortés was believed to be the feathered serpent Quetzalcoatl, returned from the East to stop the practice of human sacrifice. Despite the fact that this story was very likely a post-conquest invention – a combination of European arrogance and Indigenous belief in cyclical and metaphysical histories – the image of Cortés as Quetzalcoatl still dominates popular accounts of the conquest. It is a neat explanation which fits stereotypical assumptions and makes for a good story, as well as providing a comprehensible explanation for the fall of the great Aztec-Mexica empire.[28]

But academic and popular accounts which are built on Indigenous credulity ignore the much more interesting reality – that each side was busy sounding the other out, assessing their opponents, and attempting to understand what they wanted. From the moment a lookout had rushed from 'the shores of the great sea' to tell Moctezuma that he had seen floating 'in the middle of the sea something like a mountain range or large hill, that moved here and there and did not reach the shore', the ruler sent lookouts and emissaries, attempting to understand these new arrivals. It is typical to give the agency in this exchange to the Spanish, but the Aztec-Mexica too were seeking information, testing out their opponents, possibly even feeding them human blood to check their divine status.[29]

Before Cortés ever arrived in Tenochtitlan, he had met with the leaders of Indigenous cities, fought with them, negotiated with them, allied with them, and talked repeatedly with the emissaries of Moctezuma, who – despite their lavish gifts – made clear that he was not wanted in the capital city. By the time Cortés arrived in the Valley of Mexico, some ten months after he left Cuba, he had tens of thousands of Tlaxcalan allies. So how did all this happen? How did a group of Spaniards conduct detailed negotiations with Mexican rulers who largely spoke an entirely different – utterly unfamiliar – language? The answer is simple, and at the same time surprising; it is one of those coincidences which determine the course of history – and it lies with not one translator but two.

In early 1519, after landing in the Yucatán, Cortés heard tell

of white men with beards among one of the nearby tribes. There
he found two Spaniards who had been shipwrecked eight years
earlier: Gonzalo Guerrero and Gerónimo de Aguilar. Both had been
enslaved by the Maya and learned the language, but Guerrero had
prospered in his new life, winning fame as a war chief for Nachan
Can, Lord of Chactemal, and marrying his daughter Zazil Há; their
three children are believed to be the first *mestizo* children born
in Mexico. He not only rejected Cortés's offer of 'rescue' but also
later campaigned against the Spanish, leading Maya forces against
his former compatriots. His naked tattooed body was found dead
on a battlefield in 1536. Guerrero had apparently been part of a
large force of war canoes attempting to help prevent the Spanish
colonising Maya lands near Ticamaya in Honduras.[30]

Aguilar, on the other hand, despised Maya life and clung to his
faith, so was keen to join Cortés as his interpreter. But Cortés had
an even greater stroke of luck. As he continued through the Maya
region, a chief 'gave' him a group of enslaved women, among whom
was a woman who has passed into legend: Malintzin, doña Marina,
La Malinche – she has many names, but the one that best encapsulates her role is La Lengua (the tongue). A Nahua woman, possibly
of noble birth, enslaved to the Maya, Malintzin was the perfect
go-between for Cortés. In the early days, she and Aguilar translated
for him in a laborious chain of communication: Spanish to Chontal
Maya through Aguilar; Maya to Nahuatl through Malintzin, and
back again, Nahuatl to Maya to Spanish. As if this wasn't convo-
luted enough, the coastal Totonac region spoke another language
entirely, and so two *Nahuatlatos* (Nahuatl interpreters) translated
the Totonac speech of their chief into Nahuatl for Malintzin, who
then switched it into Maya for Aguilar, who then rendered the
words in Spanish for Cortés.[31] The possibilities for mistranslation
and misunderstanding in this tortuous and protracted chain of
translations are endless. A quick and clever woman, Malintzin
swiftly learned Spanish and became Cortés's primary translator and
aide, interpreting not only language, but also customs and culture.
Although barely mentioned by Cortés in his letters, she was at the
heart of events, and also of his life. She stayed by him through

several campaigns and, in 1522, gave birth to Cortés's son, Martín, who took the conquistador's name and was later legitimised by his father and grew up in Spain, finally becoming a page to Philip II.

Malintzin never crossed the Atlantic herself – she died of unknown causes in the winter of 1528/9 – but her son Martín (whose trail we will pick up later) was one of the first *mestizo* children of conquistadors to travel to Spain, becoming part of the Indigenous diaspora which gradually filtered across the Atlantic and penetrated everyday life in Europe.[32] Malintzin is a tangible symbol of the often-hidden Indigenous agents who are at the centre of this story and the way in which their lives and blood ties were entwined in a web of relationships spanning continents and oceans. The fact that transatlantic migration is typically seen as a westward movement has led us to see Europe as the centre, the hub and the starting point. We need to invert our understanding of encounter to see transatlantic migration and connection not just as stretching to the west, but also as originating there. Indigenous peoples did not need to cross the Atlantic to have interests which bridged it and yet, as we will see, many Native people – mostly young men – would travel east in pursuit of their ambitions, and those of their families and communities. The European sources tell a tale of Indigenous people being 'used' as go-betweens by the explorers and invaders who encroached on their lands, but these intermediaries were often as much diplomats and brokers for their own people as they were agents of the intruders. A surprising number travelled voluntarily, and found themselves negotiating the challenges of a dual identity and querying their loyalties; they were truly *nepantleras* – people caught between worlds.

Even the Indigenous people who were involuntary go-betweens – seized by invaders and forced to provide information – held considerable influence in these early years of encounter. The way Malintzin appears in pictographic texts of this period peels back the Spanish mask to expose the real speaker beneath. Rather than being a bit-part player, Indigenous sources show Malintzin as a leader and orator, standing in front of Cortés, or at his shoulder, as events unfold. She is the negotiator and instigator: the mouthpiece of the invading force, a force that was largely comprised of Indigenous warriors, especially Tlaxcalans. There were not just two sides to this conflict; Malintzin was leading complex, multilateral negotiations. According to the conquistador Bernal Díaz, who wrote a richly detailed account of the expedition, Cortés himself even came to be known as 'Malinche' among the Indigenous people because 'Doña Marina was always in his company, particularly when any Ambassadors arrived, and she spoke to them in the Mexican language'. The captain and his interpreter became almost as one person.[33] But in a situation where the language is entirely unfamiliar – who is to say whether the translation was an accurate one? Is it possible that Malintzin, sold into bondage by the Nahua people, deliberately inflamed the situation in Mexico, encouraging a violent confrontation with her former enslavers? It is certainly not an impossibility. Malintzin remains a controversial figure today in Mexico – where her name has become synonymous with those who betray their culture: *malinchistas* – at least partly because of such ambiguities. Was she the ultimate traitor? Or the coerced mother of the *mestizo* nation? The name of Felipillo – one of the youthful Indigenous interpreters used by Pizarro during his conquest of Peru* – also implies corruption today; *felipillo* is a popular media nickname for lying politicians.[34] The reality is that we have very little idea of the precise details of most early exchanges. Even when interpreters were present, we cannot be confident that the understanding of events was shared by both sides, and the records rarely note the laborious process of translation. Although frequently invisible in the sources, the decoding and rephrasing of information from one language to another provided considerable opportunity for go-betweens to exploit their unique perspective. And many intermediaries proved to be agile in capitalising on their role, seeing an opportunity to gain influence between the cracks, and finding ways to promote

---

*   Felipillo's exact heritage is unknown, with sources disagreeing about whether he is from Poechos, Tumbes, Púna or Huancavilca. His will declares he was a nephew of the *cacique* of Chincha, so he likely originated from the western coast of what is now Peru.

themselves and their families by manoeuvring within the fault lines of encounter.

Language learning was at the heart of early encounter. But the nature of the sources means that our discussions of translation tend to focus on the ways in which it was useful to Europeans and how they attempted to manage these new languages. Frequently that struggle is made visible to us via texts: alphabets, dictionaries, orthographies, lists of alien terms tamed by forcing them into a familiar structure. The process of transforming Indigenous, non-alphabetic, languages into our familiar Latin script is itself a subtle form of colonisation: rich, flexible, adaptable sounds and other forms of communication wrestled into the constraints of twenty-six neat European characters.[35] But what is often forgotten in this discussion is the contribution of Indigenous people themselves.

As usual, the focus is on great white men. Like the, undoubtedly extraordinary, Franciscan friar Bernardino de Sahagún – known as the 'first anthropologist' – who dedicated his life to understanding Nahua culture, religion and language: word lists, interviews, inform-ants. Like the English polymath Thomas Hariot who published *A Brief and True Account of the New Found Land of Virginia* in 1588, and is credited with producing the first Algonquian alphabet. But if we shift our focus just slightly, and look over the shoulder of these 'great men' to those standing behind them, the picture is suddenly rather different. It seems that behind every successful European invader or writer in this period is an Indigenous collaborator. For these men were not working alone but surrounded by Native people, men and women whose labour – whether freely given or not – should not be forgotten.

The story of the Algonquian alphabet is a wonderful example of the ways in which refocusing on Indigenous travellers can transform our understanding of history. The traditional rendition of this tale begins with a white man – Thomas Hariot* – born and

---

* His name is often spelled 'Harriot', but I am going to stick with how he spelled it in his own publications.

educated in Oxford who, after his graduation from Oriel College in 1580, started to study navigation. Hired by Walter Ralegh* as a mathematics tutor, Hariot distinguished himself for his remarkable astronomical and navigational expertise and ended up accompanying Ralegh on his first expedition to Roanoke, where they would found a doomed colony. While in Ralegh's household, Hariot met with two Algonquian-speaking men – Manteo and Wanchese – who had been brought to England by the 1584 expedition Ralegh funded to scope out the possibilities for settlement in the Americas. So the story goes, Hariot 'taught them English while he learned their Algonquian dialect' and then 'invented a phonetic alphabet'.[36] All the agency, all the credit is given to Hariot; the focus is on *his* originality, curiosity, and intelligence. But, with just a slight shift in focus, we can transform this story and tell it in a totally different way.

In 1584, an expedition to the outer banks of present-day North Carolina returned to England and – according to the first published account of the voyage – 'brought with them two sauage [savage] men of that countrie'. It's not at all clear how these 'lustie men, whose names were Wanchese and Manteo', ended up travelling to London – did they volunteer? were they kidnapped? – but the scant evidence suggests they were probably convinced rather than coerced to travel to London.[37] Both men, who were likely of high status, were from small islands off the coast, but they may well have been strangers to each other. Wanchese was from Roanoke, which later became the site of the infamous 'lost colony', and Manteo was Croatan, a person of the 'Talking Town': an appropriate name for a man who later became a translator.[38] Given the efforts made by the local elite to trade and build amicable connections with the English, it seems plausible they were willing emissaries, perhaps tasked with trying to understand the English technologies which Hariot claimed 'so farre exceeded their capacities to comprehend

---

* Although he's popularly known as Raleigh, that's not a spelling which he is ever known to have used in his lifetime, despite the fact he had a huge number of different variations.

. . . that they thought they were rather the works of gods than of men, or at the leastwise they had been given and taught us of the gods'. Although Hariot's hint at yet another belief in the 'white gods' is unlikely, there is some truth in this statement because the peoples of the Eastern Woodlands certainly inhabited a sophisticated meta-physical world that would have shaped the way they understood the European intruders.[39] It is easy enough to imagine that Indigenous peoples were keen to learn more about the intruders who had appeared at their borders, possessing remarkable instruments and abilities: 'Mathematicall instruments, sea compasses, the virtue of the lodestone in drawing iron, a perspective glasse whereby was showed manie strange sightes . . . gunnes, books, writing and reading, spring clocks that seemed to goe of themselves, and manie other things that wee had'.[40] These marvels would have been just a few of the novelties that Manteo and Wanchese experienced after they arrived on English shores in early autumn.

According to Lupold von Wedel, a German travel writer who saw them in London in October 1584 and has a reputation for volu-minous curiosity rather than accuracy: 'They were in countenance and stature like white Moors. Their usual habit was a mantle of rudely tanned skins of wild animals, no shirts, and a pelt before their privy parts. Now, however, they were clad in brown taffeta. No one was able to understand them and they made a most childish and silly figure'.[41] A mercenary who had fought against the Turks, von Wedel was hardly a sympathetic observer of 'foreigners', but his views reflect the prejudice and curiosity that often shaped the way white people saw Indigenous visitors to Europe. We have no pictures of these early travellers, but they had obviously adopted English dress, perhaps as much to cope with the chill of London as to conform to local expectations. Most Algonquin men and women of the coastal Carolinas wore an apron-like skirt made of deerskin, covering from waist to mid-thigh at the front (and sometimes the back). Men usually wore their hair long and knotted behind the ear at the side or back of their head, with the other side scraped short with a shell, possibly to avoid it becoming entangled in their bow. Tattooing was usually for women, men preferring to paint their bodies and faces on ceremonial occasions, so one wonders whether Manteo and Wanchese blended into the London crowds, or chose to keep their distinctive hair, feather and shell adornments.[42] It's impossible to know how much their appearance was controlled by their patron Ralegh, but von Wedel's disparaging comment gives a clue about how they were regarded in London. Fortunately for us, Queen Elizabeth I was deeply preoccupied with how her subjects dressed, and so the fact that Manteo and Wanchese were dressed in crisp, rustling taffeta – probably breeches, with a linen shirt and doublet, maybe with a cloak – tells us they were treated as at least equivalent to the son of a knight or rich man: someone who was seen as part of society, comfortably off, though not necessarily fabulously wealthy or important.[43]

What little we know of Manteo and Wanchese's time in London suggests they were kept busy by Hariot and Ralegh, for the two were vital to the explorer's plans for a second expedition to Ossomocomuck territory. They became part of Ralegh's household, moving into Durham House, a beautiful palace on the Strand granted to him by Elizabeth I. In this impressive mansion, on the north bank of the Thames, Manteo and Wanchese spent the winter, learning English, getting to know London, and exciting the House of Commons by revealing their knowledge of America's 'singuler great comodities'. The 1591 plea of one Thomas Harvey, 'cape [chief] merchant', suggests that Ralegh may have been using Manteo and Wanchese to promote his American endeavours. Harvey complained that he had lost a lot of money investing in an expedition under false pretences, because of the claims of two 'Inhabitants of the same foreign Nation': Manteo and Wanchese. It seems that the travellers had become not just informants but also involuntary propagandists.[44]

Manteo and Wanchese were only the first of many Algonquian-speaking people to set foot in the Tudor capital, and their faint-but-discernible footprints lead us through a London that has largely now melted away: from Durham House Street near Charing Cross Station – the name of the narrow thoroughfare the last remnant of the huge palace that once stood there – to Victoria

Embankment on the river, which once marked the boundary wall to Ralegh's estate.* Although today in the heart of the metropolis, in the 1580s Durham House lay in the genteel countryside near the recently renovated Whitehall palace, to the west of the grimy, busy centre.

On at least one occasion, on 18 October, Ralegh took Manteo and Wanchese outside the city to Hampton Court, where they met Lupold von Wedel and were probably presented to the queen.† It being a Sunday, Elizabeth and her retinue attended church, sumptuously attired and with tremendous ceremony. Manteo and Wanchese's brown taffeta would have been in striking contrast to the fabulous affluence of the court, making us wonder why Ralegh had chosen it. Perhaps they were, on this occasion, merely part of the explorer's retinue, the humble brown meant to indicate their submission to Ralegh as he sought to persuade the Crown to support his endeavours. Or maybe he did not want them to prove a distraction from his own considerable charms. The queen reputedly adored Ralegh and, only three months later, she knighted her favourite, and bestowed upon him the title of Lord and Governor of Virginia. Manteo and Wanchese might even have witnessed the ceremony. Coming from a society in which careful ritual was important, Manteo and Wanchese were perhaps able to decode some of the meticulous etiquette surrounding Queen Elizabeth, although they may have been surprised by her chalk-white face (makeup covering smallpox scars) and by the extreme deference of so many strong, effective men to this slight, if impressively arrayed, woman. Algonquin women were tough and respected, holding considerable influence and autonomy, even acting as political leaders. What would Manteo and Wanchese have

---

* Coll Thrush's marvellous book, *Indigenous London*, has walking tours of the capital which allow you to follow in the footsteps of Indigenous travellers.

† Scholars often claim that Manteo and Wanchese were never presented at court, but Lupold von Wedel saw them there with Ralegh on 18 October 1584, when the queen was in residence, and it seems highly unlikely that Ralegh would not have taken the opportunity to show off the two men.

made of the sharp distinction between the male-dominated society they saw in London, and among the politicians and investors they met, and the obeisance to Elizabeth I? The bulk of Hampton Court must also have made quite an impression. If even the well-travelled Lupold von Wedel thought the palace looked like a town from a distance, it must have loomed large in the minds of two men from the Eastern Woodlands. Would they have been awed, or just appalled?

London itself would likely have astonished the two men. They came from a culture that was mobile in the summer, with twenty or thirty *wigwams* for one clan, and which erected villages with shared longhouses in the winter. Even remembering that coastal Algonquin dwellings often housed large extended families, the English capital – with its population nudging towards 200,000 – must have made a remarkable impression, although not necessarily a positive one. Indigenous people were frequently struck by the noise, dirt and poverty of London, as much as by its size. When the Powhatan Uttamatomakkin (Tomocomo) accompanied Matoaka to London in 1616, he tried to keep track of the population he saw on his way from Plymouth to London by making notches on his stick, but 'his arithmetike soone failed'.[45] For Algonquin people, the looming islands of brick and stone were an alien world. But for many Mesoamericans, the busy, densely settled hubs of Europe would not have come as a surprise. These were an urban people, cities and towns scattering a landscape that was dominated by the slickly planned metropolis of Tenochtitlan whose population of over 100,000 rivalled (and possibly exceeded) that of London.*[46]

Manteo and Wanchese, born into a generation after the first Great Dying, were from a region which was by then lightly populated by modern standards, where what would now be called a 'hamlet' was a busy community hub. It seems likely that they were startled by

---

* Indigenous North American civilisations also had a long history of urban settlement – most well-known are the massive pre-invasion Cahokia and Chaco Canyon sites – but other larger cities also declined with the violence and disease spread by early encounter.

the magnitude of the city, the teeming streets, and the expansive stone structures dominating the landscape. Uttamatomakkin was reportedly astonished at the wealth of corn and trees he saw on his journey to London, the Powhatans having sensibly assumed that the English had travelled west for want of resources.[47] But we have little real evidence of the Powhatan translators' experiences in London. Were they confined by respectability, or did they frequent the local taverns and walk the alleys near Durham House, which would soon be dubbed 'The Bermudas' for their lawlessness and the narrow and serpentine straits? We do not know. Manteo and Wanchese's experiences of London remain largely in shadow.

But a shaft of light falls on the conversations they had in a likely rather dark and chilly room in Ralegh's house overlooking the river Thames, a busy waterway which would have been familiar to the island men in its thriving water traffic. There, in the winter of 1584–5, Manteo and Hariot laboured together to bridge the language barrier. The fruit of their efforts was not only understanding on both sides, but also a unique document: the first attempt to create a set of conventions for the alphabetic recording of an Algonquian language. Forgotten until the 1980s, when it was rediscovered in the archives of Westminster School among the papers of the seventeenth-century headmaster Richard Busby, this artefact is remarkable in its own right: a fragment of efforts long forgotten, of collective effort across cultures, and of attempts to grapple with new forms of linguistic recording.

But the reason it is so important to us is what looks like a curly scrawl in the bottom right-hand corner of the page, a set of loops and squiggles that the expert eye of historian Coll Thrush deciphered as saying: MATEOROIDN. This single word is in a very different hand to Hariot's neat list, carefully inscribed by someone who is new to alphabetic writing, someone who has not quite cracked the conventions of spelling and grammar. Here, in a bold, looping, distinctive hand, someone has carefully written 'MATEO ROIDN' (Manteo roi done), or 'King Manteo did this'.[48] Here, on this sheet, it seems we have the signature of Manteo himself. And not just a signature – a claim to authorship. In calling this document 'John

Hariot's Alphabet', we erase the work of his Indigenous partners. This text is not the product of European research, a white man's hard work of observation; this was a collaboration between Manteo and Hariot (and perhaps also Wanchese).*

We know that every time Europeans and Americans met, and learned a new language, the process *must* have been collaborative. Columbus's kidnapped translators must, in some sense, have worked *with* their captors (even if under duress) to learn to penetrate each others' gibberish. But here, for once, the reciprocal nature of that process is explicitly recognised and recorded, by Manteo himself. In just eleven letters, the mark of Native travellers to Europe becomes visible. Sliding between the cracks of understanding, helping to bridge gaps in comprehension and knowledge, go-betweens were often translators and interpreters, but they could also be creators of knowledge and channels of power.

In April 1585, Manteo and Wanchese crossed the Atlantic for the second time, sailing from Plymouth as part of a fleet under the command of Sir Richard Grenville. This expedition of some six hundred men took advantage of a generous concession granted by Queen Elizabeth I to her favourite Walter Ralegh and his heirs, who were granted the right 'to discover, search, find out, and view' (as well as settle, trade with, and exploit) 'remote, heathen and barbarous lands, countries, and territories, not actually possessed of any Christian prince, nor inhabited by Christian people'. Manteo and Wanchese, as translators and potential intermediaries, were a vital part of these plans, and were specifically mentioned in the patent granted to Ralegh – the earliest record of their transatlantic voyage – which references people 'brought home into this our Realme of England' by whom 'great comodities of that Lande are revealed & made knowen unto us'.[49] This hints at the importance of Indigenous travellers in shaping European expeditions and aspirations. They were revealing their world and making it known to the invaders, who – with tragic

---

* Or perhaps not. As later events show, although he learned English, Wanchese was far from enamoured of his trip to England.

consequences – saw it firstly as a 'commodity' to be exploited.

We cannot be sure which of the seven ships in the fleet carried the men back to Roanoke, but it seems likely they were on the flagship, the *Tiger,* a 'great ship' of some 160 tons, which Queen Elizabeth had either loaned or hired to the fleet. It would make sense for these valuable translators to be kept close to the leader of the expedition where they could advise on events, and, when the *Tiger* captured a Spanish frigate near the island of San Juan, Hernando de Altamirano reported that the English were accompanied by 'two tall Indians, whom they treated well, and who spoke English'. The warden of Havana, writing to Philip II of Spain, also mentioned that the English had 'two well-attired Indians' among their company.[50]

If Manteo and Wanchese *were* on board the *Tiger,* they may have got more than they bargained for on their arrival back in Ossomocomuck territory. While anchoring near Wococon Island (now known as Ocracoke, North Carolina) on 29 June, the *Tiger* 'struck on ground, and sunk', according to the ship's log.[51] Ralph Lane, the leader of the expedition, describes the ordeal in a letter to the queen's secretary. The entire fleet temporarily grounded on entering the inlet, but – perhaps because of her greater bulk – the *Tiger* was battered repeatedly on the shoals for hours on end; they struck eighty-nine times according to Lane, which must have been terrifying for all those on board. We can only imagine the feelings of Manteo and Wanchese, after nearly a year away, fearing that they would die only metres from the soil of their homeland.

Lane feared that 'we were all in extreme hazard of being cast away'. But through incredible luck, or divine favour, the *Tiger* eventually ran aground, and the passengers were able to drag themselves to shore. Unfortunately for the prospective colonists, all but a few of their provisions – corn, salt, meal, rice, biscuit – were ruined by water damage, and so they suddenly found themselves dependent on Indigenous aid. On 3 July, the English 'sent word of our arriving at Wococon, to Wingino at Roanoke'. Wanchese probably accompanied these messengers, because we know soon he slipped away to rejoin his people at Roanoke. He had apparently had enough of English hospitality. Three days later, Manteo accompanied the ship's master John Arundell to the mainland, perhaps to look for supplies, or even to search for his compatriot Wanchese, who never returned to the ship. As the expedition's only remaining interpreter, he must have been an invaluable part of the explorations which followed.[52]

On 11 July, a large group of Englishmen went to the mainland, where they visited the villages of Pomeiooc, Aquascogoc and Secotan. Manteo's collaborator Thomas Hariot was part of this expedition, along with the painter John White, who drew meticulous images of the people they met. These fabulously detailed pictures still shape European views of Indigenous Americans today, and it seems certain that Manteo helped White and Hariot in their communication with the Indigenous people. Europeans like to think of themselves as the teachers of 'childlike natives', but often they were the pupils. Hariot hinted at this when he said his understanding 'of the nature and manners of the [Roanoke] people' came from 'special familiarity with some of their priests' (which can only have come through Manteo). As the Wampanoag chief Metacom (often known as King Philip) explained, in the early days it was the Indigenous peoples who were the protectors and teachers. His father Massasoit was 'as a great man and the English as a litell Child'.[53]

The initially cordial relationships between the English and the people of Ossomocomuck (a word which may mean something like 'the land that we inhabit' or 'the dwelling house') did not last. Wanchese was among those who vociferously opposed the English attempts to establish a settlement, being denounced by Ralph Lane among those who conspired against the colonists: he was one of 'our great enemies'. There is a lot of speculation about what might have turned Wanchese against the English – disillusionment or disgust, irritation at Manteo's preferential treatment, allegiance to his people – but there is no evidence for any of these speculations. One aspect which is sometimes overlooked is the possibility that Wanchese had simply fulfilled his mission. On returning to Roanoke, Wanchese became a close aide of Wingina (later Pemisapan), a *weroance* (leader) who held authority over a group of communities around Roanoke, including Croatan and a coastal village called Dasemunkepeuc.[54] As a Roanoke warrior, it is entirely possible that Wanchese had agreed to cross the Atlantic as Wingina's emissary and scout, returning to his home once the ship reached Native shores.

Once Wanchese leaves the oversight of the English, he also largely disappears from the sources, making it hard to trace his later life, but it's quite clear that he saw the English as a threat rather than an ally, and it seems he fomented Indigenous resistance to Ralegh's plans. His trip to London likely brought him sooner than most to the realisation that the English were just men, albeit with warriors and resources in abundance. If Wanchese realised that this hapless cluster of men and women was just an advance party for a much larger invading force, it could explain his hostility. Certainly he abandoned the Europeans at the first opportunity, returning to his people on Roanoke where he put his knowledge of the English to defiant use. Such defections were not uncommon. In 1590, two young men 'which were the chief Caciques sons of that Countrey and part of Dominica' took ship with John White (by then 'governor' of Roanoke and on a 'rescue' mission to his long-abandoned colony). While the ship was taking on ballast at St Croix, in the Virgin Islands, they fled, presumably with hopes of returning home.[55]

Manteo, on the other hand, remained loyal to the English, crossing and recrossing the Atlantic in support of their endeavours. He became the first recorded Indigenous American to become a Protestant Christian, perhaps converted by Ralegh, and by March 1586 he had even been granted his own 'peece' (gun), an item usually jealously guarded from Indigenous hands. Manteo returned to London when the English hastily evacuated Roanoke in 1586 before braving the Atlantic for the fourth and last time a year later, as part of Ralegh's disastrous final attempt at founding a 'city' on Roanoke. According to John White, Manteo proved himself to be 'a most faithfull English man'.[56]

During his last trip to London, Manteo probably mingled with intellectuals from Ralegh and Hariot's circle, such as the mathematician and geographer Robert Hues (who circumnavigated the world with Thomas Cavendish), the globe-maker Emery Molyneux, and Henry Percy, the 9th Earl of Northumberland – called the 'Wizard Earl' for his scientific and cartographic prowess.[57] These men would likely have flocked to learn from Manteo, who not only had privileged geographical knowledge of 'new lands', but had also proved his capacity for scholarship working with Hariot and White. What the shrewd Manteo made of these men and their enthusiasms we cannot know, but when he returned to Ossomocomuck in 1587 his steadfast support of the English was rewarded.

> The 13. of August, our Savage Manteo, by the commandment of Sir Walter Ralegh, was christened in Roanok, and called Lord thereof, and of Dasamongueponke, in reward of his faithfull service.[58]

Although Ralegh's claim to the land was dubious, it is nonetheless remarkable that he should 'grant sovereignty' over the region to Manteo. It seems likely that Manteo's baptism was symbolic: the first Indigenous American welcomed into the Church of England on Virginian soil. Whether Manteo was truly converted by his time with the English or simply observing the ritual to please his allies, we do not know, just as we cannot know to what extent the new Lord of Roanoke and Dasamongueponke had manoeuvred himself into a position of power, or was rather a pawn of the English. Certainly, his rule did not last. When White returned to the Roanoke colony in 1590 after three years away, he found the site abandoned and the only sign of life was the word 'CROATOAN' scratched into the palisade. This so-called 'Lost Colony' has become a mystery that has baffled and fascinated ever since. There was no sign of death or violence, so scholars have speculated that the message was a clue to the location of the settlers. Did Manteo take his allies from England home to his Croatan community? Perhaps, in the end, it was the English who assimilated to Indigenous ways.

Manteo and Wanchese were not the only Indigenous travellers entangled with the ill-fated Roanoke colony. Often seen as exceptions, they are just the most visible members of a wider circle of

Native people who were embroiled with Ralegh and his associates. At the very bottom of a list of 'all the men, women and Children, which safely arrived in Virginia, and remained to inhabite there. 1587', appears the name Towaye, alongside Manteo, in a category reserved for Native people 'That were in Englande and returned home into Virginia with them'. This glimpse of an otherwise unknown Indigenous voyager makes us wonder how many more lie unseen below the surface of recorded history.[59]

Several others pop up fleetingly. In 1586, Grenville made a supply run to Roanoke, only to discover the island deserted and two bodies – one English, one Indigenous – hanging from a tree. Finding only three local people remaining, Grenville's crew managed to 'seize' one of them and extract the information that Francis Drake had evacuated the remaining people from the island. The Spanish pilot who testified to these events doesn't mention whether the Roanokan was able to speak English or if there was an interpreter among the crew, but it seems likely that he was familiar with the English who had attempted to appropriate his island.[60] If this man were a potential interpreter, then it would explain why he was then taken to England, where it seems he became part of Grenville's household in the coastal town of Bideford in Devon. The only record we have of his life there comes from two blunt entries in the parish record:

Anno Domini 1588 Christenings . . .

Raleigh, A Wynganditoian . . . xxvj day of March

Anno Domini 1589 Buryings . . .
Rawly A man of Wynganditoia the vijth day of Aprile sepultus fuit [was buried][61]

'Raleigh', named for Grenville's cousin, was baptised more than a year after landing in England, which suggests this may have been a voluntary conversion, or at least an educated one. Like other abductees, he probably also adopted other English behaviours during this time, and he may have been a source of curiosity for local people, as well as a resource for his kidnappers, as Grenville quickly began planning another expedition.

Bideford in the 1580s was a thriving port town. It was at Bideford that Ralegh's first shipment of tobacco was landed although, contrary to popular belief, this was not the first tobacco to arrive in England. Sailors had been smoking tobacco pipes for years, and so this was a place where an Indigenous visitor might have seen goods or even people from home, which makes it somehow all the more stark that, almost exactly a year after his Christian baptism, the Algonquin baptised 'Raleigh' (or 'Rawly') died – probably of the flu which took Grenville's teenage daughter a few weeks later. He was buried at St Mary's Church in Bideford, close by the river. Like so many others, his remains lie unmarked in foreign soil.

Bideford is two hundred miles from London. They may have been relatively few, but – by the 1580s – Indigenous people pervaded Tudor England and a cobweb of transatlantic connections was beginning to emerge. In the 1590s Ralegh, having fallen out of the queen's favour and been disgraced at court,* turned his attention south to Guiana (modern-day Guyana), which he had become convinced was a fabulous land of gold that could transform his fortunes. In 1594, Ralegh's agent, Jacob Whiddon, was sent to scout the region and returned home with four Indigenous Guianans, at least two of whom were 'familiar with the English language'. These men returned with Ralegh to Guiana in 1595, at the start of another intricate dance with the local people. The English were not the first Europeans to invade their territory; Spanish crews seeking to enslave Indigenous people had been harassing the coast and Orinoco Valley, and so – likely hearing rumours that the new arrivals had destroyed the Spanish base on Trinidad – local rulers spotted a welcome opportunity to ally with the English against these tormentors. They were helped in the negotiations by Ralegh's 'Indian interpreter, which I carried out of England'. This was probably 'John Provost' or 'John of Trinidad' who later accompanied Lawrence Keymis when he led the second expedition commissioned by Ralegh in 1596 and was vital in obtaining detailed

---

* Elizabeth was unsurprisingly unimpressed by her favourite secretly marrying one of her maids of honour, after getting her pregnant.

ethnographic and geographic information about the region. On meeting the *caciques*, Ralegh expounded on the benevolence of his Virgin Queen, who was there to free them from the 'tyranny of the Spaniards'. The interpreter, John, was key to these negotiations – explicitly acknowledged on multiple occasions – and was also responsible for ensuring that local people were compensated for any theft or damage caused by 'the meaner sort' among Ralegh's company. It seems that John was not just a mouthpiece for the English, but also an aide and trusted associate.

Topiawari, the chief of a region called Aromaia, was so persuaded of the advantages of allying with Ralegh's company that – in exchange for two young English hostages – he voluntarily sent his only son Cayowaroco (and another royal youth) to England, because 'he himself had but a short time to live' and he hoped that 'by our means his son should be established after his death'. Another 'Indian interpreter' named Henry pops up on a 1596 voyage, and French and Spanish sources suggest that Ralegh also coerced the son of a Trinidadian ruler, and three others, to accompany him across the Atlantic. A small but significant cluster of Native people were thus travelling regularly to England in the 1590s, some of whom became experienced voyagers, crossing the Atlantic on multiple occasions, becoming known among Ralegh's associates and at court. In July 1596, Ralegh's wife Bess wrote to the statesman Robert Cecil that 'TOPEAWARE the King, that was her Majesty's subject, is dead, and his son returned.' I very much doubt that Topiawari would have understood himself as a 'subject' of Elizabeth, but – likely because of his son's presence at court – he was recognised in elite circles. We don't know what Cayowaroco did in England – it is possible he appeared before the queen in a performance organised by the Earl of Essex – but he seems to have remained allied to Ralegh and the English throughout his life. Transatlantic diplomacy was strengthened by personal connections, and Ralegh's Indigenous circle was to have far-reaching influence.[62]

In 1604, when white men turned up at the mouth of the Wiapoco River (now the Oyapock), the local Iayos (or Yayoas) and Sapayos rulers used two interpreters who 'had been before in England, and could speake some English' to negotiate with the new arrivals, led by Captain Charles Leigh. The Indigenous people clearly recognised the potential value of alliance with the English, and encouraged Charles Leigh and company to settle in their territory, on condition that they aid them against their enemies. Leigh, no doubt feeling somewhat precarious in his position, 'demanded pledges of them to be sent into England' and was perhaps surprised that so many Indigenous people willingly agreed to accompany him. According to Leigh's letter to his brother, the locals pestered him every day about when he was going to England, and four 'principal men' ended up on the first ship back in June. The Guianans had learned the value of transatlantic diplomacy and Leigh the value of a good interpreter; he begged that they should send him 'Sir Walter Rawleighes Indian or my Lord Admirals', for the locals – Pluainma (by now a local leader) and William – either proved no help or 'understandeth but little to any purpose'.[63] Indigenous translators and negotiators were an established feature of transatlantic networks by the turn of the seventeenth century.

When Robert Harcourt* landed in the same region in 1609, he was unexpectedly greeted not only by a couple of men in European dress (in sharp contrast to the rest who were mostly 'starke belly naked') but also by a local man who spoke English well because he had 'beene in England, and served Sir *John Gilbert* [Ralegh's nephew] many years'. This is almost certainly Ralegh's interpreter, John Provost (doubtless named after the man he had served, like so many others). John had returned home to his people, but his identity remained profoundly transatlantic. As he lay dying, John begged that some of the Englishmen would sing a psalm with him, confessing 'that he had been a wicked sinner: but did hope that he should be saved by the precious blood of our Saviour Jesus Christ'. At the very end of his life, John asked that all present should 'beare witness that he died a Christian, yea (as

---

* A man billed by the *Oxford Dictionary of National Biography* as a 'colonial adventurer and author', but who might better be described as a bad investor and a failed colonist.

he added) a Christian of *England*. If Harcourt's account can be trusted, John may have returned home, but he had been deeply affected by his time in England. One wonders how John felt about the arrival of Harcourt's expedition, especially as it included two other Indigenous *nepantleras*, in-betweeners: 'Martin', a local lord who had been in England for four years, and 'Anthony Canabre'.* While Canabre had spent fourteen years in England, becoming a Christian, Martin seems to have understood his transatlantic trip as a temporary arrangement and was 'joyfull that he had againe recovered his owne home'.† Harcourt makes much of announcing to the local people that 'he had brought home their Countryman Martin, whome they all thought to be dead', but it must have been deeply disorientating for the Indigenous communities and families left behind by these travellers.

The ways in which Native peoples framed, understood and managed these voyages are an important and often-neglected part of the story. How were these voyages seen by Indigenous society? Were the travellers eagerly awaited, or assumed to be definitively departed? How long did you wait before assuming your son, brother, father or husband was dead? Martin's brother had become chief in his absence, so we have to wonder whether the traveller's return was entirely welcome. If we read Harcourt's account carefully, there are hints at the way in which Martin reasserted his authority as chief upon his return. There was feasting in the house that had 'belonged unto his brother as chiefe Lord in his absence', and Martin's humble speech of welcome to the English was 'approved by the rest of the Indians present', each taking it in turn to give official welcome. Harcourt, as usual, sees these formalities only in relation to himself, but it seems likely that this deliberate approbation indicates that

---

* We cannot be sure exactly which Indigenous groups these people belonged to, but they were very likely Arawak or Tupi speakers. Harcourt describes some of them as 'Yaios', a word that some have claimed to be the origin of Jonathan Swift's 'Yahoos'.

† There is no record of Martin becoming Christian, but Harcourt does claim at one point that the chief laughed at Indigenous people's 'simplicitie' in their beliefs about the eclipse, so he was not wholly immune to English forms of knowledge.

Martin was restored to his place as chief. Harcourt stops mentioning Martin as among his interpreters after this event, noting only
the help of John and Anthony Canabre. It seems Martin had come
home to stay.[64]

We can only wonder what led an Indigenous noble to risk his
life and his influence by undertaking a dangerous crossing to a
strange land. Was it curiosity, or a desire to meet the English rulers
about whom he had heard so much? Perhaps he hoped to take the
initiative in the increasingly frequent interactions with white men.
At the river Conawini, yet another transatlantic chief appears in
Harcourt's story: Leonard Ragapo was a knowledgeable Christian
who understood and spoke some English, having travelled to
England with Walter Ralegh, of whom he appears to have been
very fond.* Ragapo had spent three or four years in England with
Ralegh, becoming a cosmopolitan celebrity known as 'Captain
Leonard' by his people. According to Harcourt, he loved England
'with all his heart', and helped Harcourt's cousin find valuable topaz
gems, as well as offering him excellent hospitality: 'not after the
ordinarie rude manner of the Indians, but in a more civill fashion,
and with much respect and love'. Yet behind all this 'civilised' facade
lay some careful manoeuvring, for Ragapo finally persuaded Harcourt to leave four Englishmen in his territory, possibly as a form of
resistance against Anaki-v-ry, the chief to whom he was currently
'subjected' having 'seized' the territory. Maybe he thought the
presence of these strangers would consolidate his power locally, as
well as offer some resistance to the opponents against whom he kept
having to defend his territory. 'The policy of the Indian *Leonard*',
wrote Harcourt, was 'to take advantage by their fear and make
our men his Guard, and chief protection'. Leonard had learned to
exploit his transatlantic connections.

Anthony Canabre, meanwhile, was also taking advantage of his
time in England, for Harcourt rewarded him for his faithful service
by giving him a mountain that he had blithely 'taken possession of'
on behalf of the king. 'I delivered the possession of that Mountaine

---

*   Everywhere Harcourt went, people seemed disappointed he was not Ralegh.

to my Indian, *Anthony Canabre, To have, holde, possess,* and *enjoy the same, to him, and to his heires for ever*', provided he paid his taxes as proof his family would be 'true Subjects unto the King's Majesty'. Harcourt's 'gift' was clearly an attempt to solidify English claims to the territory and bind the local nobility into 'vassalage' with James I. Such concepts were often alien to Indigenous peoples, and it is likely that they saw these exchanges as consolidating partnership rather than submission, but one has to wonder whether Canabre – with fourteen years' experience in Ralegh's household – might have seen it differently. Far from a naïve surrender of autonomy, what we see here is a man exploiting his English allies to ensure a prosperous future in a land where he had become a stranger to his own people. Certainly, this crop of travellers saw the best opportunities for themselves in their homelands. None of the men chose to return with Harcourt, although he may have been seeking to replace their translating skills with 'an Indian boy, who died at Sea in our returne'.

More than a decade before the Pilgrims landed in Wampanoag territory, and thousands of miles to the south, Indigenous people were making meaningful transatlantic connections. London would likely have been a rather different experience for this second wave of visitors as, when Elizabeth I died in 1603, Ralegh was thrown into the Tower of London on unlikely conspiracy charges. With Durham House confiscated, along with the rest of his estate, 'Ralegh's Indians' would have been dependent on the generosity and support of his wider circle during their stay in London. It seems that two Indigenous men – a *cacique* known only as Harry, and Leonard Ragapo – served, and even lived with, Ralegh in the Tower, where he was confined in some comfort and also considerable despair, even attempting suicide on one occasion. Harry spent two years living in the Tower, presumably as one of Ralegh's two permitted servants, 'one to attend in the Chamber, the other to go about their business'.[65] Given Harry's imperfect English, he was probably Ralegh's chamber servant, attending to his personal needs and those of his wife and son. This was no dungeon – Ralegh received regular visits from other associates and friends, as well as his son's tutor

– but the household was crowded into just two rooms, and one wonders what the Guianans would have made of this incarceration, and of their energetic patron being controlled and confined. How did it affect their view of Ralegh that the man they had seen as so powerful and so dynamic was restricted to pottering around the garden of his prison and cultivating American plants? Accounts of Ralegh's incarceration frequently talk of his intellectual pursuits, his scientific explorations and horticultural experiments. But they never mention the Indigenous man who accompanied him throughout these enterprises. When Ralegh was attempting to grow tobacco and sassafras in his tiny garden, Harry was alongside him. When he wrote his *History of the World*, Harry was at his shoulder. Like Manteo with Hariot, Harry was an unacknowledged partner in Ralegh's enterprises in this period. It is quite remarkable that Ralegh would choose an Indigenous man to form one of his tiny household in this period. Perhaps he sought to continue to explore worlds unknown, through discussion and collaboration, even while confined. The Tower must surely have been an unsettling environment to a man of the river, farm and forest, and whether Harry served Ralegh willingly is unclear, although they had a respectful relationship in later years which suggests he at least became reconciled to living in the massive Bloody Tower* that overlooks the Thames.

London beyond the walls of the Tower would also have been a disconcerting experience for Indigenous visitors during Ralegh's imprisonment for, in 1603, two great transformations wrought the capital. Elizabeth I had died, after almost half a century on the throne. Were Native people among the 'multitudes of all sorts of people in their streets, houses, windows, leads, and gutters' who watched Elizabeth's body carried down the Thames on a torchlit barge, and joined the 'sighing, groaning and weeping' for the queen as she lay in state at Whitehall?[66] Perhaps they came to gawk, but not to mourn; to pay their respects to the woman who meant so

---

* Originally, more attractively, called the Garden Tower, but later nicknamed for the suspected murder of the two 'Princes in the Tower'.

much to their patron Ralegh; or out of curiosity at the scene. Maybe they were driven indoors by the overwhelming crowds.

There was another good reason to stay indoors and avoid the crowds that year. By the summer of 1603, London was suffering from a dreadful outbreak of the plague which would ultimately kill some 30,000 people. Attempting to protect his subjects, James I ordered that houses where anyone was known to have contracted the plague were 'to be closed up' for six weeks 'after the sickness be ceased' and infected people were to be 'restrained from resorting into the company of others, either publicly or privately'. Anyone who infringed the rules was to be put into the stocks on the road next to their house, as a warning to others. After the quarantine period was over, all the 'clothes, bedding and other stuff as hath been worn and occupied by the infected' was to be burned.[67] Early modern people may not have known about germs, but they had seen what infection could do. The plague is a possible reason that we do not hear the eventual fate of many Indigenous Guianans in London; those that did not sail west may have perished like so many travellers before them.

Ralegh was finally freed by the new King James I in 1616 and, a year later, he returned to Guiana in one last search for gold and glory. His story is beyond the scope of our tale, but it deserves a brief mention for the remarkable way in which Ralegh sought out not only riches, but also the Indigenous men who had been his go-betweens and allies in earlier years. In early November, confined to his cabin with sickness, Ralegh attempted to contact his old associate, Leonard Ragapo. 'I sent in my skiff to enquire for my old sarvant Leonard the Indien who [had] bine with me in Ingland 3 or 4 yeers.' Learning that Ragapo had moved 30 miles inland and, much too ill to make the journey or wait for him to be summoned, Ralegh headed for Caliana (the Cayenne River) 'where the Cassique [*cacique*] was also my sarvant and had lived with mee in the tower 2 yeers'. There, he 'sent my barge ashore to enquire for my servant Harry the Indien'. Harry – a noble in his own right, and maybe not prepared to appear at Ralegh's beck and call – sent his brother and two other *caciques*, promising to come himself with provisions if Ralegh remained incapacitated. A day or two later 'my sarvant Harry came to me, who had almost forgotten his Inglish', bringing plentiful provisions, enough to feed the company for more than a week. Ralegh was carried ashore, where he rested under a tent, and – after a day or two – he allowed himself to be tempted to eat refreshing pineapples and roasted peccary and armadillo, and he 'began to gather a little strength'. Harry's willingness to care not only for Ralegh, but his entire ship's company, providing lavish hospitality, suggests a desire to ensure that the shift in power was clear to Ralegh – Harry was the benefactor and leader here, he was not a servant – and also a genuine connection between the two men. Ralegh famously seems to have inspired great loyalty in those around him, and his letters speak warmly of 'being fedd and assisted by the Indyans of my ould acquaintance, with a greate deale of love and respect'. From being servants and interpreters, these men seem to have become something more: allies, comrades, perhaps even friends.[68]

Tracing the Indigenous people who came to England, from the earliest days of attempted English colonisation in the 1580s until the settlement at Jamestown in 1607, shows a tangible 'circle' of Indigenous associates who were tied to Ralegh's household and contacts. These men were vital not only as go-betweens for exploration, but also to intellectual enquiry. Ralegh's circle included prominent scholars, politicians and businessmen. Even in the Tower, he dabbled in science, botany and medicine, and wrote influential political and historical tracts. Through his network, Indigenous people would have become widely known in London society, and they seem to have exploited these opportunities confidently where they could. The frequency of such connections suggests extensive cross-cultural networks branching out from most early voyages, even where they are not recorded. When Epenow, a Nauset man from what is now Martha's Vineyard, was abducted to London in 1611, he was taught English by an Abenaki named Assacumet, who had been living in the city since 1605. Transatlantic understandings were not just built in the colonies, but also on European shores.[69]

Although often coerced into becoming interpreters, go-betweens were not merely tools of the colonisers, 'trapped' between 'two worlds'. Once they had learned to slide across cultures and languages, the 'in-betweeners' were in a middle ground which gave them access to unique opportunities and insights. The experiences of these nimble translators – hopping between cultural systems, negotiating, and interpreting – show the opportunities which transatlantic experience could open up for some individuals. Some, such as Manteo, took advantage of cultural mobility to further their own ambitions. Others, like Wanchese, turned their transatlantic experience to the advantage of their own communities. Many simply clung on, hoping to survive long enough to return to their families, or making the best of their situation. Felipillo and another of Pizarro's interpreters – a young man from Poechos known as don Martín – travelled to Spain with the conquistador in 1528 and returned with him to Panama, before being involved in the campaign against the Inkas. Felipillo was later executed for supposed treason, but don Martín was rewarded for his loyalty, earning the title of 'interpreter general' and becoming a wealthy citizen of Lima until Spanish infighting left him without a patron, and he was lashed and stripped of his property. Martín died in Seville in 1549, where he was petitioning for the return of his lands. Two decades later, his *mestiza* daughter Francisca was among the nobles of Indigenous descent appealing for grants at the royal court.[70]

Though constrained both by her enslaved status and her gender, Cortés's interpreter Malintzin seized the opportunity offered by her linguistic skills to secure her fortunes and those of her children. In 1528, she saw the son fathered by Cortés depart on a ship bound for Spain. Tragically, that was the last time they would see each other. By the time Martín returned to Mexico in 1540, his mother had been dead for a decade. Like so many who crossed the vast ocean, he returned a changed man, transformed by his time in Europe.

3

Kith and Kin

On 16 June 1505, a young Carijó man landed at Honfleur in France. Known to us as Essomericq, he was probably born with the name Içá-Mirim (small chief)* because he was the son of the chief Arosca, who ruled over a region of southern Brazil inhabited by the people now known to us as Guaraní. The Guaraní were deeply spiritual, agricultural people, who simply called themselves *abá* (men) or *ñande ore* (all of us).[1] But in January of the previous year, a strange sailor had arrived in their lands in a peculiar boat, larger than their dugout canoes, and made from pieces of wood. This Frenchman, Binot Paulmier de Gonneville, brought all kinds of curiosities – metal tube weapons which fired balls at devastating speed across long distances, small mirrors, glass beads, and knives and axes stronger than their own. Arosca and his people tolerated the French, watching closely and even helping when the strangers raised two wooden crosses with great ceremony, music, and noise from their weapons: a huge one, some thirty-five feet high, on a mound overlooking the sea; and another in front of their very own burial grounds. We do not know whether – as Paulmier claimed – the Guaraní feared the French, but the display of artillery on Easter Day 1504, must certainly have given them pause and may have hinted at the foreigners' potential as allies.

If Paulmier's account can be believed, the chief seized his opportunity to learn how to make these new technologies and

---

* As this is a tentative identification and not widely used, I will stick with the established Francophone version of his Indigenous name: Essomericq.

to 'be able to control their enemies', willingly allowing his young son Essomericq to accompany Gonneville to France, escorted by an older man called Namoa, who was perhaps thirty-five to forty years of age. Arosca supplied the French ship *Espoir* (Hope) lavishly with food and beautiful treasures, including many glorious feathers, as presents for the French king. He also 'made the captain swear to return in twenty moons'. Arosca clearly had no intention of losing his son – he was sending his kin as an explorer and emissary. Namoa seems likely to have been attendant, bodyguard and companion, an experienced aide to guide and accompany the young man, who was probably around fifteen. But disaster struck, and Essomericq would be left to cope alone.

On the troubled voyage to France, many of the crew were 'tormented by a malignant fever' and four men, including Namoa, died. This tragedy prompted an intense philosophical discussion among the French as to whether the Guaraní should be baptised, to 'save their souls' from damnation. The consensus was that Namoa would have been baptised in vain, for he died in ignorance of Catholic beliefs, but that Essomericq – also dangerously ill – should be baptised, with the captain and two other crew members as his godfathers, there being no women available to act as godmother. And so, on 14 September, Essomericq 'was named Binot, after the baptismal name of the captain' and confirmed the French in their convictions by making a miraculous recovery, proving that his 'baptism served as medicine to the soul and the body'.

Driven up the coast of Brazil, the *Espoir* was forced to make two more stops before attempting the transatlantic crossing. To the north of the Guaraní regions the company intruded on the lands of the Tupi, whom the French considered 'boorish' people, 'eaters of men'. These warrior people were much less welcoming to the French, and their nakedness did not match European expectations of 'civility'. Nonetheless, Gonneville and his men kidnapped 'two Indians that they wanted to bring to France'. But the Tupi, excellent swimmers, both dived overboard and escaped on the first night. What did Essomericq make of all this? He would not have considered these men to be kin, but it might have given him pause to see familiar faces seized against their will and forced on board. Did the young man try to hide any horror he felt, now alone and vulnerable? Or perhaps the prince, used to captives being taken in war, was unmoved.

After a long journey home, via a much-contested route, the *Espoir* finally found itself in familiar waters near the islands of Jersey and Guernsey, only to be attacked by pirates; many on board were slaughtered and the ship wrecked. Twenty-eight of the crew survived, including the captain, 'plus the Indian, Essomericq, otherwise called Binot, who in Honfleur, and all the other places where they passed, was well regarded, because they had never before had in France a character from such a distant country'.[2] Although this implies that Essomericq became a spectacle, and he would have certainly been the object of curiosity, the young Carijó's experience of Europe was rather unusual. Far from being exploited, paraded or ogled, he became one of the family.

Gonneville, finding himself unable to mount another expedition and keep his promise to Arosca to return his son safely home, seems to have sought another way to discharge his obligations. In 1521, when Essomericq had been living as Binot for more than a decade, and would have been a well-established man of about thirty years old, Gonneville found him an eligible bride from among his own relatives (perhaps a niece). Essomericq had fourteen children with Marie Moulin, including two sons named Binot and Olivier. This prolific parent is also reputed to have had seven daughters from a second marriage, after he was widowed late in life. When Gonneville died without an heir, Essomericq inherited the family name – Paulmier – along with his arms and some of his property. Essomericq-Binot Paulmier lived a long life, settled in Lisieux in northern France. Documents uncovered by Jean Leblond show a 'Bynot Paulmier' listed in 1523 among the 'masters and workers of the said profession and merchandise of hosiery' in Lisieux. Two decades later, three different Paulmier households appear in the Lisieux tax records: one seems to be headed by Essomericq, who is taxed 55 *sols*, and it seems likely that Jehan Paulmier – another hosier, who has newly entered the tax rolls – is his son, just married and setting up his household. Binot Paulmier (or 'Binot the Elder' as he starts to be called in the 1560s) pops up in the archives several more times, including many times in the deliberations of the town council, and twice signing notarial acts in Courtonne-la-Meurdrac, a village not far from Lisieux, where he perhaps held land. Essomericq died in 1583, probably at more than ninety years of age, and his descendants lived in the region for generations, often also bearing the names Binot and Olivier. The family was clearly respectable, for his eldest son Binot married a noblewoman, Jeanne de Robillard. The couple carried on the family tradition of fertility, having an impressive eleven children together, and their eldest son Jean Baptiste became a regional official for the royal treasury and married a marquise.[3] If we assume that the eldest Binot Paulmier in the Calvados Archives is Essomericq, then he was an active member of the local community, a successful businessman, and the father of a large and prosperous family. In just two generations, his descendants had moved from the relatively wealthy, upper-middling ranks of European society, through the local elite, into the higher echelons of the nobility. We have to wonder whether the cachet of marrying the descendants of a royal foreigner might have helped the family ambitions. Or maybe Essomericq was just an extraordinarily successful patriarch.

This Carijó-French dynasty continued to flourish quietly in Normandy in the following years until, in 1658, members of the Paulmier family were outraged to be ordered to pay a tax on foreign families living in France. This seemed an unfair imposition, given that their ancestor was not only stranded in France against his will, but was also a prince himself. So Jean Paulmier, a canon at Lisieux Cathedral at only twenty-six, determined to prove the family's ancestry and gain exemption from the taxes, went through various legal contortions to obtain a copy of Gonneville's account of his voyage from the Admiralty. In 1659, Jean explained all this in a treatise which boasted of his descent from Essomericq, as demonstrated by copies of various documents, promoting a form of humane evangelisation at a moment when France was seeking to establish its own colonies in modern-day Canada. Unfortunately for us, this text – which exists in four known versions – is the earliest evidence for Gonneville's voyage, and for Essomericq's arrival in France. Spurred by inconsistencies and elaborations in Paulmier's account, as well as later spurious claims that Gonneville was the first to reach Australia, some scholars have argued that Jean Paulmier's account was a fantasy, conjured up to burnish his lineage. In this reading, Essomericq never existed. And the trouble for us, as historians, is that – if he did exist – the Carijó 'prince' adapted so well to his adopted home and family, that he became indistinguishable in the records from any other Frenchman.[4]

But for some people today, on both sides of the Atlantic, Essomericq still holds a special significance. In 2018, Dorothée de Linares, a Frenchwoman who – according to her family records – is fourteen-generations descended from Essomericq, travelled to Brazil to look for traces of her ancestor. In São Francisco do Sul, the Brazilian region which claims Gonneville's landing, she was greeted by a delegation of local officials, was interviewed on the radio, and visited Indigenous communities. A road and a school are named after Içá-Mirim (Essomericq) and, in the local nature park, he is represented by a statue of a small boy in a feather skirt, clutching a parrot and holding a monkey by the hand. Thousands of miles away, the town of Courtonne-la-Meurdrac, which claims to be Essomericq's possible burial site, also considers him part of their history, mounting a spirited defence of his authenticity on the municipal website, claiming that his absence from their local archives can be easily explained by the fact he died two years before their records begin. They nonetheless traced the descendants of 'Binot Paulmier' all the way to 7 January 1743, when Marie-Anne Paulmier was married to a lord, in a ceremony conducted by her uncle, the canon Rocques Jean-Baptiste II Paulmier. Essomericq has slipped into family, local and national heritage, symbolising encounter, curiosity and identity.[5]

Did Essomericq really exist? There is no way of knowing for sure. But were there Indigenous people living quietly among the citizens of sixteenth-century France? The answer is certainly yes. Snippets in the archives show their presence as early as 1511, when a man from what is now Newfoundland was baptised in Tréguier with the name 'Tudgoal'. Take, for example, the six 'Indians' who returned to Dieppe in 1529 aboard *La Pensée* (The Thought) owned by the merchant Jean Ango. These people – likely from what is now Brazil – had been abandoned on the island of Saint Helena by the Portuguese. The Honfleur sailor Guillaume Lefèvre, recounting the voyage in 1575, remembered that 'it is only six years ago that the last one died, who was married in . . . Dieppe'. In 1539, at least three of the Stadaconans abducted by Jacques Cartier had been baptised and were living in France – most likely Brittany – at the expense of the Crown. According to André Thevet, the Franciscan traveller and geographer – who claimed the *agouhanna* (leader) Donnacona had informed his writing about Canadian religious practices – he died 'a good Christian, speaking French, for having been kept there four years'. It is hard to imagine that his new faith was of much comfort.[6]

In 1552, the Portuguese Jesuit Manuel da Nóbrega, one of the first missionaries in Brazil, wrote to the head of the Jesuit order that he would shortly be sending to him two Indigenous boys, probably coastal Tupiniquim or Tupinambá given the date, 'to learn the virtues [for] a year and a little bit of Latin . . . and the King will enjoy seeing them, as they are the first from this land'. According to Nóbrega, the French were so impressed with this strategy that they copied it and sent some Indigenous people (most likely Tamoio or Tupiniquim) from Guanabara Bay to Geneva so that Calvin himself could turn them into Protestant priests. The French chronicler-pastor Jean de Léry, who famously spent time among the Tupinambá, recounted meeting a Portuguese-speaking man from the neighbouring Margaia tribe, imprisoned in chains. The man told how he had been to Portugal, where he had become a Christian baptised 'Antoni', and 'shed some of his barbarian ways'. Antoni was a prisoner of war, and he begged the Europeans to rescue him from the Tupi, the traditional enemy of the Margaia.[7] Léry shows no surprise at meeting Antoni: Native voyagers were commonplace by the mid-sixteenth century.

*

Around the turn of the sixteenth century, a daughter was born to a Tupinambá *morubixaba* (ruler). Her father Taparica named her Guaibimpará (Great Sea) and, as the young girl entered the world, a disruptive force shimmered on the horizon. In 1500, a fleet of thirteen ships, led by Pedro Álvares Cabral had entered Tupinambá territory, and claimed their lands in the name of Portugal. The Tupi resisted colonisation from the beginning. They were not prepared to relinquish Pindorama, the land of palms, so easily, and Guaibimpará would have grown up experiencing intrusions from white men from the east, who regularly arrived in search of the treasures of their imagination.

Only a few years after the first European ships appeared in Tupi waters, a Portuguese sailor named Diogo Álvares Correia was shipwrecked off what is now Bahia in Brazil, probably a casualty of the dark reefs which lay waiting to catch out unwary invaders. Struggling ashore into tropical Tupinambá territory with little more than an arquebus and ammunition, Correia somehow managed to impress the Indigenous people sufficiently for them to keep him alive and adopt him into their community. Religious chroniclers of the Portuguese enterprise in Brazil, like the Jesuit Simão de Vasconcelos, tell a dramatic tale of European superiority, casting Correia as a heroic figure who overwhelms the timid locals:

> As soon as those savages learned that the man of fire (as they called him) was coming against them, and that from far away he hurt and killed, they fainted as if they had seen the fury of a volcano and fled into the forest, thus proving the valour and superhuman art (in the opinion of those people) of Diogo Álvares, whose fame soon spread through the backlands. He was taken for a powerful man, against whom their bows were no use. And here they gave him the name, calling him the great Caramuru . . . in a brief time he rose from captive to lord, who governed everything.

Taparica, perhaps recognising an opportunity to ally himself with the intruders from a position of strength, offered his daughter

Guaibimpará in marriage to the marooned sailor, drawing him into Tupinambá lineage and heritage. Correia was also given the name Caramuru – a reference to the moray eel, 'a dragon vomited out of the sea' in one evocative translation.[8] His marriage to Guaibimpará is often implausibly romanticised, with some stories even suggesting the besotted girl saved his life.*

Guaibimpará was likely a child at the time of her marriage, but would have been a young woman by the time that Caramuru (as he has become known) decided to hop on a ship returning to France in 1528.[9] There, on 30 July, in Saint-Malo, Guaibimpará was baptised 'Catherine du Brasil'.† A baptismal record preserved in the municipal archives shows that her godmother and namesake was Catherine des Granches, a daughter of one of the most influential local families, and the wife of the explorer Jacques Cartier.[10] And here some of our threads unexpectedly entwine: ten years later, Catherine des Granches would also stand as godmother to Charles, one of the three men from the St Lawrence Iroquoian village of Stadacona brought from 'parts of Canada' by her husband. Five years before Jacques Cartier ever ventured west, his wife was godmother to a young Tupinambá woman visiting France. Did Cartier meet her? Might Caramuru's acculturation, fluency in Tupi and partnership with his wife have led Cartier to believe the Stadaconans would be more persuadable than they proved? Did their tales of 'new lands' fuel his desire to voyage west? Why did Catherine agree to sponsor Guaibimpará's baptism? One wonders if this moment influenced Guaibimpará's later life. Could meeting

---

* It's hard to ignore the similarities with the heavily Disneyfied story of John Smith and 'Pocahontas' (Matoaka), in which she is (wrongly) believed to have fallen in love with the Englishman and rescued him from her father's wrath.

† There are references to 'another *india*' named Perrine – perhaps one of Caramuru's other Indigenous wives – being baptised alongside 'Catherine', but I have not been able to verify this. While Caramuru almost certainly had several 'wives' in Brazil, and some other Tupinambá may have accompanied them on the ship, it seems unlikely he would have wanted to look like a polygamist in France. It's possible this is a confusion with 'Moema', an Indigenous woman invented by Durão in his epic poem on the subject.

Catherine, a noblewoman who extended her influence through religion, have inspired Guaibimpará to do the same?

This is pure conjecture, but then so is much of what we 'know' of Guaibimpará's life, which has been written and rewritten to the point that even her original name has become shrouded. She is now usually known as Paraguaçu ('great water'), a name taken from a local river and imposed on her by the Jesuit Vasconcelos in the seventeenth century, metaphorically tying her to the Brazilian landscape and its fertility. This invented identity is often described as her 'real name' in accounts of 'Catherine of Brazil' or 'Catarina Álvares Caramuru', and her life is fiendishly difficult to disentangle from this cobweb of myth. Guaibimpará appears in multiple identities, languages, eras and sources, but there are few documents from her lifetime.[11]

The earliest accounts of Caramuru do not mention his wife at all, and we first get an outline of her life in 1627 in the work of the Franciscan, Frei Vincente do Salvador, who claimed to have met her in person. The friar says that after her baptism Guaibimpará started calling herself 'Luisa Álvares' after her husband, which is certainly not impossible – many people used a different everyday name to their formal baptismal title – but this is unattested in other sources. The couple married in France before returning to Brazil, where Catherine founded a hermitage dedicated to Our Lady of Grace, forming the basis for the oldest Marian chapel in Brazil, which stands in the city the Portuguese named for their 'saviour', São Salvador da Bahia.[12] Building on this sparse outline, in 1663 Vasconcelos created the image of 'Catherine Álvares Paraguaçu' as a devout woman who was inspired by religious visions, and stumbled upon an image of Our Lady of Grace, provoking her to found the chapel of Mary on a headland high above the bay. Guaibimpará and Caramuru (and his other wives, who are rarely mentioned in these priestly accounts) were influential intermediaries in early colonial politics, and had lots of children and grandchildren, many of whom married into the Portuguese nobility in Brazil. A widow for the last three decades of her life, Guabimpará remained dedicated to Mary, and her chapel became an important centre of pilgrimage, especially after the pope bestowed on it several relics. Not long before her death, she willed the chapel and its land to the Benedictine Order. A memorial for her still stands at the church.[13]

The image of an Indigenous woman favoured by Our Lady appealed profoundly to Christian chroniclers across the centuries and, starting with Vasconcelos, they wrote a mythology of colonisation that saw Caramuru and Paraguaçu as the Adam and Eve of Brazil. In this heroic tale – which was promoted by the messianic epic poem *Caramuru*, published by the Augustinian friar Santa Rita Durão in 1781 – the couple met King Henri II and Queen Catherine in Paris, where they had glittering nuptials arranged by the royal couple, and 'Paraguaçu' was baptised and named after her godmother: Catherine de' Medici.[14] This royal connection is a particularly sticky myth, which appears even in scholarly accounts of Guaibimpará's life, despite the existence of her baptismal record. Europeans and their descendants probably prefer the story of an 'Indian princess', a tropical adopted daughter to the queen, to the idea that a Tupinambá woman married a Portuguese sailor and travelled to Brittany, only to be baptised in the rocky port of Saint-Malo, among the robust mariners and merchants who regularly passed through its streets. Quietly, and with little fanfare, Indigenous people were making space for themselves in Europe, shifting perspectives, and becoming part of transatlantic families.

It is the very ordinariness of this connection which is interesting. Native people were walking French streets and being baptised in European churches before even Cortés reached Mexico. But for many in Brazil today, Guaibimpará, the Tupinambá woman who became a religious pioneer, holds a more dramatic place in their history. Her marriage to Caramuru was the first recorded Christian marriage in Brazil, a symbolic joining of Portugal and its new colony, and a demonstration of the value of 'civilisation' to the Indigenous peoples. This has become a story that extols hybridity, with Paraguaçu being lauded as the mother of an idealised blended nation.[15] According to the meticulous research of her thirteen-greats grandson Christovão de Avila, Guaibimpará had four daughters with Caramuru – Ana, Genebra, Apolônia and Grácia – all of whom became known, like their mother, by their father's surname 'Álvares' and married into prominent Portuguese families. What little we can see of Guaibimpará's life suggests she was an active and successful matriarch after her husband's death. The records of the Monastery of Saint Benedict of Bahia show her litigating over an inheritance, and she lived long enough to see her grandson Diogo – Genebra's eldest child – married to the half-Tupinambá granddaughter of Tomé de Sousa, the first governor-general of Brazil. Guaibimpará is often also mistakenly labelled as the mother of Madalena Caramuru, who is famous as the first literate Brazilian woman. In fact, Madalena was the daughter of one of Caramuru's other 'wives', who have been strategically erased from much of the historical record. Although they were not blood relatives – it's entirely possible that Madalena was inspired by her devout stepmother, for she later became an advocate for Indigenous education and child welfare.[16]

In 1999, more than four hundred years after Guaibimpará's death, a mass was held at the church where her body was buried. There, in the presence of her descendants, 'Catarina Paraguaçu' was celebrated as 'one of the greatest female symbols' in Brazil's history, who had 'played a fundamental role in the integration of the races that formed the Brazilian people'. The young Tupinambá woman, handed over to a Portuguese man as part of a strategic alliance, has become a 'heroine' who stood at the birth of Brazilian society, even while contemporary Indigenous peoples face prejudice and erasure. In 2012, the mayor of Salvador declared a 'Municipal Day of Catharina Paraguassu', celebrating 500 years since her birth. The contours of Guaibimpará's life are hard to trace. We can sketch her outline only in fragments of paper: a baptismal certificate; some legal records; her will and testament.[17] But her legacy as the Indigenous mother of Brazil is boundless.

Malintzin's son, Martín, the illegitimate child of Hernando Cortés, was born in 1522 in a former Aztec-Mexica palace in what is now the pretty district of Coyoacan in Mexico City. Martín was one of the first mixed-heritage children born in Mexico, and people started to call him 'El Mestizo' when his half-brother (confusingly also called Martín)* was born ten years later.[18] The conquistador's son certainly lived a complex life – both Indigenous and Spanish, he existed between his mother's and father's cultures, and is an important example of the ways in which some Native people inhabited a transatlantic space in the sixteenth century.

In 1528, with Martín barely more than a toddler, Hernando Cortés took his son to Spain when he returned for the first time after the conquest. Given the flashy entourage of nobles, entertainers and enslaved people, one small child would probably have gone largely unnoticed, and he is rarely mentioned in accounts of this voyage, but it transformed Martín's place in the world. In 1529, not long after their arrival in Spain, his father appealed to Pope Clement VII to legitimise Martín, and the pope granted the request, making Martín a full legal member of the Cortés family and removing the stain of his birth in the eyes of society. Clement VII was himself an illegitimate child of Giuliano de' Medici, of the famous Florentine family, who had been murdered before his son was born. He was even rumoured to have an illegitimate son of his own – nineteen-year-old Alessandro, whose mother was an African servant. By 1529, this African-Italian was already Duke of Penne, and would soon be elevated to even loftier heights, so it seems possible that the pope sympathised with the conquistador's son. He may also have been predisposed to grant Cortés's request after seeing the pageantry of the Mexican entertainers, representatives of the multitude of new converts Cortés's expedition had secured for Christian evangelisation. Whatever the pope's motives, in 1529 Cortés's lawyer returned from the papal court with a bull declaring that Martín Cortés, along with another half-brother and half-sister in Mexico, 'are legitimate and that in this no other laws, neither imperial nor municipal, take precedence over apostolic law'.[19]

It took Cortés some time to establish himself in Spain – during which he and Martín rested at the friary of Santa María de la

---

* The younger Martín was known as 'El Criollo' (the 'creole', a term for Mexican-born Spaniards). Both Martíns were named after Cortés's own father, another marker of Hernando Cortés's personal connection to his illegitimate son.

Rabída in Palos de la Frontera. It was here that, in 1490, Columbus had left his own small son in the care of the Franciscans while he appealed to the Crown to back his proposed search for a westward route to India. We know that Cortés took his son with him when he kissed the king's hands in Barcelona and was awarded the newly created title of Marqués del Valle de Oaxaca. And in July 1529, with the aid of four witnesses, Cortés also convinced the master and prior of the Order of Santiago that seven-year-old Martín should be admitted as a knight of the Order, one of the most prestigious military fraternities in Spain. Unlike his father, who had been con- sidered unworthy of this accolade, Martín – the son of a marqués and a 'principal Indian', both of whom had played leading roles in the conquest of Mexico – was considered to possess sufficient virtue and reason to uphold the banner and values of Saint James. The testimony presented in support of Martín's application high- lights his mother's Indigenous birth: she is 'doña Marina *india* of the nation of *indios*', a 'very honorable and senior person', and, with Aguilar, 'the true interpreter between us and those of that land'. Martín's Indigenous blood was clearly considered no bar to receiving this high social honour; in fact his mother's claimed nobility of blood was emphasised, as was the fact that she was one of 'the first Christians baptised in all of New Spain'. In the earliest years of encounter, Indigenous status – when deployed in the right way – could be an advantage, especially when it happened to align with imperial priorities.[20]

Thus Cortés's *mestizo* son Martín became firmly established in Spanish society. When the conquistador returned to Mexico, he left his son at court, where he became a page in the household of the emperor's wife, Isabella of Portugal. In the archives at Simancas, the historian Anna Lanyon found a tantalising reference to his early life, a receipt that reads 'I, Diego Pérez de Vargas, tutor to don Martyn Cortés . . . confirm that I have this day received fees in full for my services to the said don Martyn Cortés . . . In Madrid, the first of September, fifteen hundred and thirty'. So, at the age of eight, Martín was living in the royal household, and being tutored alongside many other aristocratic boys. His father, occupied in Mexico with political affairs and a new wife and child, nonetheless found time to write occasionally to Martín and remained concerned for his welfare. Writing to his cousin in Spain in 1533, he pleaded for more information, having heard that his first son had fallen ill: 'I tell you that I don't love him any less than the other [boy] whom God has given me with the Marquesa, and thus I always want to know about him'. In a model noble upbringing, Martín seems to have lived at court for most of his early life, as he is one of the seventy young noblemen listed among the pages transferred to Isabella's son Felipe (the future Philip II of Spain) when she tragically died as a result of an infection following a miscarriage in 1539. At that time, Martín would have been seventeen years old. It does not seem to have been especially difficult for Indigenous and *mestizo* people of noble birth, or who were close to power, to fit into Spanish society, and Martín's life is typical of the transatlantic ties which were formed by those with the wealth and status to seek their fortunes in Spain.[21]

A year later, Cortés returned to Spain again, bringing with him his younger son. This is the first time that Martín met the brother who shared his name and, for some reason, only a year later, he decided to leave his father and brother in Spain and return to Mexico. Perhaps the arrival of his family made Martín wonder about his heritage, for we believe he visited María, his *mestiza* half-sister on his mother's side. Whatever Martín was looking for, he did not find contentment in Mexico, for only a year later he returned to Spain and to life in the palace and fighting for the Crown across Europe. This Indigenous knight campaigned as far afield as France, Germany, northern Italy and Algiers. The younger Martín also joined Philip's household, and when the prince married Queen Mary I of England in 1554, both brothers were almost certainly among the giant retinue accompanying the bridegroom to England. According to one chronicler, 'at this time there was so many Spaniards in London that a man should have met in the streets for one Englishman above four Spaniards, to the great discomfort of the English nation'. If Martín, El Mestizo, was among them, he would have been only the fifth Indigenous person whom we know set foot on English shores.[22]

*

Tracing family bonds that criss-crossed the Atlantic is not easy, especially in the case of 'ordinary' people. Elite figures are usually named on licences giving permission for travel to and from the Americas, but many others, including families, arrived in Europe as unnamed *criados* (dependants) of nobles, priests and administrators, and sometimes as prisoners, tricked or coerced into travelling. Records show the Council of the Indies periodically attempting to recover the return costs of unfortunate people who had ended up in poverty in Spain after being deceived by unscrupulous masters. In one typical case from 1555, Francisco Becerra from Toro in Castile was ordered to pay for Francisco Martín, '*indio*', his wife and son, to return to Chincha in Peru, as well as 30 ducats in compensation for his unpaid labour after he had been convinced into coming to Spain 'with deceit'.[23]

When Sebastian Cabot returned to Spain in 1530 after a rather chaotic expedition, he brought with him a clutch of Indigenous people. As well as fifty or sixty enslaved people purchased from the Portuguese at San Vincente, including two known as Pedro and Juana who were likely Carijó or Tapés, there were also some Indigenous nobles and their wives, including a *cacique* of Paraguay and his three sons. Also among the company was the Portuguese Henrique Montes, a shipwrecked sailor who had been living among the Guaraní for more than a decade. Defying sensationalist rumours that he – along with all the men from his expedition – had been devoured by the locals, Montes married an Indigenous woman and had a family, later becoming a translator for Cabot and returning with him to Europe. On the ship, Montes 'brought two *indias horras* [freed enslaved women] of the nation of the Guaranís, and a [male] slave, that is from the port of San Vincente and was bought from the Portuguese'. According to one informant, Montes left one woman in Castile and took the other with him to Portugal.[24] Was the woman who stayed with him his wife? Or did Montes abandon his family in Patos and casually acquire two women at one of the stops on the return? What of his children? Is this a story of affection or coercion? Or both?

While the Indigenous women are treated as appendages to Montes in the brief accounts we have, this forced 'beachcomber' would have been at the mercy of the Guaraní after his ship ran aground near Lagoa dos Patos, the sheltered, sand-rimmed lagoon which sprawls along the humid coast of southern Brazil. When Cabot found Montes, and his shipmate Melchor Ramírez, they boasted of the wealthy lands to the south. Did the castaways still clutch the European dream of a river of riches, or just confirm Cabot's prejudices in hope of proving their worth? Maybe Montes's wife helped to guide Cabot's crew, or perhaps she refused to leave, clinging instead to her children and home. The threads of such family histories are ephemeral, slipping out of our grasp as we reach for them. But together they hint at a rich emotional and intellectual universe, with bonds which tied families and households together, even across the rough seas of the Atlantic. This is something particularly typical of the Spanish empire in this period. In early British and French North America, Church-sanctioned marriage or sexual contact between white men and Native women was rare, while intermarriage was more common in sixteenth-century Spanish America.[25]

The data is patchy, but our evidence suggests that about a third of Spanish men in the Americas may have been married to Indigenous women in the early colonial period, although not all would have been consensual unions and many more women were subjected to sexual violence.[26] Given that so few Spanish women migrated to the Americas in the early years, it's not surprising that so many men chose (or took) Indigenous wives. But however comfortable they may have felt with the kaleidoscope of relationships in the colonies, returning to Europe with an Indigenous wife or lover was an entirely different prospect. There was plenty of warm rhetoric about treating *indios* as full vassals and Christians, but Spanish men rarely risked bringing their Indigenous partners to Europe and in practice it was difficult for any but the highest-status Native women to be accepted as members of Spanish society.[27]

Informal relationships were probably more common than marriages – Indigenous partners and victims of abuse hiding among everyday household relationships. These cases are hard to trace, but sometimes pop up in legal records. In 1539, a Venezuelan woman, Beatríz – perhaps of Cumanagato origin – crossed the Atlantic with a Spaniard called Alonso Ponce, and their *mestiza* daughter Juana, who was likely about four or five when they made the long voyage to Spain. Having been enslaved as a young girl herself, Beatríz showed the marks of her bondage on her face, with the royal brand unmistakable on her chin, so her transition to Spanish society cannot have been easy. Ponce was her third enslaver, and true consent cannot be given under the conditions of enslavement, but we know that Beatríz was an adult when she became pregnant not long after entering Alonso's household. As Ponce was unmarried, and had no real property he might have wanted to pass on to a legitimate heir, he perhaps had fewer reasons to make strategic relationship choices and, when he returned to his village, he risked his community's condemnation by taking his small family with him. Sadly, Beatríz, like many Native people, died not long after setting foot on European soil. If she had survived just one more year, she would have become eligible to apply for her freedom under the New Laws of 1542, but instead her body was laid to rest in the Church of San Agustín in Alcalá de Guadaíra, where a mass was said for her soul.

Following Beatríz's death, Alonso cared for their daughter Juana with his sister's help, until she neared adulthood, when he placed her in domestic service – just as he might have a legitimate child – and returned to Puerto Rico by himself. Juana de Vera became a maid in a Seville household; in the cosmopolitan atmosphere of the city, with ships from the Indies coming and going, and too young to have known her Venezuelan mother, it seems likely Juana largely blended into Spanish society. She reappears in 1552 in a remarkable case uncovered by Nancy van Deusen, in which an enslaved 'mulatta' named Violante tried to pass as Beatríz, in an attempt to secure her freedom. Violante, who had arrived in Ponce's home shortly after Beatríz died, had begged and bribed Juana to support her story, but aged just seventeen, Juana gave a devastating testimony denouncing Violante as 'a liar and an imposter'. Months later, Violante, who had been confined, beaten and humiliated, gave up her appeal, having been forced to concede: 'I am a captive and of the nation and generation of blacks . . . and I ask to be turned over to Alonso López, my lord, in order to serve him and to remain under his control as a slave'. In the entangled world of six-teenth-century Castile, identities could both liberate and ensnare.[28]

Mixed households were common and presumably included some loving families, but the legal records also reveal the dangerous instability of Native women's lives. Often unmarried, they were vulnerable to changes in circumstances, and the death of a partner could have dire consequences, especially in noble families, where the stakes were higher. For Isabel, an Indigenous Peruvian woman who came to Castile with her Spanish partner Pedro de Oropesa, their *mestizo* son Lorenço, and adopted son Gaspar, her lack of legal standing proved disastrous. Isabel would presumably have felt herself to be secure. She was recognised as Pedro's *amiga* (lover or concubine) and – when she arrived in Spain – had apparently ridden 'on a mule, seated on a pillow with a chain of gold around her neck'. It must have been quite a shock when, after nine years living with his Indigenous family in Spain, Pedro unexpectedly married a Spanish woman called Isabel Gutiérrez. The life of Pedro's Indigenous partner was thrown even further into turmoil when he abruptly died only four months later, and his new wife declared Isabel and her children to be enslaved, Pedro having apparently lost Isabel's letter of freedom. What domestic machinations led to this turn of events we do not know, but it is easy to imagine Pedro's Spanish wife's jealousy of her husband's existing partner and family, especially as Pedro left a quite substantial bequest to Lorenço in his will. Fortunately, Lorenço and Gaspar (who was outraged at having been 'treated like a black slave' and called a 'Moorish dog' by Pedro's new wife) were able to bring their case before the Council of the Indies and, in 1570, King Philip II ruled Isabel and her sons to be free and eligible for compensation.[29]

Isabel's relationship with Pedro appears to have been consensual, at least by the time they arrived in Spain, but these kinds of cases are obviously complicated by inevitable, and often murky, power dynamics. We know that exploitation, sexual assault, and abuse were rife, but emotional ties also drew Native people across the Atlantic and Spaniards sometimes went to considerable lengths to keep the Indigenous members of their households with them when they sailed home. Indigenous women were commonly domestic servants and care workers, to whom children particularly developed strong attachments. In 1540, Luis de la Serna pleaded on behalf of his five-year-old granddaughter, Maria, to be reunited with Elena, an *india* servant who had raised her and been taken away after travelling to Spain without a licence. In 1536, another *india*, Juana, was entrusted with bringing a young Spanish girl to her family in Spain.[30]

Such relationships did not always survive the Atlantic crossing. *Patria potestas* (the father's legal right to his children under six-teenth-century Spanish law) was often used to cleave families in two. *Mestizo* children – legitimised by their fathers – appear frequently in the records of Atlantic travel, sometimes tragically ripped away from Indigenous mothers when Spanish fathers wished to send their children 'home'. Nancy van Deusen's remarkable archival work has uncovered both the emotional ties and the deep violence which shaped household relationships between Spanish men and Native servants and enslaved women, caught in the 'triple bind of being Indigenous, female, and servile'. When Juan Flores died, his will ordered that his five *mestizo* children be taken to his family home in Spain, regardless of the wishes of their two Indigenous mothers. María, a Native woman from Cueva in Panama, found herself similarly bereft. Despite a conspicuous bond with her partner, who provided for María's care in his will, her infant daughter was nonetheless entrusted to a custodian who would send her to Spain when she was old enough. The Crown actively encouraged this kind of separation in order to indoctrinate mixed-heritage children, who were exempted from prohibitions on Indigenous travel and allowed to accompany their parents to the peninsula after 1524.[31]

We cannot be sure exactly how many Indigenous people – enslaved or free – eventually settled in the Iberian peninsula, but it is clear

value is measured by wealth, financial worth, and usefulness. The dawning of globalisation – the entanglement of cultures, ecologies, peoples, and ideologies as a result of the violence of empire, invasion, enslavement and appropriation – is often understood as synonymous with the rise of capitalism and the development of a 'world economy'. But, while capitalist systems of exploitation did inexorably shape global systems after 1492, by intrinsically commodifying the transatlantic exchange of goods and ideas we implicitly assume a Eurocentric stance. Just as Indigenous peoples have often been erased from this period of history, so their values have been stripped from the story.[4]

There is no such thing as a single 'Indigenous' belief system, any more than there is a 'European' one. The United States has 567 federally recognised and 63 state-recognised tribes; around 600 distinct languages are spoken across Central and South America; and there are more than 630 First Nations in Canada, each with its own particular heritage. And, of course, Indigenous people are individuals, with varying attitudes and values. But, though there are many differences among these surviving peoples, before the European incursion the majority of Native cultures held a world view informed by a spirit of reciprocity between the land and its inhabitants, between community and individual – a spirit antithetical to the invaders' exploitative and individualistic mindset.[*5]

Indigenous cosmologies across the Western Hemisphere acknowledged the potency and participation of spiritual powers in everyday life, and held a transcendent belief in a 'sacred circle of life, wherein all beings, material and immaterial, are equal and interdependent'. Across the Americas, Indigenous traditions differ in their substance, stories and practice, but most remain

---

*   As in any historical analysis of the big-picture, I am inevitably simplifying here, as Europeans were no more identical than Indigenous peoples and many ordinary people held views of the natural world that were profoundly shaped by spiritual and social concerns, while some Native peoples had more individualistic value systems.

committed to a reciprocity that grounds them in relationships with deities, beings and forces representing the manifold aspects of the earth and all life upon it. The Maya creation story recorded in the sixteenth-century K'iche' Popol Vuh, depicted in two-thousand-year-old stucco panels, and held in oral histories, tells the story of the gods' repeated attempts to create humans who would appreciate the earth. Finally, Xmucane, the Grandmother, ground yellow and white corn to form the figures of the first humans. 'It was staples alone that made up their flesh.' From maize the humans were born and through maize they would be sustained. For the Nahua, we are living in the last of five cycles of creation and destruction, ages of the sun, bound to nourish the gods with blood in exchange for the sacrifice made by the gods to create the world. Though the sun stood at the heart of public Aztec-Mexica rituals, in the home and at the hearth women paid constant respect to maize, heedful always of the obligation to this sacred staple grain. The Diné (Navajo) also tell of four worlds of creation, with the First People emerging alongside animals and plants, and corn at the heart of the story. Such cycles of learning, emphasising harmony and balance, as well as our obligation to the earth and the living things upon it, reappear across the Americas. Often called 'myths' – an implicitly disparaging term that tends to suggest falsity – the phrase 'empowering stories' coined by Klara Kelley and Harris Francis (Diné) better captures the spirit of these potent and respected stories which speak to Indigenous survivance,* 'the truth or falsity of which lies in the interpretation'.[6]

Many Indigenous traditions also tell of a world covered with water, where either animals or gods forged the land, creating a place for humans to rest. For the Nahua, the earth was *cemana-huac* (the place surrounded by water), the disc of the earth resting on the back of Cipactli, the giant alligator, who sacrificed herself to form the land. Many peoples from the Eastern Woodlands

---

* 'Survivance' is a term coined by the Anishinaabe scholar Gerald Vizenor to describe the active and dynamic presence of Native peoples and their traditions as an ongoing presence and process in the contemporary world.

FIGURE 1. The first Indigenous people at the Spanish court were Totonacs. The pope's representative insulted the women as 'small and of ugly expression' but, as this exquisite ceramic shows, they had a deserved reputation for their elegant appearance, with magnificent adornments and beautiful clothing.

FIGURE 2. Many Indigenous people lived and worked in Seville. This painting by Alonso Sánchez Coello depicts the view of the late-sixteenth-century city from the Triana district, showing where the fleets arrived from the Indies.

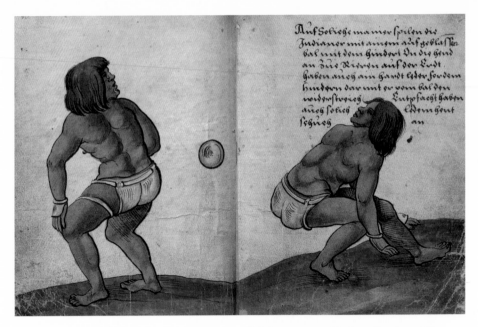

FIGURE 3. In 1528, a large group of Nahuas travelled to Spain with Cortés, including these men, who played the Mesoamerican ball game. While at court they were seen by Christoph Weiditz, who produced these images inspired by them for a costume book.

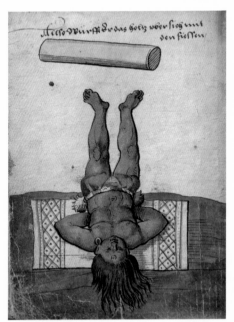

FIGURE 4. Among the 1528 group were jugglers, who impressed the court by tossing logs into the air with their feet. The warriors drawn by Weiditz seem to have had feathers added later for modesty, and as a marker of their 'Indigenousness'.

FIGURE 5. This painting supposedly depicts the only Indigenous woman to travel to court in 1528. Her hair and clothing are not typical of Nahua Mexico, casting doubt on whether only her appearance, or her entire presence, was invented by the artist.

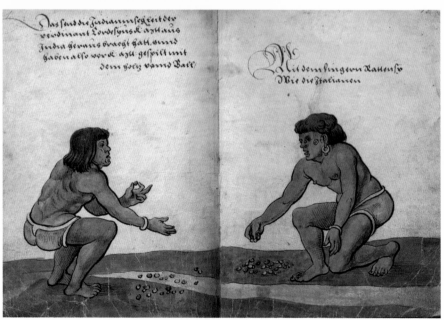

FIGURE 6. These Nahua men appear to be playing *patolli*, a popular Mesoamerican gambling game. Among the most realistic figures in Weiditz's costume book, they allow us a glimpse at the everyday lives of Indigenous people in Europe.

FIGURE 7. Indigenous peoples, especially Tupi and Guaraní, would have been among the vibrant throng in Lisbon, captured in this anonymous oil painting of the 'King's Fountain' in Lisbon. In 1551, Native people were ordered to collect drinking water from the same spouts as women of Black African descent.

FIGURE 8. Malintzin (left), shown here interpreting for Cortés (middle) and Xicotencatl (right), the ruler of Tlaxcala, was a vital go-between during the Spanish invasion. Her son with Cortés lived most of his life in Spain and became a respected nobleman, courtier, and soldier.

The manner of theirattire and
painting them selues when
they goe to their generall
huntings, or at theire
Solemne feasts.

FIGURE 9. In 1584, Manteo and Wanchese, two men from the coast of present-day North Carolina, travelled to London. Their attire and adornments likely resembled those of this *weroance* (leader) drawn from life by John White the following year.

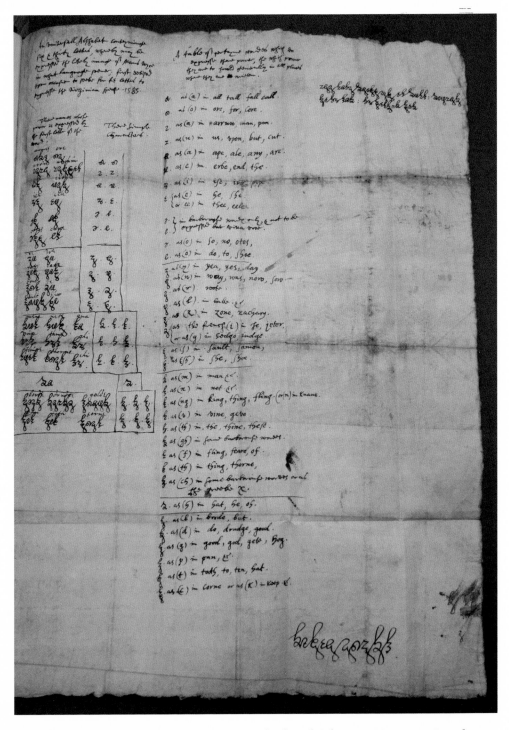

FIGURE 10. The Croatoan Manteo worked with Thomas Hariot in London to produce an Ossomocomuck 'alphabet', the first set of conventions for the alphabetic recording of an Algonquian language. His signature is the curly text in the lower-right corner: 'MATEOROIDN' (Manteo king done).

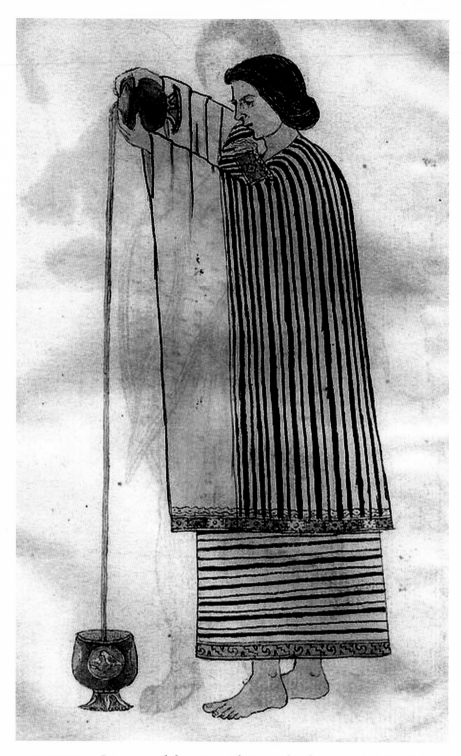

FIGURE 11. In 1545, a delegation of Maya chiefs presented the first 'containers of whisked chocolate' recorded in Europe to Prince Philip of Spain. Indigenous women were vital to the preparation of drinking chocolate, which was frothed by beating or pouring it between containers.

FIGURE 12. The quetzal bird was sacred to Mesoamericans, and its shimmering plumage – here in a replica of 'Moctezuma's headdress' – was highly prized. As well as chocolate and other foods, the Maya chiefs of Tuzulutlán presented two thousand feathers to Prince Philip as part of their diplomatic embassy.

FIGURE 13. Antonio Ponce's *A still life of peaches, fish, chestnuts, a tin plate, sweet box, chocolate grinder and Mexican lacquer cups and shawl* shows the normalisation of Indigenous tastes in Spain. A *molinillo* chocolate whisk sits on top of a round cacao container with two Mexican gourd cups.

FIGURE 14. The preparation of food and drink was and remains a distinctively female activity in many Indigenous communities. Here a Maya woman whisks chocolate with a *molinillo*, continuing a tradition that reaches back to her ancestors – in both Europe and the Americas.

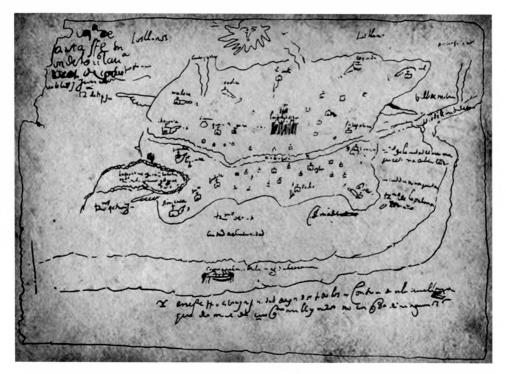

FIGURE 15. The *mestizo* chief Diego de Torres y Moyachoque, an early advocate of Indigenous rights, spent several years living in Madrid. This is one of two remarkable maps of the territory around Turmequé that he enclosed with his petition to the king appealing against abuses of the Muisca people.

FIGURE 16. *The Virgin of the Navigators* by Alejo Fernández (who had an '*indio*' servant in his workshop as early as 1523) shows Indigenous converts sheltering under Mary's cloak. Some of these converts would have seen the picture in the House of Trade in Seville.

FIGURE 17. A descendant of Inka royalty, Francisca Pizarro Yupanqui was exiled to Spain. In 1562, she and her conquistador husband (who appear on this façade) built the Palace of the Conquest in Trujillo, a town that became home to a cluster of Inka nobility.

FIGURE 18. Like many Native people, the Mississauga Chippewa chief Maungwudaus (second from left) came to Europe as part of a travelling show. His sharply cynical observations on European society – published in a short pamphlet in 1848 – mirror those of Indigenous travellers down the centuries.

FIGURE 19. Indigenous peoples were often exploited as part of spectacles of power. In 1550, fifty Tupi people inhabited a faux 'Brazilian village' created for the benefit of Henri II and Catherine de' Medici on the banks of the Seine in Rouen.

FIGURE 20. *Wunderkammern* ('cabinets of curiosities'), like this one from the Danish physician Ole Worm, are part of the long history of collecting and display that has colonised the heritage, and sometimes even the bodies, of Native peoples across the world.

FIGURE 21. Abducted Indigenous peoples were often dehumanised and treated as objects for 'curiosity' and entertainment. This pamphlet (1567) advertises the display of an Inuk woman and her seven-year-old daughter, who were transported to Antwerp after the murder of her husband.

FIGURE 22. In 1576, a kidnapped Inuk man proved a 'wonder' in London and artists such as Adriaen Coenen rushed to depict him. He died, possibly of pneumonia, after only two weeks in England and was buried in St Olave's churchyard in London.

FIGURES 23 and 24. In 1577, three captured Inuit became celebrities in Bristol, but all died soon after their arrival on English shores. Baby Nutaaq, here seen peeking from his mother's hood, died and was buried near his compatriot at St Olave's church in London.

FIGURE 25. The presence of Indigenous peoples in Europe, many of whom were buried far from home, has often been forgotten or erased. Although the remains of two Inuit lie in the graveyard behind St Olave's, their names do not appear in the parish record.

including the Haudenosaunee, Lenape and Anishinaabeg, tell of the Great Turtle, on whose shell was laid the first soil by a muskrat who gave his life to bring the earth from the depths of the ocean. Calling the Americas 'Turtle Island' is a way of evoking this Indigenous way of seeing the world, rejecting the name imposed by colonisers, and reorienting our view of the continent. Abya Yala, a term meaning 'land of life' or 'mature land' in the language of the Gunadule (Kuna) people of what is now Panama and Colombia, is used in a similar way by some Indigenous activists in South America.[7]

When the Europeans set foot on Turtle Island, Abya Yala, *Cemanahuac*, a process of exchange began that would transform the world through avaricious commodification. When Columbus met the Taíno people – after planting the royal standard, symbolically claiming the land for Spain, taking ownership of this territory with no regard for its inhabitants – nearly the first thing he did was to trade with them. In a letter to the royal treasurer, Columbus wrote that the Taínos 'bartered, like idiots', exchanging valuable cotton and gold for broken bows and glass. 'They exhibit great love towards all others in preference to themselves: they also give objects of great value for trifles, and content themselves with very little or nothing in return', he wrote. In 1607, one of the Jamestown expedition similarly recorded that the Powhatans of Tsenacomoco had 'no commerce with any nation, no respect of profit'. The idea that Indigenous peoples lacked a concept of private non-communal property has long been used to justify stripping them of their rights and territory, despite the fact that, even in the sixteenth century, scholars such as Francisco de Vitoria demonstrated that Native people held 'full *dominium*' in their lands. Indigenous peoples had a clear sense of what was theirs, and understood perfectly well the value of things *to them*. But, unlike Europeans, they did not bow down to commerce. Captain John Smith came close to appreciating their world view when he told Powhatan, 'by the gifts you bestowe on me, you gaine more then by trade'.[8]

Indigenous peoples across the Americas held (and hold) complex and varied systems of value. There was no universal utopia where *all* things were held in common and conflict did not exist. The Māori (Ngāti Awa and Ngāti Porou) scholar Linda Tuhiwai Smith mentions her caution of what she calls 'the mystical, misty-eyed discourse that is sometimes employed by Indigenous people to describe our relationships with the land and the universe'. For Tuhiwai Smith, 'our survival as peoples has come from our knowledge of our contexts, our environment, not from some active beneficence of our Earth Mother'. But whether spiritual or practical, a deep knowledge of the land and the natural environment lies at the heart of most Indigenous ideologies. In Potawatomi, the land is *emingoyak*, 'that which has been given to us' and Native peoples have long understood the need for what the Citizen Potawatomi scientist Robin Wall Kimmerer calls the 'Honourable Harvest': a relationship with the land based on an ethic of reciprocity and sustainability. The so-called 'Three Sisters' of maize, beans and squash – seen across North America, from the gardens of the Haudenosaunee in the Northeast to the *milpas* of the Yucatán – exemplify this approach. When planted close together in clusters, the maize supports the growth of the beans, the squash shades the ground, preventing weeds and retaining moisture, and the beans restore the nitrogen that would otherwise be stripped from the soil. Europeans failed to recognise the value of this labour-intensive but land-rich farming style, and introduced large agricultural mono-cultures, which (along with the land- and water-intensive practice of cattle-grazing) stripped the soil and impoverished the earth. European value-systems tended to extraction and profit, rather than sustainability and the sharing of resources.[9]

Even in Tenochtitlan, a city dependent on tribute to survive, land was theoretically held in common with rights based on effective cultivation; most luxury items were used as demonstrations of status rather than wealth; *pochteca* (merchants) redistributed their wealth through public feasts; and society was designed to ensure communal success, with shared grain stores and other forms of resource redistribution. This has some similarities with the potlach: a gift-giving and feasting ceremony practised by Indigenous peoples of the north-west coast of what is now Canada and the United States, who used the potlach to mark important events, impart cultural knowledge, establish reputation, share bounty and celebrate their associations with the land. For Native people the 'giving away' of the potlach increased one's wealth, not diminished it. As the 'Namgis elder Axu Alfred, speaking of the living significance of the potlach, said: 'Many people believe that a rich and powerful person is someone who has a lot. The people who speak Kwak'wala, the Kwakwaka'wakw, believe that a rich and powerful person is someone who gives the most away.'[10]

By contrast, the European invaders were driven by what the Wyandot chief of the Turtle Clan, Kandiaronk, called 'the notions of Mine and Thine, those two great Disturbers of the World'. This was a fictionalised conversation from 1703, in which the chief, in the guise of Adario (meaning 'great and noble friend'), demonstrates the superior values of Indigenous cultures over supposed European 'civilisation'. Written by the Baron de Lahontan – who lived among the Algonquian – and Iroquoian-speaking peoples of what is now Quebec – the dialogue is often dismissed as simply a rehearsal of the 'noble savage' trope, but it was also a clear-eyed critique of the 'savage' qualities of European society, which often shocked Indigenous travellers to Europe. When Adario contrasts French society, where 'the only happy Frenchman' is the wealthy king, to the Wyandot who 'even though naked have a contented soul', he echoes the words of other Native people, both earlier and later, who were baffled at the vast inequalities they found in Europe. As with many of our sources, we again have to be cautious at the ways in which this text 'ventriloquises' the Indigenous informant, a European 'giving voice' to Native people rather than allowing them to speak directly for themselves, but – given Kandiaronk's famed wit, intellect and eloquence – we also have every reason to believe the dialogues could be genuine. This revolutionary text, embraced by some Native scholars, offers one starting point for centring an Indigenous perspective.[11]

How did Indigenous peoples understand their early exchanges with Europeans? How can we tell the story of the early globalisation of Indigenous stuff* without commodifying it? Native peoples may have held very different views from the white men who invaded their lands, planting flags and claiming ownership, but their beliefs were neither static nor homogeneous. Many communities chose (or were forced) to engage with the new trade networks, becoming producers, suppliers or traders of desirable goods, in particular furs in the Northeast, cochineal across Mesoamerica, and brazilwood further south. Native people were the source of most of the 'novelties' that appeared in Europe during the sixteenth century; they taught Europeans how to consume plants like tobacco and cacao, passing on their knowledge and skills; and they were deeply enmeshed in the tenuous commercial networks which gradually clawed their way across the globe. To idealise Indigenous peoples as being above such things as trade and commerce is to ignore their enterprising and determined involvement in these fields. To do history justice, we must recognise this involvement, while remembering the Indigenous belief systems that often informed it.

The smoking of tobacco is perhaps the most obvious instance of an Indigenous practice that circulated around the Atlantic basin and has become an inextricable – if sometimes regrettable – aspect of our modern world. But it dramatises how difficult it is to trace Native people in the material exchange, for tobacco appears in European annals largely detached from its Indigenous context. Although its use quickly became widespread among Europeans and Africans, it was regarded simply as a plant or a product, devoid of Indigenous ritual or material significance, despite the fact that circulation and production were driven for the most part by Native people. Europeans did not recognise the economic potential of

---

* 'Stuff' is not, I realise, the most elegant word, but what are we to call these things without implicitly embroiling them in a mesh of commercial connections? 'Products' implies 'production' for a market. 'Goods' feels like 'merchandise', and things to be transported for the purpose of trade. 'Commodities' are obviously commodified and 'objects' obscures the spirit and life of the flora and fauna of the Americas. So, stuff it is.

tobacco until after the 1590s, when the British got their hooks firmly into the Caribbean.[12]

The ways in which Europeans adopted tobacco depended on the peoples they encountered, for the plant was consumed and understood in very different ways across the continent. In Meso-america, the ceremonial and elite practice was to inhale smoke through pipes and cigars, while chewing tobacco laced with lime was popular among workers to relieve tiredness, thirst and hunger. In parts of the Caribbean and the highlands of South Amer-ica, sniffing powdered, dried tobacco was the norm. Stone pipes found at archaeological sites of the Northeastern coasts attest to ritual smoking long before the arrival of Europeans, although not always of tobacco. In the Eurocentric appropriation of Indigenous histories, it is often claimed that fur traders were responsible for introducing tobacco smoking to the Native peoples of the Amer-ican Northwest. But recent archaeological research – conducted in collaboration with the Nez Perce Tribe and on their ancestral territory in Southeastern Washington State – analysed pipe frag-ments to confirm long-held Native oral histories that tobacco smoking was part of Indigenous culture for at least two thousand years before the arrival of Europeans. Medicinal use of tobacco as smoke, ointment, potion and poultice was also widespread for illnesses from headaches to open wounds. There was no single way of appreciating or using tobacco; many forms of consumption crossed the Atlantic at different moments, insinuating Indigenous ways of being and knowing into European society. The difficulty is in finding the actual Indigenous people who shaped this story.[13]

Tobacco played (and still plays) an important ceremonial role in many Indigenous communities and so often formed part of the setting in European chronicles.* In 1518, Indigenous leaders from the Yucatán peninsula engaged the conquistador Juan de Grijalva

---

* Perhaps the most famous example is the *calumet* (often oversimplified by Europeans as a 'peace pipe'), which was a sacred object used alongside prayer and dance in the *calumet* ceremony to seal agreements, prevent warfare, and create or affirm bonds of kinship.

in a tobacco ceremony which was clearly designed to establish friendship and alliance. Seated under the trees on broad leaves, Grijalva and his men were each given 'a pipe (or tube) lit by one end' which burned slowly 'without raising a flame' and 'they smelt very good as did the smoke that came out of them'. This ritual was followed by the exchange of valuable gifts and signs of friendship before the Christians, in typical uncivilised and ungrateful fashion, demanded gold.[14]

Tobacco, and Indigenous ways of consuming it – smoke, snuff and chewing – were well established in Europe, especially the Iberian peninsula, by the 1570s. A widely spread, but unsourced, story claims that in 1566, a sailor caused a stir in Bristol by 'emitting smoke from his nostrils'. But whether this is true or not, it is certain that sailors of all stripes were early enthusiasts, along with naturalists and physicians. In 1560, dried leaves and seeds were presented to King Charles IX in Paris by the ambassador to Portugal, Jean Nicot (for whom 'nicotine' was named); this 'very beautiful' and medicinal plant was being discussed in France and Italy only a few years later. In 1571, Nicolás Monardes, a Sevillian physician, reported that tobacco had become a common way for enslaved Black people from the Americas to alleviate their exhaustion. The practice seemed to be so popular that enslaved people were sometimes punished for sneaking off for a smoke.[15] It seems inconceivable that enslaved Indigenous people were not also easing their burdens by using tobacco to socialise and relax in traditional ways.

As in Mesoamerica and the Eastern Woodlands, smoking also became a ritual and social practice in Europe, a way of confirming friendships and marking important occasions. By the early 1600s, wealthy Spanish men were smoking *zigarillos* (from the highland-Maya word *sikar*, meaning cigar or tobacco) to open their 'feasts'. Native understandings of tobacco, as a medicinal, recreational and psychotropic substance, were being recorded and disseminated, and Indigenous habits were being adopted by people across the social spectrum throughout the world. By the end of the sixteenth century, smoking had reached west Africa and the Philippines, and in 1642 a visitor to Beijing noticed there were 'tobacconists on every street corner'. Tobacco – usually pipe smoking – also became integral to the coffee-house culture of seventeenth- and eighteenth-century Europe, in the service of relaxation, socialisation and showing off. The world had adopted Indigenous habits.[16]

It is certain that Indigenous people, enslaved and free, were part of the flows introducing smoking to Seville, but to find them we have to read between the lines of our sources. Living in Seville, and a regular visitor to the House of Trade, where he dealt not only in resources such as cochineal dye but also in enslaved Africans, Monardes must have been aware of the presence of Indigenous people in the city: he would have seen them being sold at the block, walking the streets, and working in businesses. Yet the only reference to them in his voluminous treatise, which shows deep knowledge of Indigenous medicinal and therapeutic practices, is that Black people in Seville smoked 'in the same way' as the *indios*. In his widely published natural history of 1535, Gonzalo Fernández de Oviedo y Valdés noted that Black people in the Caribbean – presumably living alongside oppressed Indigenous populations – had adopted the 'very bad' local vice of smoking, cultivating the plant and using it to take away their fatigue.[17] Black and Indigenous histories are deeply entwined in this region, with blended Afro-Caribbean culture being responsible for the survival and transmission of many Taíno and Carib customs that might otherwise have been obliterated with the decimation of their people.

Vital though these cultural and commercial exchanges are, they show how easily Indigenous peoples have been erased from the story of exchange. Where they do appear, they are silenced, never venturing beyond their own shores, dependent on European conduits of communication, though tobacco was principally supplied by Native peoples and continued to be closely associated with Indigenous ways. Knowledge was often abstracted from Native cultures, Europeanised and appropriated, even while Indigenous people themselves were vital to the currents of information which criss-crossed the Atlantic. From 1536, the College of Santa Cruz

at Tlatelolco in Mexico City educated many sons of the Indigenous nobility, teaching them to read and write in Spanish, Latin
and Nahuatl. Most famous for collaborating with Bernardino de
Sahagún to produce the *Florentine Codex*, such Indigenous intellectuals also produced work in their own right. Long known as the
Libellus de Medicinalibus Indorum Herbis (the Book of Medicinal
Herbs of the Indies), the *Codex de la Cruz Badiano* was recently
renamed in recognition of Martín de la Cruz and Juan Badiano,
the Nahua men who wrote and translated the text at the College
of Santa Cruz. An experienced doctor, Martín de la Cruz wrote
the 'little book of Indian herbs and medicine' as a favour for the
son of the viceroy, who sent it to Philip II along with a shipment
of botanical specimens. This gorgeously illustrated herbal then
made its way to the library of the wealthy Barberini family in Rome
before being absorbed into the Vatican collections. The original was
repatriated to Mexico by Pope John Paul II, but an early copy has
emerged in the library of the British royal family at Windsor Castle,
in testament to its influence and interest in European circles.[18]

Another Mesoamerican sacred plant with stimulant properties,
cacao, found its niche more quickly in Europe. The habit of drinking
chocolate was swiftly adopted by enthusiastic consumers, although
it did not become the irresistible blocks of smooth creaminess we
now imagine until much later. Without the sugar and milk which
later transformed the concoction, Mesoamerican peoples ground
the beans and mixed them with water to make a thick foamy
liquid which could be drunk either hot (the Maya preference) or
cold (the Nahua) with the addition of your favourite flavours. The
most popular ingredient was powdered chillies, which came in
such variety that the afterburn ranged from aromatic tingling to
fiery inferno.* Poorer people added ground maize to their cacao to
make a nourishing gruel, while the elite could hope to add flowers,
vanilla, honey and spices. The *Florentine Codex* describes at length

---

*   Cocoa and chillies are still a popular combination across Mexico, especially in
the famously elaborate *mole* sauces which come in numerous regional varieties.

the cornucopia laid out for the Aztec-Mexica ruler at the end of
his meal:

> Then, in his house, the ruler was served his chocolate, with
> which he finished [his repast] – green, made of tender cacao;
> honeyed chocolate made with ground-up dried flowers – with
> green vanilla pods; bright-red chocolate; orange-colored choc-
> olate; rose-colored chocolate; black chocolate; white chocolate.
>
> The chocolate was served in a painted gourd vessel, with a
> stopper also painted with a design, and [having] a beater; or
> in a painted gourd, smoky [in color], from neighboring lands,
> with a gourd stopper, and a jar rest of ocelot skin or of cured
> leather. In a small net were kept the earthen jars, the strainer
> with which was purified the chocolate, a large painted gourd
> vessel in which the hands were washed, richly designed drinking
> vessels; [there were] large food baskets, sauce dishes, polished
> dishes, and wooden dishes.[19]

In Mesoamerica, only the elite could command such a feast, for
cacao was not only a piquant drink, but also a form of wealth. In
the barter economies of Central America, cacao beans – podded,
fermented, dried and roasted – were used as 'coinage'; convenient small tokens that could be used in standardised economic
exchange. At the market in Tlaxcala, one cacao bean would buy you
one large tomato or five chillies. To get a turkey egg or avocado,
or a take-home dinner of fish wrapped in maize husks, would
cost you 3 beans. Showing the relative scarcity of meat, a small
rabbit would cost you 30 beans and a turkey cock a whopping 200
(hens were half that). Cotton *quachtli* (blankets or capes) and gold
quills covered higher costs, but cacao was convenient for everyday
transactions.[20]

Cacao has been deeply embedded in Indigenous social and religious ceremonies for thousands of years, showing up in pre-Olmec
archaeology on the Gulf Coast nearly 4000 years ago. Needing a
temperate and damp climate, it grew mostly in the coastal regions,
and so was traded over long distances, with traces having been

found on pottery as far away as present-day Utah, over 1500 miles to the north. Cacao from Mesoamerica and the Gulf was also a common ingredient in the highly caffeinated 'black drink' that was consumed by Ancestral Puebloans and other cultures across what is now the American Southwest. The Aztec-Mexica relied on the Maya for their supply, increasing its desirability through scarcity. So valuable was cacao that people even tried to counterfeit beans, shaping them from wax, dough and carved avocado pits. Cacao held a sacred place in Mesoamerican cultures, strongly linked to divine creation. In the Madrid Codex, four gods are shown sprinkling blood from their ears onto cacao pods, filling them with life force. Cacao pods and chocolate were precious, often symbolically tied to hearts and blood. In Nahuatl, the phrase *yollotli, eztli* (literally, heart, blood) meant 'cacao', because it was so rare and precious. 'The common folk, the needy did not drink it . . . The heart, the blood [cacao] are to be feared', wrote Sahagún, explaining the metaphor. Like maize, cacao was tied to the earth and to fertility, featured in feasting and celebration at ritual events. This intoxicant was to be consumed with caution, even by warriors and the nobility.[21]

When a young Aztec-Mexica couple agreed to be married, the stuff of the earth was at the heart of the festivities.

> Thereupon there were preparations: the ashes were prepared, ground cacao was prepared, flowers were secured, smoking tubes were purchased, tubes of tobacco were prepared, sauce bowls and pottery cups and baskets were purchased. Then maize was ground; leavening was set out in basins. Then tamales [steamed maize dumplings] were prepared.[22]

Cacao, tobacco and maize were all precious goods valued for feasting, but also central to the Indigenous way of understanding their relationship to the land: fruits of the earth, which bound humans to the wider cosmos through their consumption. Maize was a divine staple across Mesoamerica. So important was corn that the Aztec-Mexica had deities representing it in all its different forms: the tender young maize was personified by the virgin goddess Xilonen ('hairy one', named for the silky threads on the young maize); the mature corn was Centeotl, the proud erect god of the firm, swollen, cobs; and Chicomecoatl or 'Seven Snake' (perhaps just an older incarnation of Xilonen) was his female counterpart, an older sister of the rain gods, who 'maketh all our food'. Generally shown clutching ears of maize, she embodied fertility and sustenance, and was associated with the seeds during the planting season. The Green Corn (or Great Peace) Ceremony celebrating the first harvest is a deep tradition across a wide swathe of tribes in what is now the eastern part of the United States. The Maya too recognised maize in many divine forms: from Hun Hunahpu, who was depicted as a vigorous young man with hair of cornsilk and ears of corn adorning his head; to Ah Mun, the tender shoot of the unripe maize; and Zac Uac Nal, who represented the bursting forth of the new white corn.* The cycle of nourishment was embraced and celebrated at every stage, and Indigenous peoples recognised the spirit and personality of the plants in the foods they consumed and used for celebration, repaying their debt to them through sacrificial festivals, prayer and offerings.

One wonders which of these associations were in the minds of the delegation of Maya chiefs in full regalia who, on 12 February 1545, stood before Prince (soon to become King) Philip with presents showing the richness of their lands.† In addition to two thousand quetzal feathers sent by the chiefs of Tuzulutlán, the gifts included beautiful clay pots and fruit platters, as well as 'containers of whisked chocolate'. This is the first reference to the drinking of chocolate in Europe, the chocolate brought to the Spanish court – and presumably prepared – by Native people.

Frothing chocolate was an expert skill, usually performed by

---

* The Maya peoples lived from 2000 BCE to the present day, so their range of beliefs is vast, and the sources contested by scholars.

† According to the Guatemalan historian Agustín Estrada Monroy, he was able to view the source for this meeting at the archive in front of the chief and mayor of the Q'eqchi' (formerly written K'ekchí), a Maya people originally from northern Guatemala.

women, who poured the thick liquid from head height back and forth between two jugs or pots. Who prepared the chocolate for the Q'eqchi' chiefs? Given the splendid repast, it seems likely there were women among their retinue, but they go unnoticed in the official accounts. In cultures across Mesoamerica, cacao was not only intimately associated with women, but also with marriage and betrothal agreements. In the Madrid Codex,* the longest of the surviving Maya codices, the rain god Chaak is shown marrying the earth goddess Ixik Kaab; a jar of frothy chocolate sits between them and they each hold honeycomb above, alongside a text which is usually translated: 'they were given their cacao'. The Cherokee scholar Martha Macri noted that the verb for 'they were given' (*ts' ab' a'*) is defined in the epic 'Cordemex Maya dictionary' – the product of a massive collaborative effort – as 'payment of the marriage debt': cacao and the marriage contract were almost synonymous. The Codex Tonindeye, a rare pre-invasion codex from the Ñuu Dzaui (Mixtec) people of highland Mexico, also shows foaming chocolate being given by Lady Thirteen Snake to her groom, the ruler Eight Deer, to bind their wedding in 1501. (These names originate from their birth date numbers and signs in the 260-day ritual calendar.) Similarly, when Lady Nine Crocodile marries Lord Five Wind in the Ñuu Dzaui Codex Yuta Tnoho, their union is symbolised by a jar of frothy chocolate between them.†[23]

---

*   As with many of these documents, the codex is named after the city in which it now rests after being stolen away from its Indigenous owners. Its alternative names, the 'Tro-Cortesianus' or 'Troano Codex', evoke Juan Tro y Ortelano, a professor of palaeography who is often called its 'first owner', in blithe ignorance of its original Maya possessors.

†   The Codex Tonindeye is better known as the Codex Zouche-Nuttall after the two people most connected with it in Europe, rather than its originators. And the Codex Yuta Tnoho is better known as the Codex Vindobonensis Mexicanus I after the Latin name for Vienna (Vindobona) where it rests. But as Jansen and Pérez Jiménez have rightly argued, we need to start using terms which make 'efforts to interpret this unique literary heritage in terms of the civilization that produced' it. 'Tonindeye' means 'lineage history' in the Dzaha Dzaui (Mixtec) language and 'Yuta Tnoho' is the sacred valley where the dynasties on the manuscript originated.

Eric Thompson, the famed scholar of Maya archaeology, history and language, wrote that the term *tac haa*, broadly meaning 'to serve chocolate', carries a huge currency in its brief syllables, being translated in the Motul Maya dictionary as 'to invite the father of a girl whom one's son wants to marry to discuss the marriage and serve him drink'. According to a colonial report on the Chol Maya, who lived in the forests of Chiapas, when a couple married, they exchanged five grains of cacao along with a stool (for him) and some skirts (for her) saying, 'These I give thee as a sign that I accept thee as my husband/wife.' The Awakatec Maya mountain people of Guatemala still call their traditional marriage ceremony *quicyuj*, meaning 'cacao beans', even though cacao is no longer involved. It's even possible that our word for 'chocolate' comes from the K'iche' term *chokola'j*, meaning 'drink chocolate together'. Cacao was a symbol of union, of agreement, of changing status. What would it have meant for the Maya chiefs to present whisked chocolate to Prince Philip? This often gets lost among the list of 'new commodities', but for the Maya it carried political and sacred implications.[24]

Indigenous delegations were not unusual at court by the 1540s, but the regent was nonetheless impressed, not only by their finery but also by their fortitude; seeing the Maya 'with so few clothes, in the rigours of the cold of Madrid', he said to them, 'You must be [made] of steel.' Despite the bitter weather, the four chiefs had elected to appear dressed in traditional regalia: cotton shifts and breeches decorated with rainbow-hued thread, cinched at the waist, with a bright, fringed belt hanging down in front. Calves and sandals were tasselled with thread which shone 'like a small bouquet of flowers' and their long hair was entwined with ribbons which hung behind and supported a showy headpiece composed of multicoloured tassels. Their capes were of feathers, worked with incredible skill to show scenes of parrots, flowers, jars and diamonds. It was a direct manifestation of Indigenous power on a European stage, led by a man who would later become a legend: don Juan Aj Pop B'atz', the 'chief of chiefs'.[25]

Elected as leader of Tuzulutlán (now Alta and Baja Verapaz)

after the Spanish abducted and murdered the previous ruler, Aj
Pop B'atz' is now a local hero in the Q'eqchi'-Maya town of San
Juan Chamelco in Guatemala, where he is seen as the man who
successfully protected his people from the Spanish invasion, at
first by force, and later by diplomacy.[26] Oral and textual histories,
collected by Ashley Kistler as part of a collaborative research
project with the Maya community, describe how Aj Pop B'atz',
who was renowned for his 'wisdom, bravery, faithfulness, skill,
and prudence', saw the devastation of neighbouring communities
and chose to save his people by welcoming three Dominican friars
to Chamelco and becoming the region's first Q'eqchi' Catholic,
baptised in a nearby river.[27] Not long after this important act of
accommodation, the Spanish invited Aj Pop B'atz' to visit Spain,
along with three other chiefs: don Miguel de Paz y Chun, don Juan
Rafael Ramírez Aj Sakq'uim de San Luis and don Diego de Avila
Mo y Pop.

A Q'eqchi' Maya tradition about the voyage has been faithfully
passed down through the centuries. The original manuscripts are
now almost illegible, but the leaders of the community have made
copy after copy. These transcriptions, which are seen as 'inheriting
the words', tell how the Dominican fathers, led by Diego Avila,
invited the four chiefs in the name of God, to go with them to
Spain, 'where our king is'. They set off at the start of May 1544 along
with seven priests, nine Spanish men and 'the former *chinames*'
(community leaders and elders). It seems there was some dispute
about the bounty they planned to take with them because the text
notes that 'if they don't accept our finery and gifts in the ship we
will perforce have to go to Spain, we will tell the guards, let's go
anyway'. According to Q'eqchi' oral histories, the men travelled to
Spain through caves below the earth, or even flew using super-
natural powers, but the text says that they would take ship on 4
June (though in fact the date of their journey seems to have been
later). They travelled down the Polochic river valley – famed for
its chocolate production – and through the delta to the Caribbean
coast of what is now Honduras, where they embarked at Puerto

heavy-handed attempt to confirm their authority in the region, whether it happened in reality, or only later became part of the narrative of the voyage. The Q'eqchi' were not the only ones shaping their collective identities in this story.

We know little more about the activities of the Q'eqchi' chiefs in Spain, but the sources are in agreement about the wealth of gifts bestowed on Aj Pop B'atz' by the king: two large silver bells for the church at Chamelco, silver crosses and other smaller bells, sacred implements to conduct baptisms and the mass, banners and images of saints, vestments, mantles, cloth, candleholders and altar fronts for the church, as well as more cloth, scissors, knives and hoes, to bolster the community. The task of returning this mountain of gifts to Tuzulutlán was so great that Diego de Avila Mo y Pop was appointed Leader of the Bell, a title which allowed him to command the Indigenous labour necessary to transport the treasure. (It's not clear whether this 'servitude' was enslaved, requisitioned, or paid.) The journey home was clearly arduous, and what was likely a fairly typical trip for Indigenous travellers is itemised in the records with unusual care.

The ship was loaded at the port of Muelas in Triana, Seville, on the river Guadalquivir, where inspectors checked the size, legal specifications and seaworthiness of the vessel. If all was in order, they were given a licence which specified their voyage, as well as the cargo, weapons and ammunition they were permitted to carry. Once the ships started loading, the larger ships began to struggle in the shallow waters of the Guadalquivir and could only take on a certain amount of cargo before having to set off, carefully navigating the banks of the river, though not before having their licence checked a second time. Passengers had to disembark regularly to lighten the ship's load, trekking some forty miles by land as well as water before reaching the port of Sanlúcar de Barrameda on the Atlantic coast. Finally embarking for the Americas, the chiefs had an eighteen-day sail to the Canary Islands to the southwest, where they landed at La Gomera on Gran Canaria, a gloriously mountainous island with spectacular rocky coasts. This outpost off the coast of Africa was one of Spain's earliest colonial claims, invaded in 1402, and was a common waypoint for voyagers to the Americas. One wonders if the Q'eqchi' chiefs saw any of the Indigenous Guanches,* who – though they often resisted fiercely, and had some acquired immunity to European diseases – had proven early victims of similar violence and forced labour to that later inflicted on the Maya. After leaving the Canaries, they would first travel south to avoid being becalmed in the lee of El Hierro ('the iron' island), and then strike out across the Atlantic. Leaving in the summer, the chiefs would have been likely to make an easier trip because of favourable winds, completing the transatlantic crossing in some twenty-five or so days. (A winter trip was faster, but also more dangerous, because of the strong winds and rough weather.) The first island they would spot, after weeks surrounded by nothing but ocean, was La Deseada† (the Desired, since Columbus's crew supposedly cried 'Oh desired island' at this first sight of land).

And so, on 11 February 1546, after more than five months of travelling, Aj Pop B'atz' and his company arrived back in Maya territory where the Leader of the Bell set about requisitioning Indigenous people to transport all the cargo, using rafts on the river where possible because of the damp, mountainous terrain. The base required to co-ordinate all this work was apparently so substantial that it became a village, and a commercial hub for the river. The Q'eqchi' records mention that the people there 'remember the day that they happily arrived in the land of the k'ekchí chiefs' – an interesting elision of the complicity of the Maya chiefs in the forced displacement and possible enslavement of other Indigenous peoples.[33]

For the Q'eqchi' of Chamelco, Aj Pop B'atz' is a symbol of local identity, Indigenous resistance and shared past; 'He fought so they didn't take Guatemala away from us, because if he hadn't fought, we would already have been in the hands of the Spaniards', doña

---

* Now the common term for all Indigenous inhabitants of the Canary Islands, this was originally the name of the people of the largest island: Tenerife.

† Now part of Guadeloupe and called La Désirade since the French colonisation in 1648.

Gloria told Kistler.[34] But he is also part of a transatlantic story which comprehends Indigenous histories as part of a global narrative. The voyage of the chiefs to Europe is a central part of the histories guarded by the Maya – their conceptions of identity, although strongly rooted in territory, also understand the Q'eqchi' as active and significant within a cosmos that stretched far beyond their own shores. For the Maya chiefs, the stuff they brought to court extended their own systems of value across the Atlantic, demonstrating the richness of their environment, as well as displaying the resources at their command. Aj Pop B'atz' was a renowned diplomat who clearly discerned the intricacies of colonial politics, so we must assume the performance was strategic: refusing to bow, elevating the symbolic quetzal feathers, and centring Q'eqchi' identity through dress and language, rather than Hispanising their presentation.

The Q'eqchi' chiefs brought an array of other foods and plants from their homeland, including chillies, beans and maize. The abundance of American plant life was remarkable, and fundamentally changed the European diet, while the introduction of European livestock and farming methods to the Indigenous world transformed their lived environment in myriad ways, reshaping the ecology and remaking the land. Before contact with the Americas, Europe (and indeed the rest of the world) had no potatoes, squash, maize or beans.* Many of these foodstuffs became entangled with European beliefs about America and its original inhabitants, being viewed with suspicion or curiosity. Even chocolate was at first viewed with misgivings. After spending time in the coastal regions of what is now Nicaragua and Costa Rica, Oviedo found the Nicarao practice of drinking chocolate mixed with achiote spice repellent, because it dyed the lips and mouths red. Believing that 'these people liked drinking blood', the effect was a 'horrendous thing'.[35]

The way in which potatoes filtered into European diets is fairly typical of responses to Indigenous foods. Columbus first brought sweet potatoes from Hispaniola in 1493 and, although it is

---

* Except soybeans in Asia.

frequently claimed that the common potato only made its way into European diets in the 1570s, it already formed part of many Atlantic ships' stores by the mid-sixteenth century. Indigenous foods may not have been fashionable among the elite – unless they were an extraordinary novelty – but they were seen as more than acceptable for the poor, enslaved and ordinary workers. In Seville, unsurprisingly, potatoes were common in the marketplace by the early 1570s, and they were being cultivated in gardens as far afield as Germany and Italy by the following decade. When J. G. Hawkes and J. Francisco-Ortega analysed the sixteenth-century account books of the Hospital de la Sangre – a hospital for the poor and infirm in Seville, and hardly a place for extravagance – they found potatoes, squashes, and chillies among their purchases. Potatoes in particular, seem to have been bought in quite significant quantities from the 1580s. Working people understood not only the nutritional value of these tubers, but also their relative obscurity from the authorities who often requisitioned a share of their crops. In England, the account books of the Earl of Northumberland show expensive, imported, sweet potatoes among the purchases for the supplies of Alnwick Castle in the late-sixteenth century and they were clearly common enough by the turn of the seventeenth century for Shakespeare to have Falstaff cry 'let the sky rain potatoes'! While ordinary people seized on the humble potato, and colonists quickly saw their value, in Europe the elites viewed them either as cures or causes of disease. In 1619 they were banned by Burgundy as a possible cause of leprosy (due to the marks on the skin), and just the following year they were being applauded by the English doctor Tobias Venner as a cure for consumption (tuberculosis), who found potatoes 'surpassing the nourishment of all other roots or fruits'.[36]

In 1544, the Tuscan botanist and imperial physician, Pietro Andrea Mattioli noted the arrival of 'another species of eggplant' (itself a relatively new arrival from Persia via Andalusia), that could be cooked and eaten with salt, black pepper and oil. This low-key reference marks the appearance in Italy of a fruit that would become inextricable from their culture and cuisine – what Mattioli ten years later dubbed *pomi d'oro* (golden fruits) – the tomato. Like potatoes, however, they were a member of the nightshade family and so immediately subject to intellectual suspicion. The vast folios of Francisco Hernández de Toledo, personal physician to Philip II, described the tomatillo (often confused with the green tomato) as 'horrible and obscene'. Although he acknowledged it could be used to make spicy sauces with chillies – salsa, essentially – he was repulsed by the interior's 'venereal and lascivious' similarity to the vulva. Tomatoes were also seen as an especially 'cold' and 'moist' food in the Galenic tradition which saw people as governed by the balance of four humours. Tomatoes were considered to be wetter and colder, like women, which was naturally seen by men as a *bad thing*. Yet, by the turn of the seventeenth century, tomatoes and tomatillos were ubiquitous in Italian gardens, sometimes for their exotic beauty, but also for their distinctive taste.* In 1592, the head gardener at Aranjuez, a botanical garden patronised by Philip II, wrote 'it is said [tomatoes] are good for sauces', and they appear entwined on the large bronze frieze cast for the door of Pisa Cathedral around 1600/1601.[37]

Gradual acceptance is fairly typical of European reactions to Indigenous goods. At first repelled by their 'foreignness', people gradually realised the potential of these products. Discussion of this shift in attitudes often excludes Native peoples, focusing on the elite men who wrote the scientific, medical and natural histories of the plants in question. But Indigenous peoples were vital to the ways in which parts of their traditional foods and cultures became embedded in European life.

Antonio Ponce's catchily titled painting – *A still life of peaches, fish, chestnuts, a tin plate, sweet box, chocolate grinder and Mexican lacquer cups and shawl* – shows the way that Indigenous tastes and practices were normalised in Spain. A *molinolli* whisk is perched on a round cacao container in the centre along with one of the two

---

* As early as 1546, the duke of Ferentillo, Lorenzo Cibo Malaspina, also planted some maize at his estate near Pisa. We will never know what he thought of it, because the mice ate it.

Mexican *jícaras*, lacquered gourd cups. The picture is a model of globalised ecology: mottled peeled chestnuts, a staple carbohydrate in Spain from Roman times until potatoes became fashionable; local fish; sweet, downy peaches from China, introduced by the Romans, and then again by Muslims by the twelfth century; along with sharp juicy lemons, the citrus trees now so evocative of Spain in the popular imagination; the chocolate accoutrements; and a shiny shawl made of the silk introduced to Mexico shortly after the Spanish invasion. But when we look at this picture, we can see more than changing diets and global foods. We can see the Mesoamerican women – Maya, Nahua, Totonac, Ñuu Dzaui and others – who would have frothed chocolate in Seville and Madrid, just as they had learned to do it from their mothers and grandmothers, in the mountains and forests, cities and villages, of their homelands.

For Mesoamerican people, the entire world was to be found in the household. The hearth was the heart of the world, and the woman was 'the heart of the home'.[38] So when Indigenous women stepped into the kitchen in the colonial world, they were continuing a tradition that reached back to their ancestors, taking care and charge of the chocolate as their mothers had done. The influence of these women – servants, wives, mistresses, and enslaved people, who were often illiterate – is hard to trace in the literature, but we know that they were there, in Spain and Portugal, and further afield. They are part of the European past. And they brought their traditions and languages along with them.

The wooden *molinillo* whisk – still used for frothing chocolate in Mexico and Spain today – is often claimed as a colonial invention, supposedly replacing the Nahua practice of pouring chocolate back and forth between two vessels to make it foamy. But chocolate beaters were common in Maya, Totonac and other regions, and the Aztec-Mexica had a chocolate-stirring stick made of wood. Even the name *molinillo* (typically thought to come from the Spanish for a 'little mill', *molino*) may be derived from the Nahuatl word *moliniani*, meaning an instrument that wiggles, shakes or moves. Indigenous gourd and clay cups (*jícaras* and *teocomates*) were also being imported, supposedly because they enhanced the flavour of the chocolate. Europeans were not only enjoying the novel drink, but also adopting Indigenous habits and preferences, along with their language.[39]

For a long time, it was assumed that *chocolate* (*chocolatl* in the colonial world) came from *xocoatl* (pronounced 'sho-co-at-ul'), meaning 'bitter water'. This fitted very nicely with people's expectations about European reactions to Indigenous foodstuffs. But it seems like the word may actually have come from the K'iche' *chokola'j*, the much duller Nahuatl *cacáhuatl* (cocoa water/liquid), or the combination of the Mayan word *chocol* (hot) and the Nahuatl word *atl* (meaning water or liquid).[40] And language is one area where the Indigenous influence on our understanding of the stuff of our world is undeniable. Indigenous peoples did not just form their own Atlantic patois, but also profoundly changed European languages. To give just a few examples: because of the Caribbean Arawak languages, we can *barbecue*, *canoe* or lie in a *hammock* during a *hurricane*. Quechua, spoken by the Inkas, is why we eat *jerky* and *quinoa* and perhaps even take *cocaine*. Nahuatl, the language of the Aztec-Mexica and their neighbours, gave us *avocados* and *tomatoes* to eat with *chile* and *chocolate* in a *shack*. Tupi-Guaraní is why we eat *manioc* and *tapioca* while watching *jaguars*, *piranhas* and *toucans* sitting among *petunias*. For cold weather, Inuit gave us the iconic *anorak*, and Algonquian our *moccasins* and *toboggans*.

Many of these words cut across the European linguistic map, being borrowed from one language to another: *chocolate* in English and Spanish, *chocolat* in French, *schokolade* in German, *chocola* in Dutch, *čokolada* in Croatian, *cioccolato* in Italian. And the meetings of peoples are reflected in the language. The Spanish use *tiza* (chalk) and *hule* (rubber) because of their encounter with the Nahua, while French is peppered with Tupi, thanks to their trade with Brazil, where we get words like *ananas* (pineapple, from *nanas* meaning 'excellent fruit') and *boucanier* (buccaneer) from *boucan* (smoking meat) after the food eaten by these corsairs in the Caribbean. Some of these new concepts fundamentally changed European ways of doing things. *Hammocks* (Taíno) revolutionised shipboard life from the late-sixteenth century onwards, allowing for safer and more comfortable sleeping in crowded quarters. The value of the light-weight *canoes* (from Carib/Arawakan) was quickly recognised by European invaders and became a critical part of their expeditions on inland waterways.

Indigenous words filled the gaps in European perception, silently (or audibly but furtively) setting contours in their understanding. How we speak of things helps determine how we see them. As the twentieth-century Māori community leader Sir James Henare put it: 'The language is like a cloak which clothes, envelops, and adorns the myriad of one's thoughts.'[41] This is why it is so vital to revitalise Indigenous languages, to preserve their cultures, and to listen to their unique perspectives.[42] I cannot 'think' within the languages of Native peoples, but I *can* try to hear their words, and to avoid making assumptions about value that are rooted in modern, western, preconceptions.

In 1526, the Venetian author and orator Andrea Navagero travelled to Spain as ambassador to the court of Charles V. Ending up in Seville in late spring, which he found unbearably hot, he wrote of how entangled the city was with the Atlantic: 'so many people have left for the Indies, that the city is sparsely populated and is almost in the power of women'.* He also 'saw in Seville many things of the Indies and ate the roots that they call *batatas* [sweet potatoes], that taste like chestnuts. I also saw and ate because they arrived fresh, a most beautiful fruit that they call [the name is omitted, likely pineapple], and they have a flavour between melon and peach, with a strong scent, and truly it is very pleasant.' As well as these delicacies, Navagero saw some young Indigenous noblemen who had accompanied a friar to Spain, 'dressed in their own way, half naked, and with only a sort of short doublet or loose trousers; they had black hair, wide face, Roman nose'. The Venetian was impressed with their 'great wit and vitality' and especially the game of *pelota*, which was played with 'a type of very light and bouncy piece of

---

*   He doesn't say whether he thinks this is a good thing, but I assume not.

wood'* that was passed between them 'with great agility' without using their hands and feet. Two years before Cortés's arrival, young Indigenous men were already playing the Mesoamerican ball game in Seville, and visitors were able to sample exotic tastes from their homelands. Both people and plants were embedded in the flows of information, goods and ideas that regularly crossed the Atlantic. Standing at a distance, it may be easier at times to detect the 'commodities' – they are valued, registered, and fixed in the records. But to follow the siren call of economics is to implicitly adopt a Eurocentric approach in which globalisation and interconnection are inextricably linked to western capitalist ways of thinking, ideas which have become so ubiquitous that they are often taken for granted. In the wise words of Linda Tuhiwai Smith: 'The term "trade" assumes at the very least a two-way transaction between those who sold and those who bought. It further assumes that human beings and other cultural items were commodities or goods and were actually available "for sale". For Indigenous peoples those assumptions are not held. From Indigenous perspectives territories, peoples and their possessions were stolen, not traded.'[43]

It is not that Native peoples did not participate in exchange. They most certainly did, both in their own internal, far-reaching, trade networks and with Europe, Asia and Africa. But that does not mean that they necessarily perceived these exchanges, or the objects of exchange, in the same way as Europeans. For many Indigenous peoples, these transactions formed part of larger networks of obligation, understanding and reciprocity. They framed friendship, diplomacy and alliances, and were freely offered, in the expectation of mutual understanding. When Moctezuma reportedly told Cortés, 'in all the land that lies in my domain, you may command as you will, for you shall be obeyed . . . you are in your own country and your own house', he was offering hospitality, not authority. But the conquistador – lacking understanding of Indigenous courtesy and mutuality – claimed the land for his own.[44]

---

* This was almost certainly rubber, which Navagero had presumably learned was from a tree and, unfamiliar with the substance, used the term *leño* (log).

The racist insult 'Indian giver' refers to someone 'who is so uncivilized to ask us to return a gift he has given'. This is rooted in a misconception of Indigenous understandings of property centring on reciprocity and sharing rather than trade and acquisition. In reality, as Lewis Hyde famously wrote: 'The opposite of "Indian giver" would be something like "white man keeper" (or maybe "capitalist"), that is, a person whose instinct is to remove property from circulation, to put it in a warehouse or museum (or, more to the point for capitalism, to lay it aside to be used for production)'.[45] Concepts of reciprocity, circulation, and sufficiency underlay much Indigenous thought, in the ideal if not always in practice.

We cannot be sure how the manifold inhabitants of sixteenth-century Turtle Island, the Alligator Disc, those who stood on the world surrounded by waters, saw the exchanges that exploded life-styles, ideas and economies after 1492, but Jean de Léry's reported account of a discussion with one elderly Tupinambá man in the 1550s gives us one rare insight. The man asked: 'What does it mean that you *Mairs* and *Peros* (that is, French and Portuguese) come so far for wood to warm yourselves? Is there none in your own country?' Yes, we have some, replied Léry, but not brazilwood, with all its uses. 'But do you need so much of it?', the Tupinambá man quickly responded. 'Yes', said Léry again, explaining that they would be able to sell the brazilwood to a rich merchant in France, whose family would inherit all his wealth if he were to die. Léry's account of the man's response is revealing: '"Truly," said my elder (who, as you will judge, was no dullard), "I see now that you *Mairs* (that is, Frenchmen) are great fools; must you labor so hard to cross the sea, on which (as you told us) you endured so many hardships, just to amass riches for your children or for those who will survive you? Will not the earth that nourishes you suffice to nourish them? We have kinsmen and children, whom, as you see, we love and cherish; but because we are certain that after our death the earth which has nourished us will nourish them, we rest easy and do not trouble ourselves further about it."' The Calvinist pastor Léry was certainly using this dialogue to critique what he saw as the excesses and avarice of European society, but his account chimes with others we have of Indigenous scepticism and incomprehension at European cultures of inequality, and the accrual of resources for their own sake. Almost four centuries later, Raoni Metuktire, chief of the Kayapó people of Brazil, echoed the Tupinambá elder in his fight against the ravaging of the Amazon: 'In the Kayapó language we call your money *piu caprim*, "sad leaves", because it is a dead and useless thing, and it brings only harm and sadness.'[46]

5

Diplomacy

Don Francisco Tenamaztle, a *cacique* from southern Zacatecas, was transported to Spain in the 1550s to account for his part as a leader of the Mixtón War, a struggle against Spanish domination which resulted in the brutal suppression of the Caxcanes, Zacatecos and other semi-nomadic peoples of northern Mexico. Having evaded capture for nearly a decade, in 1551 Tenamaztle – often called America's first guerrilla fighter – was convinced by the Bishop of Guadalajara to surrender voluntarily and seek official justice for the abuses against his people. Unfortunately, a new viceroy had taken charge and – rather than hearing the *cacique*'s complaints – he arrested Tenamaztle as a leader of the rebellion: 'Hearing that the Bishop had died, I planned to return home, but the Viceroy told me no. He placed me in irons, sent me to Veracruz, and from there I was put aboard a ship bound for Seville, traveling as a prisoner.' Imprisoned in Valladolid, before being transferred to a Dominican monastery, Tenamaztle was lucky enough to secure the services of Bartolomé de Las Casas to act on his behalf. Together, they composed a blistering denunciation of Spanish abuses and exploitation of the *indios*, arguing that Tenamaztle's actions were a 'natural act of fleeing and defending oneself' and that it was the colonial authorities who had acted illegally and tyrannically in their abuses and violent suppression of the revolt. The *memorial* also included a petition for royal support, not only for missionaries to convert the people of Tenamaztle's region in New Galicia, but also for 'funds to buy the chief some clothing and other necessities'. Even though Tenamaztle was a prisoner, facing justice for leading a rebellion, the Crown agreed to pay a substantial sum to cover his maintenance because of 'all the time that he would spend at court'.[1]

The work of José Carlos de la Puente Luna has shed light on hundreds of Andeans from across the social spectrum who travelled to Spain and took advantage of such royal patronage, while representing themselves, their families, or their communities at court. His meticulous archival work shows that it became customary for Indigenous visitors to be granted financial aid from the royal treasury to cover day-to-day expenses and travel costs. A legal loophole meant that *indios* were seen as *'miserable'* (poor and wretched), a category usually reserved for minors, and those who were unable to seek justice for themselves. The early embassies were treated on a more ad hoc basis but, by the 1560s, Indigenous visitors to Spain were routinely awarded funds in line with their station, leading to a situation where wealthy Indigenous nobles obtained huge sums from the treasury on the grounds that they were only the king's 'poor' and 'wretched' vassals, children of the monarch, and so entitled to protection, legal assistance and financial support.

Even the costs of a more ordinary traveller could run into hundreds of pesos for daily provisions and travel. In the 1560s, the Crown paid for Paquiquineo, an Algonquian-speaking (probably Kisiack or Paspahegh) noble from near what is now Chesapeake Bay, to have clothes, haircuts, trips to the theatre, masses for his soul and alms for the poor, and a new rosary, as well as the usual travel and subsistence expenses. This remarkable figure, famous for his extraordinary mobility, travelled twice to Spain, in 1561 and 1566, as well as spending time in Portugal (briefly), Havana, and Mexico City (where he was christened with his better-known name, don Luís de Velasco, after the viceroy). After a decade away, Paquiquineo persuaded the Jesuits to return him to Spanish Florida, where he killed the missionaries and disappeared into his homeland. The Crown's role as guardian of the *indios* benefited them enormously in imperial propaganda, but it also had drawbacks. Supporting Indigenous travellers according to their *calidad* (quality) could prove very expensive. In 1602, don Melchor

Carlos Inca, seen by many as the last true heir to the Inka line,* was granted a massive 6000 ducats to cover the cost of moving to Spain, where he secured a knighthood, along with extravagant expenses, and a magnificent pension of 8500 ducats for himself and his heirs.[2]

In January 1556, the imprisoned *cacique* Tenamaztle received 6000 *maravedís* toward costs, which included hiring and out-fitting his lodgings and paying his servant's salary, a grant that was repeated in July. Further awards were made in March and September, including to cover the arrival of yet another servant. Tenamaztle was not just a prisoner but also a member of the elite, who merited appropriate treatment. As a Christian vassal of the Crown, he was eligible for protection and a fair hearing, and, as the ruler of Nochistlán, he was entitled to live in a manner fitting his quality. The Crown did not want to devalue nobility, in whatever form it came. As an *indio*, who could claim protection and guardianship from the king, Tenamaztle also exploited the opportunity to petition the Crown directly about the abuses his people had suffered.[3]

> I beg Your Highness that, having before Your eyes God and true justice, you consider the incomparable grievances and injustices that I and all the *naturales* (natural inhabitants) of that province have received and were receiving at that time and that what we did was not rise and rebel but flee from the inhumane and insufferable cruelty of the Spaniards, as animals flee from those who want to kill them.[4]

On 26 September 1556 the Crown covered the expense of 'curing'

---

* In 1975, the Peruvian government adopted new official spellings which more closely reflect the original sounds of Quechua and Aymara languages, rather than using the forms of the colonisers. I will use these where possible (such as Inka, instead of Inca), but names (which were written in Spanish) will have to stay in their original form or it would get very confusing for any reader who tried to search for them.

Tenamaztle, but it seems he never recovered from his unnamed affliction. On 31 October a *cédula* (decree) orders the payment of 4 ducats to Doctor Peñaranda (quite a large sum of money – he must have been a good doctor) 'for the work he did in visiting don Francisco Tenamaztle deceased during his illness from 25 September past until the fifth of this present month of October'. Like so many Indigenous travellers, Francisco Tenamaztle – guerrilla leader, human-rights campaigner, Native voyager – died in Spain before seeing out his case.[5] A secret enquiry into the conduct of the viceroy, Antonio de Mendoza, later vindicated Tenamaztle's accusations of brutality in Zacatecas:

> After the capture of the hill of Mixtón, many of the Indians taken in the conquest of the said hill were put to death in his presence and by his orders. Some were placed in line and blown to pieces by cannon fire; others were torn to pieces by dogs; and others were given to *negros* to be killed, and these killed them with knife thrusts, while others were hung. Again, at other places, Indians were thrown to the dogs in his presence.[6]

*

While some Indigenous ambassadors came to court to seek redress for the misdeeds of conquistadors, others found themselves in Spain as a result of alliances with the invaders. In the main square of the small town of Trujillo stands the faded glory of the Palace of the Conquest. And, on the corner of the building, staring out from the façade, is the lichen-streaked face of an Inka princess: doña Francisca Pizarro Yupanqui. Along with her husband (and uncle) Hernando, Francisca ordered the palace to be built in 1562, some ten years after she landed on Spanish shores. It still stands as testimony to the Inka presence in Europe.

Mestiza daughter of the Inka *ñusta* (princess) Quispe Sisa and the conquistador Francisco Pizarro, Francisca had a strong claim to both royal lineage and Castilian authority. Her mother, baptised Iñes Yupanqui, was of impeccable birth, as daughter of the last pre-contact Inka ruler, Huayna Capac and sister to his successors Huáscar and Atahualpa. After the invasion, she had two children

– Francisca and Gonzalo – with the leading conquistador, later
Governor of New Castile (roughly present-day Peru), Francisco
Pizarro. Both children were legitimised by Charles V in 1537 and,
at the age of seventeen – and holding strong claims to her father's
inheritance after the death of her brother – Francisca was exiled to
Spain in an attempt to reduce the dynastic infighting that had been
complicating the settlement of the colony. Her request for a delay
to sort out her affairs denied,[7] Francisca – this child of Inka royalty
and colonial aristocracy, left Peru for the last time in March 1551 in
the care of her stepfather Francisco de Ampuero – a conquistador
and senior colonial official – who was ordered to ensure she arrived
in Spain, along with her twelve-year-old half-brother Francisco,
the *mestizo* son of Pizarro's second *ñusta* wife, Cuxirimay Ocllo
(baptised doña Angelina Yupanqui). Also travelling with them was
Catalina de la Cueva, Francisca's Spanish nurse and governess, as
well as Francisco de Ampuero's *mestiza* daughter Isabel, whom he
hoped to establish securely in Spain.

Catalina was probably the closest thing the young princess had
to a confidante and companion, having been with her since infancy.
Despite being married herself, Catalina would follow Francisca
faithfully until her death. She would have ensured that Francisca
was fluent in Castilian, and we know the Inka royal was literate, for
she frequently endorsed documents with an elaborately embellished
signature. This must have been a daunting journey for the young
mestiza, although she was in some ways better off away from the
intrigues of colonial politics, for suitors had been attempting to
take her hand since she was a child. Did Catalina – herself from
Segovia – help to prepare Francisca for married life, and for the
voyage, with stories of Spain? Her return would certainly have been
a more comfortable trip than Catalina was used to, for the financial
records of the voyage suggest that it was extraordinarily luxurious.
Though we know little about Francisca's inner life, the accounts
uncovered by her biographer María Rostworowski de Diez Canseco,
give us a unique insight into the conditions of her voyage which
is as fascinating as it is frustrating, allowing us only to scratch the
surface of her existence.

Having departed on 15 March 1551, the ship went first to the Guañape islands off the coast of northern Peru, where they bought two bottles of wine and hired a horse 'to call [on] the *caciques*' – we have no idea why, but it is an incredible snippet. Was Francisca bidding farewell to the lords of these islands, source of the guano (bird droppings) that fertilised the Inka lands? After this short stop, they sailed up the coast to Panama where the group paused for more than a month, preparing for the transatlantic voyage, and also perhaps because some of the company were struggling with seasickness, for there is a bill for twenty pesos for 'Martin, barber, on the order of la señora doña Francisca, because he cured us all at sea when we fell ill'. In these dispassionate records, we can see Francisca and Catalina wandering around Panama, shopping for their long voyage. Francisca bought them each a hat, a sensible precaution for the exposed deck, a table for the ship, and material for new clothes for herself and her attendants. She also bought rich gifts for some local dignitaries and gave alms to several poor women. We know she managed to lose the key to a chest on the ship, because it had to be replaced while at the dock. The grand total of Francisca's expenses when she left Panama on 9 June amounted to a very substantial 205,611 *maravedís*. When they stopped at the Azores and Sanlúcar, she remained on board, paying for laundry, fish, fruits, wine and other refreshments to be brought out to the ship. But she made up for it with an orgy of shopping on arrival in Seville, buying a wealth of silverware, including 'a jug and a salt shaker of plated silver . . . and a platter of silver . . . and two candlesticks of silver', silk and cloth for clothes and a tailor to make them, a gold necklace, a silver drinking vessel, and other luxuries, as well as the cost of having all these things delivered. Through such mundane details, we can glimpse the outline of a transatlantic life.

After arriving in Spain, Francisca fell under the influence of her uncle, Hernando Pizarro. He was now the head of the family – despite being incarcerated in La Mota Castle as part of the fall-out from the civil war in Peru – and he ordered that his niece be brought to Medina del Campo near his prison rather than placed in the care of her aunt in Trujillo as her guardian Francisco de

Ampuero suggested. By 27 October 1552, Hernando had managed to engineer a marriage to his niece, shoring up his financial and political position among the often-feuding Pizarros. Francisca cannot possibly have seen this as a love match: married to her uncle, who was three decades older and confined to prison for the foreseeable future. They likely wed at the medieval fortress, since Hernando could not leave, and she lived there with him (albeit in considerable comfort) for most of the first decade of their marriage, bearing five children. Of their three sons and two daughters, only Francisco, Juan and Iñes lived to adulthood. Perhaps Francisca's eldest daughter was named for the Inka mother from whom she was separated as a toddler, or for the surrogate parent (Iñes Muñoz) who had raised her from infancy.[8]

As soon as they were married, the couple set about consolidating their inheritance. It is hard to know exactly how active Francisca was in this process – as a legal minor to her husband and still a young woman – but a desire to handle her affairs and secure her estate is visible throughout her later life, possibly a reaction to this early period of dependence. Hernando was released in 1561, and just a year later the couple ordered the building of a grand house (now the Palace of the Conquest) in the main square at Trujillo, where they spent much of their time. The town – famous for its conquistador connections – was also closely associated with the Inka dynasty, who had become so involuntarily entangled with the Pizarros. Several children of other royal Inka women appropriated by the Pizarro brothers were also sent to Spain. In 1557, Inés Pizarro Inquill, a descendant of Manco Inca, was married in Trujillo to her cousin Francisco, Francisca's half-brother.* The so-called 'Inka princess' was just the most visible of a small but significant circle of Inka nobles who were making space for themselves and building families in this ordinary hilltop town in western Spain.

Hernando died in 1578 and, less than three years later, on 30

---

* Francisco also lived for a few years in the castle with his family, but only survived until he was about seventeen, dying in 1557: the same year he was married.

November 1581, Francisca was remarried to Pedro Arias Dávila Portocarrero in the church of Santa María La Mayor in Trujillo, where she had lived most of her European life. In another incestuous development, typical of royalty at the time, her son had recently married her new husband's sister, making him her brother-in-law. Now forty-four years old, Francisca seems to have had enough of life in the provinces and she and her spouse relocated to the court in Madrid, where they took a house on Calle del Príncipe at the heart of the city. She continued to vigorously pursue her legal rights as the heir to Pizarro; a request from the Council president in 1588 reminded the king that 'Doña Francisca Pizarro daily requests in the Council that her lawsuit is decided upon and she is quite right, for it is now more than eight years since it was seen, and to delay justice so is a matter of conscience.' The case had gone on so long that when the king was once more reminded of the matter only three of the nine judges who had seen the case were still alive. Nonetheless, a decade later, doña Francisca Pizarro, the Inka princess who came to Spain, died on 30 May 1598 having secured her family estate. In Trujillo, home of so many conquistadors, her face still gazes across the square, largely unnoticed by the tourists who flock to see the nearby statue of her father, Francisco Pizarro, greenish-bronze and in full armour, sitting proudly astride his horse.[9]

Francisca was forced into exile in Spain, despite her conquistador father, but Indigenous allies regularly chose to cross the Atlantic to assert their privileges. The Moctezuma family's efforts to build their relationship with the Crown at court bore fruit in 1537 when his sons Martín and Francisco were granted coats of arms in recognition of Moctezuma II's 'help' in bringing about the Spanish conquest of Tenochtitlan – the history of their family had been rewritten, and its future secured.[10] The Tlaxcalans too were keen to capitalise on their privileged status as the primary allies of the Spanish conquistadors. Their first embassy to Spain – which travelled with Cortés in 1528 – consisted of five senior men, likely representing different polities in the Tlaxcalan federation: don Lorenzo Tianquiztlatohuatzin, don Valeriano Quetzalcoltzin, don

Julían Quahpiltzintli, don Juan Citlalihuitzin de Avalos and Antonio Huitlalotzin. For a long time, it was believed that this voyage proved fruitless, but Jovita Baber – whose research in the archives has shed much-needed light on Tlaxcala in this early period – discovered the grant of 10 August 1529 which ordered that the city should be self-governing, reporting directly to the Crown, and free from *encomienda*. The city was required to pay 8000 bushels of corn annually to the Crown; all other tributes were controlled by the local nobility. From the earliest days of colonisation, Indigenous diplomats worked to promote the interests of their peoples on the periphery and at the heart of empire.

In the following years, Tlaxcala – setting a precedent for Indigenous peoples all over the Americas – campaigned actively for the confirmation, renewal and extension of their rights, using intermediaries, official missives, and direct diplomacy at court. Originally a confederacy of four *teccalli* (noble houses), the Tlaxcalan elites quickly reframed themselves as a single municipality to conform to Castilian expectations and legal codes, establishing an urban centre and building it on a European model in Spanish style with a central plaza, church, and *cabildo* (council) building. Chosen by the Franciscans for one of their first missions, and confirmed as Mexico's first bishopric in 1525, the Tlaxcalans quickly committed to the missionary endeavour and thereafter sold themselves as devoted Christians and emissaries of the Catholic faith. In the 1530s, concerned by the ominous establishment of the Spanish settlement of Puebla on their doorstep, the Tlaxcalans determined to confirm their royal entitlements and sent another embassy to Spain. In 1534, the governor of Tlaxcala, don Diego Maxixcatzin Tlilquiya-huatzin – a man described by Las Casas as 'very courageous and tough' – led their second delegation to Europe, taking with him a prominent judge from the local *audiencia*, Juan de Salmerón, and two other leading Tlaxcalans: Sebastián Yaotequihua and (another) don Martín.[11]

Salmerón's presence at court is another marker of how deeply the Tlaxcalans had committed to their alliance with the Castilians, building on their local alliances and bringing them to a transatlantic stage. Having obtained an audience with Charles V in Madrid, the Tlaxcalan lords – long experienced in their own federal negotiations – again showed capability in Castilian law and court protocol. Having presented a petition asserting their faithful service as Christians and staunch allies, they secured for their city the title of 'La Leal Ciudad de Tlaxcala' (the loyal city of Tlaxcala), a coat of arms, and a guarantee that it would remain perpetually self-governing under direct Crown control, free from local interference. When the embassy returned to Tlaxcala in 1535, they were fortunate to travel on the same ship as the newly appointed Viceroy of New Spain, Antonio de Mendoza, Count of Tendilla, one of the most respected noble families in Spain. Diego de Maxixcatzin, the Tlaxcalan governor, almost certainly used the voyage as an opportunity to get to know the new viceroy and cement his diplomatic progress. In 1547, the viceroy noted that Diego and Martín (now deceased) and don Sebastian who 'came with Licenciado Salmeron to Spain, only to see and to know Your Majesty . . . are honourable people and good Christians and friends of the Spanish'.[12]

Tlaxcala sent several more embassies to court, aiming to consolidate its relationship with the Crown and secure new privileges. The first, in 1540, led by Leonardo Cortés and Felipe Ortiz, may have prompted the *cédula* (decree) of 1541 that confirms Tlaxcala may never be alienated from the Crown 'for any cause nor reason' and praising their service 'as loyal and good vassals'. They sent ambassadors again two years later, and the records show campaigning throughout the century, some in person and some through correspondence and representatives. In 1550, the local nobility even aimed to impress the Crown by sending a profusion of artificial flowers along with a missive carried by a Spanish priest. Regular *cédulas* ordering funds and personnel testify to the Crown's interest in the local cathedral, and the Tlaxcalan elite clearly cultivated their close relationship with the Spanish. As Las Casas, who must have met many of these ambassadors, wrote:

> This lineage worked hard to be kept inviolable, because they very jealously preserved their aristocracy and nobility, and for

this reason, after they had converted to our Catholic faith, they sent agents to the Emperor, of themselves, in the year 1540, begging him to favour that province by confirming their ancient customs and laws, and so he did.[13]

Sometime after 1552, the Tlaxcalans decided to record their own history of the conquest to support their campaign for colonial influence. 'It will be written', recorded the council, 'so that it can be taken to Spain, it will be seen by the emperor'. The so-called *Lienzo de Tlaxcala* (Canvas of Tlaxcala) was a huge canvas that framed the current, privileged status of the city within a narrative of the joint Tlaxcalan and Spanish conquest of the Aztec-Mexica.[14] The story is told through a sequence of pictures, some with alphabetic labels, mostly for people and places. The original has been lost, but an eighteenth-century copy shows the astute construction of Tlaxcala's heritage as an Indigenous seat of power within the Catholic Habsburg empire. Heading the *lienzo* is a green peak signifying Tlaxcala, topped by a large rendering of Charles V's coat of arms: the city was answerable only to the emperor, who sat directly above them. The mountain is rich with symbolism, containing the Tlaxcalan coat of arms, the Virgin of the Assumption, and a church, and crowded round are figures representing the different components of the state before the invasion. In the foreground, three Europeans and four Tlaxcalans together erect a cross, surrounded by settlements and religious buildings, densely peopled with Tlaxcalan and European lords and Indigenous noble 'houses' showing family allegiances. This is a vision of Tlaxcala as an ideal Christian city and imperial vassal, leading the conquest and evangelisation of Mexico shown in the panels below. The council minutes of 17 June 1552 dictate that this magnificent piece of propaganda was intended to be sent with a delegation to Spain, but it disappears from the historical record until a copy was made in the late-eighteenth century. The fate of the original is unknown.

On 4 January 1552, the *cabildo* of Tlaxcala determined to 'kiss the hands of the viceroy and to beg him for a licence for some of the principal people of this city to go to Spain'. This was just the start of the preparations for this important embassy, which was carefully planned and equipped. In June, the council talked again about the 'trip to Spain to the emperor ... to notify him of all the things that concern Tlaxcala'. It was clearly a collective undertaking, involving the whole community, for 'every Tlaxcalan person will help with the funds that they will take to Spain, for the provisioning and to pay there in Spain for the solicitor, and what will be given to the lawyer, etc.' The licence to travel seems to have been granted by October 1554, a full two years later, but in 1557 they were still deciding on the details of the trip, talking about making feather pictures and capes to take with them and naming representatives. If this voyage was ever completed, it must have made a sumptuous entrance, with all the plumage and the huge *lienzo*.[15]

Such campaigns continued throughout the sixteenth century, gradually accruing privileges such as exemptions from tribute, protection from external interference, and coats of arms for noble families across the region. The *mestizo* historian Diego Muñoz Camargo – son of a conquistador and a Tlaxcalan mother – advocated for the city's influence in his work as well as in person, being received regularly at court during the 1580s after travelling to Spain as the interpreter for a Tlaxcalan embassy.[*][16] The Tlaxcalans cleverly deployed both transatlantic diplomacy and local connections to secure their position in the shifting sands of colonial politics. Once the threat of Puebla was neutralised, the city became increasingly established as an independent centre, holding a powerful council and key religious institutions, and continuing to fight alongside the Spanish in expeditions to the north. Eventually, the Tlaxcalans themselves became settlers, forming frontier towns that were intended as models of religious and cultural 'civilisation', outposts of imperial power which would set an example to the Chichimec peoples. Since 1981, the *Salida* festival in Tlaxcala has re-enacted

---

[*] Camargo's *Historia de Tlaxcala*, a lavish collection of pictographic and alphabetic texts that was presented to the king in 1586, somehow found its way from the royal library of El Escorial to the collections of Glasgow University, Scotland, where it is held today.

the 1591 'departure' of 400 families to colonise what is now northern Mexico. The Spanish Crown stood at the apex of the hierarchy – the hub and heart of the legal and political systems – so creating transatlantic networks that provided direct access to royal authority was vital to Indigenous communities' success in the colonial world. Tlaxcala played the game so effectively that – despite suffering the same precipitous population decline as everywhere else – they managed to cling onto their independence and trumpet their victory over Tenochtitlan for centuries to come. The flag of the Tlaxcalan state today still shows the coat of arms granted in 1535, along with a piratical-but-poignant skull and crossbones in memory of the many who died during the invasion.[17]

Tlaxcala was particularly successful at leveraging its alliance with Spain into tangible benefits, but other Indigenous nobles also travelled constantly to court in the attempt to secure their own or their family's fortunes. Some played on their historic privilege, and others on Spanish law or colonial pursuits; this transatlantic elite was a constant presence at court, and an often-overlooked part of the ways in which Indigenous peoples understood the world in which they lived and operated. But such long-distance networks could be risky – this was a densely knotted web, and a fragile one at times.

When the K'iche' Maya lord don Juan Cortés travelled to Spain in 1557 to plead for the restoration of his historic tribute rights, his ship was attacked by French pirates and he lost all the evidence he had been planning to present to the Crown. While many Indigenous people relied on heavily elaborated personal testimonies to make their appeals, appellants increasingly understood the value of documentary evidence – pictographic and alphabetic – in making their case. Often incorrectly viewed as 'illiterate', Indigenous peoples had complex systems of verbal and textual recording that they quickly adapted to colonial requirements. Many surviving sixteenth-century Maya texts were written as legal claims to nobility and territory, signed and witnessed by Indigenous rulers, and intended to be used as evidence before the Crown. Based on long oral and glyphic traditions, composed in the new alphabetic script, these *títulos* (titles) modified Indigenous forms to suit colonial requirements and contest newcomers' claims to the land. Because these texts appeared after the Spanish invasion and often celebrated Catholicism, some scholars have argued that these *títulos* are 'forgeries', invented after the fact to justify Indigenous claims. But they can also be seen as a creative adaptation to colonial expectations, Indigenous peoples finding a way to record ancestral knowledge in a way which was both meaningful to outsiders and useful to the community.[18]

According to Dennis Tedlock, the *Popol Vuh* – the sacred text telling the history and mythology of the K'iche' Maya people which concludes with a list of 'the generations, the sequences of lordships, so that all of them will be clear' – may have been one of the *títulos* carried to court by the K'iche' lord Juan Cortés. He is named 'in the fourteenth generation of lords' as 'Keeper of the Reception House Mat', a role that included the rights to tribute collection he was attempting to reclaim. This may or may not be true, but there would certainly have been a *título* of some form among Juan's papers when he left Santa Cruz, the colonial centre built of stone looted from the nearby Maya capital of Q'umarkaj. His signature appears on both the *Título Totonicapán* (28 September 1554) and the *Royal Title of Don Francisco Izquin Nehaib* (22 November 1558), so we know it was a form with which he was well familiar. Unfortunately for Juan, the king was not persuaded by his appeal. The loss of his papers certainly did not help, but local officials in the region were also wary of returning power to Maya rulers. Widely dispersed, and with a faith that was deeply rooted in the landscape, the Maya were proving a tougher target for forced conversion than the urban peoples of Central Mexico. It would take 'very little to restore their ceremonies and attract their former subjects to himself', warned a missionary writing to Philip II.[19] Juan returned home empty-handed.

In recent years, archaeology has shown us the awesome diversity and complexity of the Indigenous peoples of Colombia, and has also given some support to the idea that the myth of El Dorado originated in the lands of the Muisca people. In 1969, a stunning gold model was found in a cave by three farmers. This miniature woven raft, bearing intricately moulded figures, almost certainly represents the religious ceremony that inflamed the search for El Dorado. Muisca histories are difficult to access, having been simplified and ignored by the colonisers,* but according to Juan Rodríguez Freyle, a writer born in Bogotá (a name taken from the nearby Muisca settlement of Bacata) in the 1560s, when a new *zipa* (the ruler of the southern Muisca territories) was appointed, his naked body was covered with gold dust and placed on a raft heaped with 'a great mountain of gold and emeralds to offer to their gods'. He was then pushed out into Lake Guatavita with four other senior lords, also covered with 'feathers, crowns of gold, arm, nose and ear ornaments of gold, also naked and each carrying another offering'. When they reached the centre of the lake, these riches were all cast into the water along with the *zipa*'s gold dust, which was rinsed into the sacred lake.[20] Such accounts fuelled the frenzy of Spanish exploration into Muisca territory, and also drove three attempts to drain the lake, the last in 1898, none of which found more than a few artefacts. It is now a protected site of ecological importance; any treasures are buried forever in the silt of the lake bed. With its rich mineral resources and developed economy, the Muisca realm was an enticing prospect for the acquisitive Spaniards and it was in this complex political context – with gold fever sweeping the region and Indigenous people being driven into forced labour, seized and sold into slavery in defiance of royal law – that a certain don Diego de Torres y Moyachoque crossed the Atlantic on a diplomatic mission to the Spanish court in 1575.

Diego was a *cacique* from Turmequé in what is now central Colombia. He was a *mestizo*: the son of Spanish conquistador Juan de Torres and a Muisca noblewoman, doña Catalina de

---

*   The form of the Chibcha language which they spoke was declared extinct, after Charles III banned its use in 1770 – a law which officially remained in force until 1991. Nonetheless, words from Muysccubun (language of the people – 'Muisca' comes from 'Myusca', person) are common in the area, and the language is in daily use at the Jizcamox school in Cota, home to one of five recognised Muisca councils.

Moyachoque. Educated in a religious school, and fluent in both Spanish and Muisca, Diego was highly literate and seemingly a true *caballero* – a gentleman – trained in archery, horse-riding and jousting, yet his Spanish half-brother attempted to debase his authority by accusing him of being a '*mestizo* in the dress of an *indio*'. Being *mestizo* was often seen by Spanish authorities as a troublesome quality leading to 'bad tendencies'. Mixed heritage was tied to illegitimacy and the potential to corrupt, and *mestizo* nobility were recognised as neither fully Indigenous *caciques* nor as Spaniards.[21]

So although Diego was in many ways highly privileged, he also occupied an ambivalent space in the colonial world. Diego's half-brother Pedro held the local *encomienda* and, in 1574, Diego had brought a formal complaint against him for mistreating the Muisca people in his care. It is hard to know whether this was a principled charge, or just a tactic in an ongoing power struggle, but when the local authorities ruled against him, Diego decided to travel to Spain to plead his case, and this *mestizo* began the journey which would transform him into an advocate for Indigenous rights.

We know little of the two Muisca who volunteered to accompany him. These Chibcha-speaking people may well also have spoken Spanish, and would have been used to the vagaries of the colonisers after thirty years of rule, but the journey must have been a memorable experience for the men from the high plateau. Did they hope to ensure that their favoured leader would be successful? Or to petition on their own behalf for better treatment? Both objectives seem likely, and would befit men from the Muisca Confederation, a highly organised if loosely structured realm with clear understandings of hierarchy and allegiance. These Indigenous ambassadors would have wanted to represent their own affairs at court, rather than having to rely on a *mestizo* representative.[22]

In 1575, outraged at being stripped of his authority as *cacique* of Turmequé by the *audiencia* (high court and council of state) of Santa Fé on the grounds of his *mestizo* heritage, Diego set out for court, most likely sailing from Havana in one of the well-armed fleets that dominated transatlantic traffic from the 1560s onwards, intent on deterring pirates and privateers. But before he could even reach the fleet, Diego found himself shipwrecked on Santo Domingo by a storm. There, in the Caribbean, he saw towns standing vacant, abandoned as Taíno people died in huge numbers. 'I was amazed', he wrote, 'to understand that in such a short time so many natives had ended and considering this terrible spectacle, it gave me great pity to think that the same was to come to my homeland'.²³ For two years Diego struggled to complete his voyage, lost and short of funds, but the *cacique* made good use of his time studying the works of Bartolomé de Las Casas, who advocated protection of Indigenous peoples. By the time he made it to court, Diego was fighting for the good treatment of *all* the Indigenous peoples of Nuevo Reino, the 'New Kingdom' of Granada, not just for himself and those who had been in his charge.

While his half-brother had more local clout, and anti-*mestizo* rhetoric could be compelling in the febrile atmosphere of colonial Santa Fé de Bogotá, Diego's argument proved persuasive at court, and in 1578 Philip II reversed the decision of the *audiencia*, restoring Diego's authority.²⁴ Here we see the different systems of colonial authority clashing with each other: one brother held the *cacicazgo*, the inherited authority over the Muisca community in the region; the other was the *encomendero*, who represented the will of the Spanish Crown. Both power structures operated concurrently, which sometimes worked to the advantage of Indigenous people if their *cacique* was prepared to advocate for them, and sometimes to their detriment if the Native people found themselves caught in disputes between the different authorities.

When Diego, the *cacique*, returned to the New Kingdom of Granada in 1579, he was accompanied by a *visitador* (literally visitor, an inspector holding enormous powers to investigate the affairs of the province). Diego's transatlantic diplomacy had been critical in bringing about this intervention, which was intended to reform the *encomiendas* and improve the treatment of the Muisca people, but it backfired spectacularly. The *visitador*, Juan Bautista Monzón, was so wildly unpopular that he ended up in prison for conspiracy, along with Diego, who was accused of plotting an armed rebellion. Where

What is most interesting about the man baptised Pedro is how typical he was. Educated in a Franciscan college, he spoke (and probably wrote) excellent Spanish, having acted as official interpreter to the royal *audiencia* in Quito.[29] He was a *ladino*, a Hispanised *indio*, someone who spoke Spanish and tended to adopt European dress and behaviour. In the eyes of the colonisers, these critical intermediaries helped to further the imperial project by spreading Catholicism and adopting Spanish norms. Like many Indigenous people who found themselves inhabiting this in-between state – often subject to suspicion from all sides – Pedro played a careful game, deploying both his knowledge of Spanish law and custom, and his authority as a descendant of (most likely) Pastuso nobility, to negotiate adeptly for his family and community. For elites in the sixteenth century, international negotiations were unavoidable. And, while it is tempting to follow the contemporary chroniclers in focusing on the most high-profile ambassadors, men like Pedro and Diego were everywhere and must have been common sights not only at court but also in the cities and towns linked to the transatlantic networks.

Pedro was lodging at an inn near the waterfront, just five minutes' walk from the newly completed Seville Cathedral, an elaborately pinnacled edifice, which was at that time the largest church in the world. As a fervent Christian, who sang and taught religious music and had gathered 10,000 bricks to build the new church in his village, Pedro would surely have visited this Gothic masterpiece with its five naves, eighty side chapels and soaring Giralda: the minaret of the mosque that had formerly stood on the site and was repurposed as a bell tower in a lofty display of Christian conquest and cultural assimilation.* An even more obvious sign of the city's diverse past stood just beyond the cathedral:

---

* The tomb of Christopher Columbus is now a major tourist attraction in the cathedral, but at that time Columbus's body lay in the cathedral in Santo Domingo (now the Dominican Republic). His remains have travelled almost as much as the man himself, having been laid in Valladolid, Seville, Santo Domingo, Havana and finally Seville again.

the Alcázar, the royal palace built on the remains of a Muslim fortress. One wonders if the glorious 'Mudéjar' architecture of the palace, blending Muslim and Christian styles, inspired Pedro when he asked for permission to bring an *azulejo* tile-maker home to decorate his own church. Lying between the cathedral and the Alcázar is the Casa Lonja de Mercaderes (the Merchants' Exchange, now the Archive of the Indies), which was commissioned in 1572, after the archbishop begged Philip II to stop the sullying of the cathedral by merchants and bankers trading on the steps behind the Giralda courtyard. These three buildings – the Cathedral, the Royal Alcázar and the Exchange – together form a UNESCO world heritage site, singular in its evocation of the so-called 'Golden Age' of Spain, when Catholic and royal grandeur jostled with traces of Islamic influence and the bustling commerce of the Indies trade, which included the brutal traffic in enslaved people. Inside the Alcázar in the Sala de los Almirantes (the Admirals' Room) was the Casa de Contratación (House of Trade), hub of the transatlantic exchange. We know the *cacique*, Pedro, spent many hours here, petitioning officials alongside hundreds of other Indigenous men and women of all stripes, from enslaved people to the children of royalty.

In the chapel of the Casa de Contratación, above the altar, stands a painting which encapsulates the spirit of the age (at least, from a Spanish perspective). *The Virgin of the Navigators* by Alejo Fernández was installed in the 1530s and shows the Virgin Mary, with spiked halo and brocaded, gold-patterned dress, gathering the faithful under her dark cloak. Visible among the throng are Spanish navigators and conquistadors, including Columbus, Cortés, and Vespucci. But if you look harder, behind the richly dressed men clustering on clouds, you can see shadowy figures in simple white clothes: the multitude of Indigenous converts brought to baptism by the richly dressed invaders. In the foreground of the picture floats an array of the ships that carried these men (as well as many African and Indigenous people) across the Atlantic. The merciful Virgin and all the faithful stand on clouds above the ocean; she inclines her head gracefully to look down at the Atlantic endeavours, while mortals kneel in wonder. This altarpiece projected an idealised vision of the empire as a devout (and profitable) enterprise, the powerful gathering the meek in their apostolic embrace.

Did the Indigenous lords who travelled to Spain see the painting? And did they see themselves among the meek converts or the triumphant leaders of evangelisation? The neophytes in the picture are clad in a European vision of simple, baptismal dress, and their features are hard to distinguish, but we have every reason to think that the faces looking back may reflect some of those who travelled from their homes across the great water, for the painter's workshop included both Black and Indigenous enslaved people. Among them was Juan de Güejar, an *indio* man who was recorded as a *vecino* (resident) of Seville. In August 1523, the painter Alejo granted Juan power of attorney to collect debts on his behalf; clearly, despite his enslaved status, Juan was a senior and well-trusted agent, who ranged widely in the painter's service and must have spoken Spanish. The artist did not have to imagine the faces of Indigenous converts, for he lived and worked alongside them.[30]

The *cacique* Pedro de Henao found himself spending far more time in Spain than he had intended, relying on charity. When he returned to court in 1584 to beg for his lost grants to be awarded a second time, a customs officer, Juan Gonzalez, testified that Pedro had only survived through the compassion of his acquaintances. Two Franciscans had given him some new clothes and solicited donations for him. And several people, including his landlady Ana Sanchez, had extended him credit on the basis that such a noble servant of the king must be trustworthy.[31]

In January 1584, he was given permission to travel to Quito at the Crown's expense, but was unable to get his affairs in order. In August that year he returned to Madrid to plead successfully for the reissuing of his grants, and for more Franciscans to return to Ipiales to spread the faith. He also took the opportunity to complain about the grazing of Spanish animals encroaching on Indigenous lands. In the end, the Crown may have been keen to get rid of Pedro, for on 18 August 1584 they granted him 100 ducats, only 10 of which would be paid up front. The other 90 were to be handed

out when he reached Tierra Firme (the 'mainland' of the Indies).
The officials of the House of Trade also seem to have tired of the
cacique's pleas, proving extremely awkward when it came to issuing
his funds. The judges refused to hand over 500 ducats awarded by
the Crown for church supplies, and only after considerable effort
did they grudgingly give 200 ducats to the *factor*, the king's agent,
to hold on his behalf. Maybe they feared he would lose it again. All
this administrative bickering sounds petty, but for a minor noble
with few assets it could have serious consequences. Pedro again
missed the fleet and found himself in dire financial straits, telling a
priest in Seville that he would return to Madrid to complain to the
king, even if he had to walk there barefoot. Documents uncovered
by José Carlos Pérez Morales suggest a reason for his desperation.[32]

In January 1585, Pedro had hired a sculptor and a gilder in
Seville to make beautiful images of Our Lady of the Rosary and
Our Lady of Antiquity, as well as two candlesticks, a crucifix, six
angels and an altarpiece. He clearly had glorious ambitions for the
Ipiales church. The craftsmen were given five months to complete
the commission, but in the winter of 1585–6 Pedro still lacked the
funds to pay for the church ornaments and so he went to beg the
king for a third time. Sadly, Pedro's vision for the church in Ipiales
would never be fulfilled. On 28 December 1585, the Crown yet
again ordered the officials of the House of Trade to pay the
remainder of the debt. It seems unlikely Pedro ever received it, for
that winter he was again granted travelling expenses and, perhaps
finally worn down by wrestling the bureaucracy of royal adminis-
tration, it seems this time he conceded, and went home. We can't
be sure he travelled immediately, but when we next hear of him, in
1589, the Crown is attempting to sort out what to do with some of
the commissioned objects 'that the said don Pedro went without
and [he] is dead'. Resolving that it was too difficult and expensive
to send them to Peru, the Crown orders that they should be sold
and the money used for other things for the Ipiales church. Pedro
de Henao, the great ambassador for his church and his people – we
have records of him lodging complaints of ongoing issues right up
to January 1586, almost certainly prompted by reports from home

– died without seeing his dream realised.* But one tiny fragment may have survived.[33]

In 1600, a royal decree notes that an image of Christ from among those 'certain images that were made for don Pedro de Henao, native *indio* from the place of Ipiales' had been lodged in the church of the nuns of the Discalced Carmelites at the convent of Sanlúcar la Mayor for the past twelve years. The letter confirms that this 'Christ of great size' belongs to the convent and can never be reclaimed. Morales, having explored the photographic records of the convent preserved at the University of Seville thinks it possible that a beautifully worked and tender figure of Christ on the cross, his head limp and face tender with blood delicately trailing on his shins and his chest, might be Pedro's Christ. The convent is closed to visitors, so it is impossible to verify the age, but even the possibility that this might be the very piece that Pedro commissioned, imagined and prayed for, more than four hundred years ago, is incredible.[34]

Once the first shocks of invasion were past, the Native men (and occasionally women) who crossed the Atlantic for political purposes were ordinarily not isolated pioneers striking out into the unknown. They were sophisticated diplomats, aware of the nuances of what we would call international law (the foundations of which were being laid in this period, often in response to the challenges of Indigenous diplomacy), and able to draw on the experience and support of previous travellers, legal advocates and colonial officials. After don Felipe Gaucrapaucar – the first Andean *cacique* recorded voyaging to court – returned home to Jauja in 1562, his brother claimed he had become very 'litigious' 'after doing business with *letrados* [lawyers] and learning to write' in Spain. When the local viceroy tried to punish him for bringing frivolous suits by

---

*   Ipiales later became the site of one of the most breath-taking churches in the Americas: Las Lajas shrine, a filigreed neo-Gothic basilica jutting organically out of a cliff at the site of a miraculous healing in 1754. Four centuries after Pedro's death, his faith flourishes in Ipiales.

forcing him to give up the trappings of a Spaniard and put on *indio* clothing', Felipe responded by launching an appeal, all while dressed in Spanish garb and carrying a sword. Felipe had used his transatlantic experience to learn the subtleties of Spanish law. Most of the Mexican and Peruvian voyagers had long experience within the colonial legal system, their names appearing on multiple petitions, before they considered crossing the Atlantic to press their case with the king himself. Letters flew back and forth across the ocean carrying news and legal requests, and some of the travellers even lived in the same houses when they came to Spain. While in Madrid in 1607, for example, don Pedro Carillo de Soto Inga, the *mestizo* great-grandson of Huayna Capac, lived 'at the rented home (*posada*) of Don Melchor Carlos Ynga'.[35]

The historian Lauri Uusitalo discovered that Pedro de Henao was part of a network of Indigenous and colonial connections that spanned the Atlantic. As well as the Franciscans, who had worked in Pedro's community and were clearly a source of relief in Spain, Pedro drew on local officials and churchmen to witness on his behalf and could also call on the assistance of two high-ranking colonial agents with whom he had travelled to Spain: Diego de Ortegón, a senior judge from Quito who was married to Columbus's great-granddaughter, and his secretary Francisco de Zuñiga. Despite being a relatively unimportant *cacique*, Pedro was able to access a considerable web of support. As a member of the nobility, he could also deploy his privilege on behalf of others. Not long after he arrived, Pedro asked the king to issue a licence for four *mestizo* soldiers to return home. Sons of a Spanish conquistador and an Indigenous mother, they had found themselves abandoned in Seville. How many more were unable to draw on such support and remained in Europe?

Shared Indigenous identity often cut across status barriers for those overseas; despite the importance of regional identities and beliefs, there was also a sense of a shared *indio* community among those far from home. Most remarkably, in 1585, one of the witnesses at a hearing asking for Pedro's title to be confirmed (again), was don Alonso Atahualpa Inca, a member of the very highest echelons of Indigenous nobility, a grandson of the last independent Inka ruler Atahualpa.[36] His descendants would fight for their rights on both sides of the Atlantic, through diplomacy, negotiation, and armed resistance. In May 1532, Atahualpa, the Sapa Inka (Only Inka, the ruler of the empire), had finally managed to assert his right to rule over Tawantinsuyu ('the four parts together', a reference to the four lineages of the realm) after almost a decade of fighting with his brothers. Barely six months later, he found himself imprisoned in the temple at Kashamarka (Cajamarca) by the Spanish invader Francisco Pizarro and his brothers, following a brutal ambush. Atahualpa, with an acute eye on the invaders' covetous intentions, offered to ransom himself in exchange for 'ten thousand ingots of gold and so many silver vessels that it would be enough to fill a large house'. Pizarro was astounded when the Inka's subjects delivered on his promise. The immense ransom has been estimated at one million pesos of *buen oro* (good gold) and more than two million silver pesos (pieces) of eight *reales*, a vast fortune, which the invaders did not hesitate to divide up among themselves, even as they prepared to break their promise. Aware of their precarious position in the mountains, far from support and fearful of rebellion, some of the senior conquistadors engineered a show trial and executed Atahualpa. On 23 August 1533, after accepting baptism to avoid being burned alive, the last independent Sapa Inka was garrotted. He died nominally a Christian, and his Catholic descendants would spend centuries alternately fighting for recognition from and resisting the Spanish.[37]

Alonso Atahualpa Inca, grandson of Atahualpa, was one of the less successful Inka supplicants to the Spanish Crown. Arrived in 1585, by the following year he was pleading with King Philip II to help him 'because he had nothing to eat, much less that which would allow him to behave [live] in accordance with his quality/rank'. Unlike Pedro, who made similar pleas, Alonso was deeply in debt as a result of his attempts to live the lifestyle he considered suitable for a young royal. While in Madrid, he had not only bought one house but also rented another. In dire straits – for debt was an imprisonable offence – the young noble became engaged to marry

María de Toledo, the niece of doña Leonor de Cárdenas, to whom he owed a large sum. It seems an Inka prince was considered more than a good enough match for a genteel woman in Spain.

In November 1586, the Crown recognised that Alonso was eligible to inherit a grant of two thousand pesos in perpetuity, 'for his merits and for the services of his father and himself'. He also received three hundred ducats to help him and 'allow him to return' because 'he is poor and suffers want'. This was just 'for once', emphasises the decree; the Crown – so generous with Pedro – maybe saw the ramshackle Alonso in a different light, and they would have been right to do so. Rather than cutting his losses and returning home, Alonso paid his debts and broke off his engagement. Three years later, at around thirty years old, this heir to the Inka throne died of an unknown illness in a Madrid prison, incarcerated for failure to pay a debt of 100 pesos.[38]

Transatlantic ambassadorial and diplomatic efforts ran broad and deep in the sixteenth century as Indigenous representatives of cities, states, families and organisations vied for attention at court. Official ambassadors with their entourage; nobles with dependants, kin and servants; sometimes individuals, alone or accompanied by Spanish officials or clerics. For elites especially, international negotiations were a necessity, but the diplomatic careers of these men (and it was usually men) have not often been recognised for their presence in European history. They tend to be seen as a sidebar to the history of colonisation, people whose lives were centred in the Americas and happened to travel to the metropole before returning home (or not). But whether accidental diplomats – victims of kidnapping who ended up speaking for their people – or voluntary ambassadors seeking redress for grievances, promoting their familial, local or individual interests, or simply seeking assurances or information from a distant ruler they had never met, these Indigenous politicians helped to shape European society and its transatlantic dealings as a conspicuous minority at court and in imperial hubs. The same patterns repeated themselves later in courts across Europe, as other powers established and consolidated colonies to the west. And, fifty years before Elizabeth I gave official impetus to English-men's imperial dabbling to the west, there was one conspicuous exception: a 'Brazilian' king, who found himself at the court of Henry VIII.

William Hawkins was one of the richest men in Plymouth, a merchant and sea captain, when he became a transatlantic trader. He was the first Englishman to trade regularly across the Atlantic, establishing a route from Guinea to Brazil, exchanging African products for American novelties. According to his son,* who told the tale to the geographer and chronicler Richard Hakluyt, Hawkins returned from his second voyage to Brazil in 1531 with 'one of the savage kings of the Countrey of Brasill'. Apparently, Hawkins – an experienced international merchant and negotia-tor – had 'behaved himself so wisely . . . that he grew into great familiarite and friendship with them'. The Native 'king' judiciously negotiated that one of Hawkins' crew – a fellow Plymouth man named Martin Cockeram – should be left behind 'as a pledge for his safetie and returne againe', and then he embarked for England on 'a tall and goodlie' ship called the *Pole*. We don't know for sure where he landed, probably at the *Pole*'s home port of Plymouth, from where he was 'brought up to London, and presented to King Henry 8' who was then at Whitehall.

The chief – almost certainly a Tupinambá from the Bahia coast – stayed in England for nearly a year, and made a considerable impression on the nobles who saw him. He had cheek piercings, from each of which a bone ornament protruded prominently: a mark of his 'great bravery'. His lower lip was also pierced and set with 'a precious stone about the bignesse of a pea: all his apparel, behaviour, and gesture, were very strange to the beholders'. The Eng-lish court would have seemed equally unusual to the Tupinambá: a

---

* Also (infuriatingly for a historian attempting to track him in the records) a seafarer called William Hawkins, who had a son who was also a well-known sea captain called, predictably, William Hawkins.

solid indoor structure, with sumptuous cloth and paint decorations, very different to the forest homes of the Tupi.[39]

Henry VIII had only just moved into the palace at Whitehall – which at that time was called York House – when he met the chief. One of the most magnificent buildings in London, York House had been acquired by Henry when he stripped Cardinal Wolsey of his property in 1530, and the king was just starting to undertake an enormous redesign which would transform and extend the building. Unfortunately, we have to imagine what it might have looked like, as pictures are scarce and the building was largely destroyed by fire in the seventeenth century. One of the few original parts that remain intact is an underground space known as Henry VIII's wine cellar. This brick-vaulted hall, with a sweeping Tudor roof, has survived largely untouched, except that it is now nineteen feet deeper and five feet farther west than it was when the Tupinambá ruler met Henry. In the 1940s, it was getting in the way of post-war reconstruction, so was encased in steel and concrete to protect the soft Tudor brick and moved lock, stock and barrel to make space for the building of Horse Guards Avenue.[40]

We have no idea if Henry ever actually kept wine in this room, but the Tupinambá visitor would certainly have been offered wine and entertained impressively in the palace above it. When the French missionary Claude d'Abbeville took a group of Tupinambá to the French court of Louis XIII in 1614, Paris went 'wild', and the English court also 'marvelled' at the visit of the 'Savage king' as 'all his apparel, behaviour, and gesture, were very strange to the beholders.' And so it must also have seemed for the chief, although – as he had seen European traders on his own shores, and lived closely with them on the transatlantic crossing – any shock would presumably have derived more from the grandeur of the court, and the oddity of his surroundings, rather than from the peculiar habits of Europeans themselves.[41]

One can only guess what the Tupinambá king made of the flamboyant Henry, then in his prime, and embroiled in negotiations with the pope over his proposed first divorce. They would likely

in 1526 alone, and in 1529 two hundred tons of brazilwood were unloaded on the docks at Honfleur. In 1541, between 30 and 40 ships left northern France for South America; in 1549 six sailed for Brazil from Rouen alone, and other ports such as Honfleur and Dieppe also saw frequent trips. The cargo of *La Pèlerine* (The Pilgrim), a French ship seized by the Portuguese in 1532 included 5000 *quintals* (about 500 tons) of brazilwood, 300 monkeys, 3000 'leopard' (likely jaguar) skins and 600 very clever parrots, all recorded as knowing how to speak French.[8]

Despite Portuguese military and diplomatic pressure, and wavering Crown support, the French trade persisted throughout this period, helped by a papal arbitration of 1536 which declared that the previous bulls of donation to the Spanish and Portuguese did not apply to lands later 'discovered' by other nations. The fabulous Vallard Atlas (1547), now held in the Huntington Library in California, shows Europeans, presumably Frenchmen, trading with the Indigenous peoples of South America. We know little about this ornate piece of early cartography, or its first owner – Nicolas Vallard de Dieppe – but the intricate illustrations show that the idea of exchange with 'Brazilians' was normalised in French coastal regions by the 1540s. The maps show us Europeans trading for brazilwood, as well as exchanging a mirror and metal tools for tame parrots and monkeys, much like those from the 'Brazilian village' on the Seine. The Native people depicted in the Vallard Atlas closely resemble those in the pictures of the Rouen gala, but this likely says more about European preconceptions and artistic conventions than it does about the actual appearance of the Tupi.

The pictures of the festival entry show the Tupi wearing small hats, or crowns, of feathers, but Hans Staden – a German soldier who was famously captured by the Tupinambá and lived among them for nearly three years – described them as shaving off their hair in a tonsure, like monks, and then tying an ornament of red feathers around the head. The houses too may not have been especially accurate; according to Staden, the Tupinambá ordinarily lived in large communal longhouses made of straw, surrounded by a palisade fence for protection. But Tupi living structures varied considerably, and the scattered wooden huts shown in Rouen may anyway have been an imaginative choice by the illustrator or just a question of practicality. Despite protestations of absolute accuracy, that it was an 'illusion of the truth', the reality is that the 'village' had to fit on a long, narrow field – large longhouses around an open plaza may not have been possible in the circumstances. It is unclear whether the Tupi themselves joined in building the village. Were they performers on a pre-prepared stage, or active participants in the way their world was displayed?[9]

Whether the village was accurate or not, knowledge about Brazil and its people was becoming ubiquitous in France by the mid-1500s, with widely read authors such as André Thevet (1557) and Jean de Léry (1575) covering the brazilwood trade,[10] and Hans Staden's account of his captivity (1557) becoming a bestseller in multiple languages. In Normandy, the connections were especially tangible. Sometime between 1530 and 1550, two heavy oak panels were erected on the facade of the Hôtel l'Isle du Brésil at 17 rue Malpalu in Rouen, which show Tupi people harvesting and loading brazilwood.[11] It is sometimes speculated that the Brazilian visitors to Rouen may have stayed at 17 rue Malpalu, but more likely it was owned by one of the many merchants who made their riches selling brazilwood. Lying near the cathedral, this impressive edifice would have been an everyday sight for the people of Rouen, normalising the idea of Brazilian people as part of their economy and even their extended social networks. A similar frieze was installed in the church of Saint-Jacques in Dieppe. Commissioned in the 1530s by the merchant Jean Ango, the frieze depicts what appear to be Indigenous figures, bearing belts, collars and shields of feathers. These carvings – now on show at the Musée des Antiquités de Seine-Maritime in Rouen – are typical of the way in which Brazil and its inhabitants were often stylised in European imagery; as we saw in the Nahua at court, feathers were part of the visual language of 'Brazilianness' by 1528.

In erecting these friezes Jean Ango was crediting the Lord with his good fortune, but his gratitude was short-lived. Ango, along with his father (again confusingly named Jean Ango), was responsible for stimulating much of the French trade with Brazil in the 1530s and 1540s, but in 1549 Henri dealt the Dieppe merchants a devastating blow, granting the cities of Rouen and Marseille the exclusive right to import brazilwood. The Ango family, favourites of the former king, shipping magnates and, coincidentally, owners of some privateer ships that pillaged a fortune from Cortés's embassy in 1522, were ruined.

For Rouen, however, the 1549 grant was a huge coup. The 'Brazilian village' at Rouen was a signal of this royal concession, as well as a celebration of local and transatlantic loyalties. This is borne out by the fact that two of the men involved in planning and funding the royal festivities – Joseph Tasserie and Pierre du Couldray – were heavily entangled in transatlantic affairs. The Tupi village at the triumphal entry was therefore more than just a celebration of royal power, it was a tangible manifestation of the connections between the Tupinambá and the city. Long before French influence was firmly established across the ocean, Native people were becoming part of their everyday reality at home. But they were not only present in Normandy. Indigenous peoples were regularly listed as part of the cavalcade of 'exotic' people paraded during royal tours of the provinces. In 1565, 'Indians', 'Savage Americans' and 'Brazilians' were all among the captive nations listed as 'haranguing the king at length' through an interpreter at Charles IX's royal entry into Bordeaux more than 300 miles to the south.[12]

The idea of Indigenous peoples 'haranguing' the king at his own triumphal party is counterintuitive, for this was mostly a ritualised performance of submission: the parade of captured nations intended to reflect the king's glory as ruler of many lands. Of course, the 'Americans' might have seized the opportunity to press their interests, but their words are not recorded, only their presence. In the French mind, they were a blank slate on which to sketch the contours of European expectation and influence. Indigenous peoples in Europe lived a refracted reality: whatever their purpose or intent, they found themselves gazed upon by Europeans whose enquiring eye not only observed, but also transformed and implicitly limited

them, framing them within European assumptions. Whether translators or rulers, enslaved entertainers or diplomats, Native travellers
often found themselves the object of curiosity in Europe, whatever
their personal purpose or intentions.

Indigenous peoples were part of the tapestry of everyday life in
some corners of Europe, especially the Iberian peninsula, where
some Indigenous and mixed-heritage people – especially servants
or those who were enslaved – may have receded into their communities, achieving a measure of anonymity. But in regions where
Indigenous visitors were relatively rare, their presence provoked
more of a stir, and people flocked to see these 'exotic' visitors,
making them part of a spectacle that most had certainly not signed
up for.

Some time between September 1501 and September 1502, three
'men taken in the New Found Island' appeared before King Henry
VII. We know of these first-known Native people in the British Isles
only through a fragment from an anonymous chronicle of 1580:

> These were clothed In beasts skins and ate Raw flesh and spake
> such speech that no man could understand them, and in their
> demeanor like to brute beasts whom the king kept a time after,
> Of the which upon two years passed (after) I saw two of them
> appareled after English men In westminster palace, which at
> that time I could not discern from Inglish men till I was learned
> what men they were, But as for speech I heard none of them
> utter one word.[13]

We do not know how these men, most likely Inuit, came to cross
the ocean.[14] Tales of rich fishing grounds to the west, and a mysterious 'Isle of Brasil', as well as contacts with Azorean traders,
had fuelled voyages even before Cabot's landing in 1497, and the
Inuit could have arrived on any one of a number of small ships.[15]
But it is clear that they were seen chiefly as objects of curiosity,
valued at court for their rarity and supposed strangeness.

For Native peoples, being a 'spectacle' is so entwined with
their European presence that a project seeking to transform our

understanding of Indigenous Americans in Britain is even called *Beyond the Spectacle*.* Displays of Native people were common enough in London by 1610 that Shakespeare could make a knowing reference to them in *The Tempest*. And, when the so-called 'Four Indian Kings' (Mohawk and Mahican chiefs) who came to London in 1710 went to the theatre to see *Macbeth*, the audience clamoured so much to see them that they ended up sitting in chairs on the stage, watching the play while the 'Mob' watched them.[16]

This fascination has barely changed over the centuries. Right up into the twentieth century, Buffalo Bill's 'Wild West' shows toured Europe, thrilling audiences with a cast of largely Lakota performers, who were displayed before crowds which regularly included royalty. In 1887, the Oglala Lakota chief and diplomat, and former US Army Scout, Red Shirt met Queen Victoria. Recalling the occasion, William 'Buffalo Bill' Cody remembered: 'He clearly felt that this was a ceremony between one ruler and another, and the dignity with which he went through the introduction was wonderful to behold. One would have thought that to watch him most of his life was spent in introduction to kings and queens, and that he was really a little bored with the effort required to go through with them.' What Cody did not seem to realise was that Red Shirt had long experience as an ambassador of his people and though he may have been 'playing Indian' for the audience, that did not erase his history as a headman and diplomat, especially in his own eyes. In this double life, Red Shirt saw himself not at all as the gawkers imagined him. The chief spoke poignantly to an English reporter about the future of his people: 'The Indian of the next generation will not be the Indian of the last. Our buffaloes are nearly all gone: the deer have entirely vanished; and the white man takes more and more of our land.'

---

*   This collaborative project, led by Professor David Stirrup of the University of Kent, brings together researchers and Native North American people to uncover and amplify the stories of Indigenous travellers, both in history and today, as well as connecting descendant communities to their cultural heritage in the UK: https://research.kent.ac.uk/beyondthespectacle/

Other Indigenous performers saw touring with Buffalo Bill as an opportunity to learn more about white society, for the benefit of their people. As the medicine man Black Elk is quoted: 'I wanted to see the great water, the great world and the ways of the white men; this is why I wanted to go.' As Linda Scarangella McNenly has put it, these performers 'gazed back' at their audiences.[17]

We do not know what happened to the fifty Tupi when the pageant at Rouen was over. Did they return to their own country, or join crews of ships participating in the Brazilian trade? Might some have stayed and become part of life in the city? It was in Rouen, only twelve years after the triumphant festival, that the philosopher Michel de Montaigne said he met three Tupinambá men who inspired him to write a famous essay 'On the Cannibals'. Although the source is brief, and problematic – as always when we are relying on Native voices filtered through a European ventriloquist – Montaigne allows us a peek at a possible Indigenous perspective on their travels to Europe.[18]

The three Tupinambá met King Charles IX in Rouen in 1562 and he 'talked with them a long time. They were shown our ways, our ceremonies, and the layout of a beautiful city.' Montaigne claims they came to Europe because of their 'desire for novelty', and it certainly seems that the French court were keen to show off their world to the American visitors.

> . . . someone asked them their opinion, in order to learn from them what they had found most admirable . . . They said that, first of all, they found it really strange that so many large men with beards – strong and armed – who surrounded the king (they were probably referring to the Swiss guards) would agree to obey a child rather than choosing one for themselves to be in command. Secondly (since in their way of speaking they call men halves of one another) they said they had noticed that among us some men were overstuffed with all sorts of rich commodities while their halves were begging at their doors, emaciated from hunger and poverty. They found it strange that

these halves in such desperate need could put up with such an injustice and did not seize the others by the throat or set fire to their houses.[19]

The Tupi emphasis on military prowess above birth is obvious: why would you follow a child when you could choose a powerful leader? Unlike Europeans, these Indigenous witnesses held primogeniture and private property in disregard. Native societies were not always the egalitarian utopia sometimes imagined in popular culture – status and hierarchy were central to many Indigenous ways of life – but the idea of a small number of people amassing immense wealth while others starved was entirely alien. The records we have of later travellers suggest that they found the vast inequalities of Europe, where extravagance and poverty sat side by side, to be one of the things that most struck Native people on their arrival.

Senontiyah, an Ioway (Báxoje) spiritual leader who was brought to London in the mid-nineteenth century, spoke to a deputation from the Temperance Society at the town hall in Birmingham:

My Friends,—If we were rich, like many white men in this country, the poor people we see around the streets in this cold weather, with their little children barefooted and begging, would soon get enough to eat, and clothes to keep them warm.

My Friends,—It has made us unhappy to see the poor begging for something to eat since we came to this country. In our country we are all poor, but the poor all have enough to eat, and clothes to keep them warm . . .

My Friends,—It makes us unhappy, in a country where there is so much wealth, to see so many poor and hungry, and so many as we see drunk.[20]

This revulsion at the inequality of European society was a common response among Indigenous travellers whose voices emerge in later years, particularly those from outside the major urban centres of Mexico and Peru. What little evidence we have suggests that earlier voyagers would have shared this response, seeing the contrast between the endemic poverty of the cities and the luxury of the royal court. A Wyandot youth named Savignon, brought to France by the navigator Samuel de Champlain in 1610, was shocked that some people had to beg for charity in Europe just to eat, as well as by the violence meted out in the name of justice and parenting.[21]

The Mississauga Chippewa chief Maungwudaus (also known as George Henry) who was part of a travelling show in the mid-nineteenth century, wrote a pamphlet about his experiences in Europe: *An Account of the Chippewa Indians who have been travelling among the whites in the United States, England, Ireland, Scotland, France and Belgium* . . . He sold himself as a 'self-taught Indian', which is a little disingenuous as he was quite well-educated, but Maungwudaus had a sharp eye, and his account is hilarious in parts, especially when discussing the airs affected by English gentlewomen. He noted that 'English women cannot walk alone; they must always be assisted by the men', who were made to carry the babies. 'When the tea got ready, the ladies were brought to the table like sick women . . . They carry their heads on one side of the shoulder; they hold the knife and fork with the two forefingers and the thumb of each hand; the two last ones are of no use to them, only sticking out like our fish-spears'. In France, the ladies were handsome, but 'the gentlemen never shave their faces; this makes them look as if they had no mouths'. Others had such luxuriant moustaches that they looked 'as if they had black squirrel's tails sticking on each side of their mouths'.

But woven among these amusing national peculiarities is a story of wealth and poverty. Maungwudaus regularly comments on the conspicuous wealth of the elites and the disparities he sees in European cities. London is a 'wonderful city', but the people are like the mosquitoes in America 'biting one another to get a living. Many very rich, and many very poor.' Queen Victoria had a house so huge that they were tired before walking through all the rooms, yet – despite having three or four others just as large – they were building her another as 'the one we saw they say is too small for her'. His awareness of the contrast between the extreme poverty he saw in Ireland, where 'the British government is over them', and the wealth of the capital is pronounced.[22] The Tupinambá 'king' would have had a very different experience, probably unable to speak the language and with little awareness of English ways, but if Maungwudaus – a converted Christian who was once considered for the priesthood – experienced culture shock, then we can only imagine what it must have been like for the Tupinambá three centuries earlier.

The men Montaigne met were of 'superior rank', one of them 'was a captain, and our sailors used to call him "King"'. This man had the privilege of leading an army of perhaps four or five thousand men into battle, and had several subject villages, which were expected to clear the forest paths so that he could walk his realm unimpeded. Montaigne spoke to this king 'for a very long time', but was seriously unimpressed with his interpreter 'who followed what I said so badly and whose stupidity prevented him from understanding my ideas so much that I could derive nothing worthwhile from the conversation'. This is an odd claim given how much detail he reveals, but maybe the essayist had hoped for a level of philosophical discussion that was simply beyond his translator, who was likely one of the sailors from the ships that ploughed the brazilwood route.

Montaigne was an exceptionally self-reflective writer for his time. After speaking with a man who had lived for 'ten or twelve years in that world which was discovered in our century', Montaigne concluded of the Tupinambá 'that there is nothing barbarous and savage about them, except that everyone calls things which he does not practise himself barbaric'. Pointing to the torture and violence in European society, he argued that 'we can call these natives barbarians . . . but not in comparison with ourselves, who surpass them in every variety of savagery'. Recognising that 'savagery' and 'civilisation' are relative and deliberately constructed concepts, Montaigne used the life of the Tupi to hold a critical mirror up to his own society.[23]

We do not know exactly where these Tupi people originated, but it is possible they were among those shipped to Europe in the 1550s by the French naval officer Nicolas Durand de Villegagnon, who led

an expedition to establish a fortified base on what became the site of
Rio de Janeiro. A tough and experienced soldier, a fervent Christian
and Huguenot sympathiser, Villegagnon bought ten Tupi boys, no
older than nine or ten, 'who had been captured in war and sold as
slaves' by an Indigenous group who were friendly to the French.
Seeking to bring these young men, who were probably Tamoio,
'to knowledge of their salvation', Villegagnon asked a local priest
to lay hands on the children, and they 'prayed God all together'
for divine grace. There is no mention of the Frenchman freeing
these children, or thinking of them as anything but objects of his
evangelism; like so many others, they were a canvas on which to
paint the potential of Christianity. The youths were sent to France
in 1557, where they were presented to Henri II as gifts – perhaps
as part of Villegagnon's attempt to secure more support for his
Brazilian venture. The king distributed them among 'several great
lords', including one Monsieur de Passy who 'had the boy baptized';
this young man was still living in France when Léry returned in
1558, but this snippet is all we know about him.[24]

When Villegagnon himself returned to France in 1559, he
brought around fifty Tupi men, women and children with him,
'through force or friendship'. Whether the Brazilians had consented
to the trip or not, they almost certainly had no choice in their
eventual fate. Most were presented to the king – it is remarkable
how common Native people must have been at the court in the
1550s – while Villegagnon 'retained some half a dozen for himself
and his brother'. This group included two young men, sixteen and
eighteen years old, who Villegagnon 'gave' to his brother Philippe, a
minor royal official in Provins, an impressive, fortified town to the
southeast of Paris. A local Catholic priest, Claude Haton, describes
in his memoirs how the boys – dubbed Donat and Doncart – having
learned a little French and gained some understanding of Christianity, were baptised in the Hôtel-Dieu (the religious hospital)
which still stands in the centre of Provins. They served Philippe,
who supposedly 'treated them very humanely', for seven or eight
years, before dying in his service. As usual, we hear little about
the lives of these young Tupi – mere silhouettes etched by a local

Edward Kelley (also known as Edward Talbot) was an English alchemist and occultist who worked with John Dee, conjuring up spirits with the aid of the glass. Their partnership has become infamous for conducting angel séances and recording a special angelic language (later known as Enochian). This is especially remarkable, given that, for the Aztecs, such mirrors were associated with the god Tezcatlipoca, whose name itself references the gleaming, dark obsidian; he was the 'Smoking Mirror', a figure linked to the fates, whose capricious will could be accessed through the obsidian discs which formed part of his regalia. He was instantly recognisable by the round mirror that replaced his left foot, lost tempting the great crocodile Cipactli to the surface of the primordial waters, where she would be sacrificed to become the earth.

In the Aztec-Mexica world, obsidian mirrors were used for divination, along with sacred texts and casting lots. The fates were interpreted by a specialist, who understood the signs within a complex calendar of multiple, interlocking cycles, each with their own precise implications. When a *tonalpouhqui* (reader of days, often translated as soothsayer) met a client, they would open the consultation by saying: 'You came to see yourself in the mirror; you came to consult the book.' This pairing of the ineffable, metaphysical meanings to be found in the smoked glass of the obsidian mirror, and the meticulous, methodical interpretation of the *tonalpohualli* (day count) with the aid of the *tonalamatl* (book of days) epitomises the Indigenous understanding of time and circumstance that ironically would have proved so appealing to Dee, despite his Christian upbringing. Dee's commitment to astrology, combined with his increasing conviction in the power of crystal divination as a medium to angelic communication, fitted closely with Aztec-Mexica beliefs about the obsidian disc. Although unequivocally appropriated as part of his own prestige and worldview, in many ways Dee was mirroring Indigenous religion in his rooms and even at court.

Those few codices whose paths to Europe we can track show how such Indigenous records were changing hands in elite circles throughout this period. We know that the Ñuu Dzaui Codex Yuta

Tnoho (formerly the Codex Vindobonensis) was at the papal court by the early 1520s, and was acquired by Duke Albrecht V of Bavaria in 1558. The Italian physician and writer Paolo Giovio had received a 'handwritten history' with 'hieroglyphic figures' as a gift by 1530 and the Florentine Codex was in the possession of Ferdinando de' Medici by the 1580s. We already know there were two pictographic texts among the treasures sent to Charles V by Cortés, one of which may have been the astonishing Codex Cihuacoatl (formerly Codex Borbonicus), a fifteen-metre-long calendrical text, that was in the possession of Philip II by 1600.[33]

The fact that so many Indigenous texts lie in European collections, and are often named after the men (and one woman) who collected or curated them, alludes to a process of intellectual colonisation that has lasted for five centuries. Although sometimes justified by claims that the European 'acquisition' of Indigenous documents 'saved' them from the conflagration following the Spanish invasion, such arguments hardly hold up as a justification for the export of such texts in the nineteenth century, and speak to a long-standing dispute about the ownership of sacred Indigenous knowledge and objects.

In 1982, the actions of a Mexican journalist named José Luis Castañeda del Valle brought the issue into sharp relief. Passing himself off as a student in Paris, he gained entry into the Bibliothèque Nationale de France (BNF), put the Tonalamatl de Aubin – an extremely rare calendrical screenfold – under his jacket and calmly walked out, returning only the empty box. By the time the loss was discovered, Castañeda had already returned to Mexico with the codex and, when he was arrested, claimed he was repatriating the manuscript: 'It was stolen from Mexico, and now we have recovered stolen property', he told one reporter. His claims of patriotism are rather undermined by the fact he had quietly held onto it for two months – it seems likely he had planned to sell it on the black market – but that did not stop Mexico from arguing the manuscript was part of their inalienable national patrimony and should remain on their shores. That summer in Mexico City, at UNESCO's 6th World Conference on Cultural Policies, Mexico was among the

nations making a strong case for the 'restitution of cultural property', but the return of the Tonalamatl de Aubin was seen as setting
a dangerous precedent. 'Can you imagine', said one diplomat, 'the
Greeks trying to steal the Elgin Marbles from the British Museum,
the Italians trying to steal the Mona Lisa from the Louvre and
so on? It could be chaos.' In 1991, the embarrassment was finally
resolved through an official loan to Mexico, to be reviewed every
three years.[34]

For more than five hundred years, Indigenous objects, peoples
and histories have been subject to European appropriation and
configuration. Four decades after the theft of the Tonalamatl de
Aubin, museums are still arguing that it is impossible to repatriate
Indigenous artefacts and remains to their descendants because of
the 'dangerous precedent' it sets. The Elgin Marbles (now renamed
the Parthenon Marbles, because it seems better to name them after
the place they were stolen from than the person who stole them) are
still in the British Museum, along with the remains of Indigenous
ancestors from all over the world.

Both policy and practice *are* changing. Since the passing of laws
such as the Native American Graves Protection and Repatriation
Act (USA, 1990) and the Human Tissue Act (UK, 2004), human
remains have increasingly been 'deaccessioned' (as the bloodless
terminology of heritage puts it) and returned to their descendant
communities. But hundreds of thousands of Indigenous remains
are still held in collections around the world, principally in the
United States, along with millions of Indigenous objects. While
many requests are approved, the humane assumption that ancestors
should be restored to their communities is far from the norm.

In 2008, the British Museum refused to return seven tattooed
Māori heads because, they claimed, it was uncertain that any mor-
tuary traditions had been interrupted, and 'it was not clear that the
importance of the remains to an original community outweighed
the significance of the remains as sources of information about
human history'. In other words, the museum thought their ability
to research these people, without their consent, was more important
than the expressed wishes of their descendants, who had said it was

vital to them that (in the words of the British Museum's minutes) the 'remains of the ancestor should be in the community'. In 2016 they refused for the same reasons to repatriate the skulls of two named individuals from the Torres Strait Island peoples, one of which had been 'collected' and the other bought by a British marine biologist named Alfred Cort Haddon in 1888. It is telling that the British Museum was sufficiently aware of their humanity to redact their names in the records, but still did not consider them human enough to be restored to their people. It is for such reasons that Linda Tuhiwai Smith famously wrote: 'the word itself, "research", is probably one of the dirtiest words in the Indigenous world's vocabulary'.[35]

From triumphal parades and cabinets of curiosities, through 'human zoos' and 'ethnographic displays', there is a long history of collecting and display which has dehumanised and disempowered people of colour* throughout history and contributed to the growth of 'scientific', as well as just garden-variety, racism. It was rare in the sixteenth century to see the display of Indigenous peoples for direct financial gain, but nonetheless they were consciously displayed for European purposes, and to their profit. While racism as we know it was only incipient in this period, the work of collectors, historians and ethnographers (often religious men interested in understanding 'other peoples', the better to convert them) sowed the seeds of later 'scientific' beliefs about race as a 'natural', fixed category serving to classify and often condemn people. Sixteenth-century collectors, in their zeal to own prestige objects, and even people, contributed to the creation of classifications and hierarchies of cultures, peoples and 'races'.[36]

Nearly fifty years before the grand pageant at Rouen, Pedro Álvares Cabral had solemnly and ceremoniously 'discovered' Brazil on behalf of Portugal. On 1 May 1500, he ordered Gaspar de Lemos to return home to inform the king. Gaspar took two 'fine' people 'from there' and, according to the prolific Jesuit writer Simão de Vasconcelos, 'He was received in Portugal with great joy by the

---

* As well as those with disabilities and congenital deformities. The history of 'human curiosities' is deeply implicated with eugenics as well as racism.

King and the Realm. Neither great nor small could get enough of seeing and hearing the speech, gesture and ways of life of that new individual of the human race. Some people even thought they might be fauns or some kind of ancient monster', mused Vasconcelos. This connection between Indigenous peoples and the monstrous races of the classical imagination was a common leap by Europeans; in 1542, Francisco de Orellana even claimed he had found the Amazons (probably in reality Tapuya people), when he almost died navigating the river he named after these female warriors of classical mythology. King Manuel was so impressed that he wrote to the Catholic monarchs in Spain about the visit of the mythologised men in 1500. The following year, two Italian diplomats living in Lisbon – Alberto Cantino and Pietro Pasqualigo – wrote of more people being shipped to the Portuguese king, this time from the north-east coast of the modern-day United States or Canada. Cantino was struck by their nakedness, green eyes, and 'rather human' language. In discussions, across Europe, Indigenous peoples were being categorised and classified, often with emphasis on their nudity or 'wildness', in direct opposition to European ideals of 'civilisation'.[37]

Whether they liked it or not, Indigenous peoples often ended up caged, metaphorically or literally, by European expectations of them. Their presence played into a wider culture of collecting, classification, and curiosity. It is easy to be dazzled by American spectacles in Europe: whirling feathers; dancing, singing and ball playing; lounging in hammocks in a village glade; pretending to sacrifice at the Spanish court. But while some of these prisoners of European expectation turned the situation to their advantage, skilfully navigating European networks and connections, others found themselves all too vulnerable.

In 1566, an Inuk* woman and her seven-year-old daughter were kidnapped from what is now the coast of Nunatsiavut (Canadian

---

* Inuit means 'the people', so – even though there are multiple groups – we don't talk about 'Inuit peoples' because it means 'the people peoples'. One person is an 'Inuk'.

Labrador) and transported to Antwerp. Her husband had been murdered defending his family and the woman, 'raving and mad' at the prospect of leaving her child behind, was permitted to draw her small daughter out of hiding and bring her on board ship. We only know about this tragedy because pamphlets were printed in Augsburg and Nuremberg advertising the 'wild woman with her daughter . . . brought to Antwerp and recently publicly seen there and still to be seen'. According to the pamphlet, the twenty-year-old woman had learned enough French in the intervening eight months to explain 'that she had eaten many men'. This should be filed under sensationalist advertising for the show (along with the claim that her husband was twelve feet tall and had singlehandedly killed and eaten twelve people in twelve days). The pamphlet shows both dressed in sealskin parka-like clothes and boots. The woman – her face tattooed with 'sky blue' – is standing with one arm protectively around her daughter, a chubby-cheeked little girl with curly hair, identical to her mother's, poking out from under her hood. We know nothing of them beyond this glimpse, but the phrasing of the pamphlet, which speaks of them as 'man-eaters', living like 'beasts', gives little confidence that they would have been humanely treated.[38]

On 9 October 1576, another 'strange man' arrived in London, along with 'his bote'. This Inuk, from Qikiqtaaluk (Baffin Island) in what is now north-eastern Canada, had been kidnapped by Martin Frobisher in retaliation for the disappearance of five of his men. Frobisher – an English privateer who was searching for a north-west passage to the Pacific – enticed him near to their ship with the offer of a loud bell and then 'caught the man fast, and plucked him with main force, boat and all into his bark [a small ship], out of the Sea'. George Best, who advised on the voyage and later recorded it, claimed that the Inuk was so furious at being captured that he bit his tongue in half, though this most likely happened in the struggle to get him on board ship. One of the investors to the voyage, Michael Lok, who saw the Inuk in London, described him in detail.

He was a very good shape and strongly pight [fixed] made his head, his neck, his breast, a very broad face and very fat and fu[ll] his body. But his legs shorter and smaller [than the pro] portion of his body required, and his hands [h]is hair coal black and long hanging and 'tyer' tied [in a knot] above his forehead. His eyes little and a little [coal] black beard. His colour of skin all over his bo[dy and fa]ce of a dark sallow, much like to the tawny Moors, [or ra]ther to the Tartar nation, whereof I think he was. [His] countenance sullen or churlish and sharp withall.

It is not surprising that the Inuit man looked 'sullen' when he was shown off in London. He was extremely ill from the injury to his tongue and died only two weeks later. Best put it down to a 'cold which he had taken at Sea' (perhaps pneumonia). One of the earliest Indigenous Americans in Britain, this Inuk man was shown off as a tremendous novelty and a success of the voyage.

Having landed in Harwich on 2 October, the Inuk man was taken to London, where he 'was such a wonder onto the whole city and to the rest of the realm that heard of it'. Despite the Inuk's malaise, portraitists were eager to capture his likeness. The Cathay Company, which had funded Frobisher's expedition, paid for the successful Flemish artist Cornelius Ketel to paint several 'great pictures' of the Inuk man, including a full-length portrait. One of the pictures was intended for Queen Elizabeth, and one for the Cathay Company; and we know from records of the commission that most of them featured the Inuk 'in his [native] garments', although in one he wears 'Englishe ap[par]ell'. The company also paid a Dutchman, William Cure, to make a wax cast of the Inuk's head. One can only assume, and hope, that it was a death mask. One wonders what he made of being forced to wear English clothing, for – according to oral accounts of Inuit first impressions of these *qallunaat* ('not Inuit') shared by esteemed elder Inookie Adamie – the clothes of the Europeans were so wildly unsuitable for the Arctic weather that the Inuit concluded they 'more or less wore rags'.[39]

Although neither the pictures nor the wax mask survive, there were many illustrations of the Inuk circulating, and two images remain that were probably drawn from the original portraits: an ink drawing by Adriaen Coenen from 1577, and a watercolour by Lucas de Heere of Ghent that appeared in a costume book. De Heere was in London during the Inuit man's visit, so it is possible this was drawn from life, but – given his brief stay – it seems more likely that he was in contact with his fellow Fleming, Ketel, and worked from his pictures. Coenen's picture shows the stocky Inuk standing with his bow above a bay in which floats the *Gabriel*, Frobisher's ship on which he was carried to England, as well as two canoes. In reality, the Inuk must have spent most of his brief visit to London bedridden. The bills for Frobisher's expedition include costs 'for bedding for him spoiled in his sickness', as well as for an apothecary and 'folk hired to tend him' when he was gravely ill.

Despite treating the Inuk like a mere curiosity in life, someone who could be seized and studied at will, the Englishmen do seem to have offered him some respect in death. The bills include the substantial sum of five pounds to a quite-prestigious London surgeon, William Crow, 'for opening of the Indian man, and [em]balming him dead, preserved to have him been sent back again in to his country' as well as charges for a coffin and bran to pack him in. For some reason, the Inuk's body was not returned to Qikiqtaaluk as they had originally intended, so the final cost to the company was a payment 'for burying the Tartar Indian man in St Olave's churchyard'. The fact that this burial went unrecorded by the parish shows the way he fell between worlds: he was recognised as a person who needed Christian burial, but was not sufficiently 'of us' to be registered as part of the community.[40]

In 1577, a year after the earliest Inuk visitor was buried in London, Frobisher returned to Inuit territory, hoping to recover his five lost crewmen, as well as to investigate a mysterious (and ultimately worthless) 'black ore' discovered on his first voyage.* Arriving at the mouth of Iqaluit (Frobisher Bay) in what is now

---

* It turned out to be iron pyrite: fool's gold.

Nunavut* in Canada, Frobisher exchanged signs with a group of Inuit on the shore, before attempting to seize two men, intending to use one to take trifles and clothes back to his people 'and to retain the other for an interpreter'. Realising they were being lured into a trap, the Inuit – better equipped on the slippery, snow-covered ground – fled, and shot Frobisher 'in the buttock with an arrow'. But while the captain made good his escape on a sled, a man called Nicholas Conger, a servant of Lord Warwick who was an especially good runner, managed to overtake one of the Inuit and wrestle him to the ground with 'a Cornish trick', injuring the Inuk so that 'he made his sides ache against the ground for a month after'.

After exploring more of the coastline, poking about in abandoned tents, and stealing a dog (presumably left behind when the Inuit fled hastily to the mountains), Frobisher and his men made one last attempt to find out what had happened to their five lost comrades. They seem seriously to have tried to communicate with the Inuit, showing one of them 'the picture of his Countryman which the last year was brought into England (whose counterfeit we had drawn, with boat, and other furniture, both as he was in his own, and also in English apparel)'. According to Inookie Adamie, who died in 2020, reportedly at 109 years old, his ancestors were 'terrified of these white men in the row boats . . . thinking they were not of this world', so we can only guess at how they interpreted the sudden appearance of a picture of the Inuk traveller in English clothing – who could have been a family member for all we know.

Frobisher's lieutenant Best claimed that, although at first the Inuk was 'much amazed', he realised 'by feeling and handling' that this was 'but a deceiving picture'. He saw the 'great noise and cries' the man made as fear, but it seems more likely to have been grief or shock. Whatever he felt about the confusing portrait, the Inuk attempted to communicate with signs, and seemed to have some knowledge of the five lost men, though he 'earnestly denied' that they had been 'slain and eaten'. Landing in a bay, hoping to take

---

* Meaning 'our land' in Inuktitut, Nunavut is a predominantly Inuit territory in northern Canada.

some of the Inuit alive, Frobisher's men found themselves fiercely assaulted by the land's inhabitants, who may have been all too aware of the previous year's kidnappings, for three died leaping desperately off the rocks into the sea, in an attempt to avoid being captured. Dionyse Settle, one of Frobisher's company, appears oblivious to the tragedy he describes:

> . . . if by any means we could have taken them alive . . . we would both have saved them, and also have sought remedy to cure their woundes, wounds received at our hands. But they, altogether void of humanity, and ignorant what mercy means, look for no other than death: and perceiving they should fall into our hands, thus miserably by drowning rather desired death, than otherwise to be saved by us: the rest, perceiving their fellows in this distress, fled into the high mountains.

Best suggests that the Inuit killed themselves rather than be taken prisoner because they believed the English to be cannibals. If this is true, we can imagine the terror that must have been felt by two women who found themselves unable to escape: an 'old wretch' and a mother 'encumbered with a young child'. The old woman was too 'ugly and deformed' to be of interest so, after assuring themselves that she was not a devil or a witch – plucking off her boots to check for cloven feet – they let her go. But the young woman and baby were a great prize. Frobisher clearly saw his three captives as a possible bargaining chip for his lost men, and wrote a letter offering to trade them for the supposed prisoners, but eventually they gave the sailors up for lost and, on 22 August 1577, they set sail for Bristol.*

The three Inuit prisoners were thrown together and, although the Englishmen crudely assumed that the woman would be 'for the comfort of our [Inuit] man', in reality the Inuit do seem to have drawn genuine comfort from each other.[41] The trio may have looked

---

* Inuit oral tradition is divided on whether the five Englishmen were killed or built a boat and were lost at sea.

like a family, but the man was a stranger to the woman and her child, and at their first meeting they showed no sign of friendship. Both adults tried multiple times to escape while the boats were still close to the coast, even as the Inuit ashore attempted to negotiate for the return of the woman and baby but, once escape was deemed impossible, the woman and the man resigned themselves to making the best of the situation, maintaining their dignity and independence, so far as they could. The baby had been injured by an arrow during their capture, and the woman rejected the surgeon's salves, preferring to heal the wound in the traditional way, by licking it with her tongue until it healed.[42]

The Inuit lived together as a household, the woman cleaning their cabin, caring for the man when he was seasick, and skinning dogs for them to eat. Best thought 'the one would hardly have lived without the comfort of the other', and all sources agree that their relationship was carefully (admirably in the eyes of the English) chaste. The man would make sure that the woman had left the cabin before he removed his clothes, and they were fastidious about keeping their 'privie parts' covered. Torn away from her husband, the woman found 'his embrace . . . abhorrent to her'. Although they slept in the same bed, 'nothing had occurred between them apart from conversation'.[43]

When they arrived in Bristol in southwest England in October 1577, the three Inuit immediately became a spectacle. Their identities remain a mystery, but for the first time they are given names in our accounts. The man was called Kalicho, and the woman and her baby were Arnaq and Nutaaq, meaning 'woman' and 'child' (or 'someone new').* It seems that the Inuit had learned a little English on the voyage, as they were able to say 'God give you good morrow' and 'farewell'.† Kalicho quickly became a local celebrity, paddling up and

---

* Some early chroniclers, wrestling with the unfamiliar language, called the man 'Cally Chough'. There are many variations of these names in the sources, so these are standardised spellings in modern Inuktitut.

† Like many of us, their first words in a foreign language were 'hello' and 'goodbye'.

down the river Avon at high tide in his canoe, and hunting ducks with his 'dart' (either an arrow or harpoon – he is shown with both in pictures). Crowds of people, including the mayor, got a taste of Inuit life, watching Kalicho carry the canoe on his back through the marshes and show off his considerable skill on the water. 'He would hit a duck a good distance off and not miss.'[44]

Arnaq was also a subject of fascination for the way she was able to breastfeed Nutaaq – now about a year old – inside her parka by 'casting her breasts over her shoulders'. The Inuit preference for raw meat caused great consternation, though they started to eat cooked meat after they arrived in England, having a keen appreciation of the broth.

Again, artists flocked to depict the three captives, and an astonishing number of pictures survive from the short period they were in Bristol, perhaps thirty in total. The best known were painted by John White, who is famous today for his watercolours of the Algonquian-speaking peoples of Virginia. He painstakingly depicted the three Inuit, with the baby Nutaaq peeking from his mother's hood. These pictures of the Inuit looking hale and hearty, Arnaq with a slight smile and her hand resting on her thigh, again disguise a painful reality.[45]

Still injured from his capture, Kalicho soon fell ill. A doctor was called for him on several occasions, and, as well as the Inuk's physical symptoms, he diagnosed what he called '"Anglophobia", which he had from when he first arrived, even though his fairly cheerful features and appearance concealed it and gave a false impression with considerable skill'. Dr Edward Dodding saw this as a physical ailment, which he thought 'betokened an incipient fatal illness', but it is an exceptionally astute description of a man who – torn away from his home and his people – was putting a brave face on the situation.

Less than a month after arriving in Bristol, Kalicho died. Dr Dodding was hired to perform an autopsy, and the account of his findings is a remarkable record of the Inuk's experience in his final days. During his time in England, Kalicho – the doctor reports – suffered constantly from 'deafness and intense head pains', but 'his strength was still unimpaired' and he was fit enough to refuse the bloodletting recommended by the doctor. Dodding saw this as evidence that the Inuk was 'uncivilised', timid, and foolish, but – even in captivity and far from home – Kalicho clearly remained capable of asserting himself. His condition declined quickly and, when the physician was called for the last time, he found Kalicho barely conscious and unable to speak properly. Close to the end, he 'came back to himself as if from a deep sleep' and recognised his companions. He was even able to speak a few words of English and answer questions. At the last, Kalicho sang what the doctor believed to be an Inuit song of mourning or departure, 'like the swans who foresee what good there is in death and die happily with a song'. Clinging to his traditions, perhaps seeking a connection to his home and family as he lay dying, Kalicho's song seems an act of resistance, as well as a poignant acknowledgement of loss. But he came back to the reality of his situation at the end, 'forcing out' the words 'God be with you' in English, before slipping away.

Dodding's autopsy showed that Kalicho had two badly broken ribs, very likely from his capture, as well as signs of a brain injury, which presumably accounted for his dreadful headaches and deafness. The rib fractures had failed to heal, causing his left lung to fill with fluid and collapse, which must have been causing him considerable pain, as well as making breathing difficult. Yet Dodding's main concern was that Queen Elizabeth I had missed her chance to see one of the Inuit visitors. In the late 1570s, Elizabeth was tentatively encouraging overseas exploration – Francis Drake would shortly set off on the voyage which would become his famous circumnavigation of the globe – and the doctor was 'grieved and saddened' that this chance to see an Inuk captive had 'slipped through her fingers'.

Kalicho was buried on 8 November 1577, at St Stephen's Church in Bristol. Keen to assure Arnaq that the English were not cannibals, Dodding forced the unwilling woman to witness the burial, taking pains to show her Kalicho's (dissected) body and other human bones dug up at the time 'in order to remove from her mind all anxiety about human flesh being eaten'. Arnaq seems to have remained impassive throughout the process. Dodding thought she was 'not in any way disturbed by his death', and her apparent lack of distress made him think that either she was the most stoic and decorous woman he had ever seen, or else that she 'was far outstripped in human sensitivity by the wild animals themselves'. It seems more likely that Arnaq was suffering from shock or trauma, unable to cope with the loss of her companion and the sight of his dissected corpse, or else that – like Kalicho – she chose to put on a brave face in front of her captors.

Arnaq herself was already seriously ill, 'troubled with boils (which broke out very densely on her skin)' the day after the burial.[46] She had probably contracted measles, or something similar: just one of the many deadly diseases to which Indigenous Americans had no natural immunity. She died just a few days after Kalicho and was buried alongside him at St Stephen's, close to the river. The parish register of burials for 1577 reads:

> Collinchang a heathen man bur*ied* the 8th of November.
> Egnock a heathen woman bur*ied* the 13th of November.

Unlike their compatriot the year before, Kalicho and Arnaq were given proper recognition as well as burial in consecrated ground, although the parish clerk made sure to note that they were heathens; they were still not quite 'one of us'. This is the first-known occasion when the deaths of two Indigenous Americans were recorded in an English parish register, and this sparse report speaks of a world that was gradually opening up. A world where 'other' peoples were starting to become visible. A place of possibility, and also of tragedy.

The baby, Nutaaq, was left to the dubious care of Frobisher and the Cathay Company. Probably only fourteen or fifteen months old, and still nursing when Arnaq died, Nutaaq must have been terrified and extremely vulnerable.* Frobisher hired a local nurse†

---

* We do not really know whether Nutaaq was a girl or a boy, but a very bad French source with lots of mistakes claims the baby was a boy, so (despite the possibility this is wrong) we will imagine him that way, to avoid dehumanising and objectifying him still further.
† Possibly a wet nurse, as we know the baby was still breastfeeding.

and displacement is both profound and ongoing. For some of those who lie in European land, the rupture cannot be repaired. Raleigh's bones will never be reunited with his people. We can never know where Nutaaq's tiny body lies. But by finding Indigenous travellers 'in unexpected places',* across the Atlantic world, at the heart of empire and in its provinces, at court and in the country, in homes and in bondage, we can help to bridge the crevasse. These stories are vital, to understanding European and global histories, and to comprehending both the Indigenous past and the present.

Like Nutaaq and his assumed family, the majority of Indigenous voyagers did not *choose* to travel to Europe. We may choose to foreground the choices they made, their agency, influence, and importance, but the reality is that Indigenous people were most often coerced into visiting a new, often-unacknowledged, imperial centre across an awesome expanse of ocean. The physical shackles, and chains of expectation, that bound so many of these pioneers must be part of our picture of their experience and of the sixteenth century. There were certainly Indigenous rulers, nobles and diplomats in the Atlantic world – glamorous kings and imposing ambassadors – but there were also many people of the most ordinary sort, people whose presence barely merited a mention in the annals of history. Only by accumulating many tiny slivers of these lives, which touched so many but have seemingly made so shallow an imprint on western traditions, can we start to build a picture of the past that sees these travellers as they were – sometimes remarkable, and at other times mundane – but above all *there*.

Too often the history of peoples of colour in Europe is marginalised or deliberately suppressed, their presence in the past ignored. Too often their contribution to the contemporary world is a footnote or a sidebar, an interesting anecdote or a local-interest story. But Indigenous people were, are, and should be, central characters in this history. As Europeans took their first steps across the world, so

---

* To paraphrase Philip Deloria (Harvard professor of History and a member of the Standing Rock Sioux tribe).

too Native explorers set out to discover new lands, their diplomats built political ties, and their traders formed commercial networks. As Christians imposed their religion on sceptical communities, Indigenous converts crossed the great water to follow (or be forced into) the faith. As European settlers migrated west, Indigenous and mixed-heritage families were also forming in the east. As enslaved peoples of African descent began to be shipped across the Atlantic in horrifying conditions, Indigenous people were branded, bonded, and enslaved alongside them.

Like so many of the travellers who grace the pages of this book, the baby Nutaaq appears only briefly in our story, and then vanishes again, not from history, but just from the part of it we can see. His experience was not insignificant because it did not merit much attention, rather his incidental appearance is a reminder of how heavily our picture of the past is shaped by the sources we have available, sources that are coloured by European and elite expectations. However hard we look, Indigenous peoples are often a marginal note, a passing reference, an object of Christian aspiration or exploitation, a silent face on a building that screams of a deep history being ignored. Through this book, I ask you to look harder for those traces, to think about their presence and significance, and to listen to the voices of their descendants.

Glossary

Abya Yala: 'land of life' in the language of the Gunadule people; a term for the Americas used by some South American Indigenous activists

agouhanna: Iroquoian term for 'chief'

Algonquian: a cultural and linguistic group belonging to the Indigenous peoples of the eastern United States and Canada

Anishinaabeg: a group of Indigenous peoples from the Great Lakes region

Arawak: a language spoken by the Lokono people of South America

audiencia: high court and council of state in a Spanish colony

Aztec-Mexica: the people who dominated much of Central Mexico from their capital city of Tenochtitlan at the time of the Spanish invasion

cabildo: Nahuatl term for 'council'

cacique: Taíno term for 'chief', widely applied by the Spanish to refer to hereditary Indigenous rulers

cantares (singular *canto*): Nahuatl songs or poems

Carib: Indigenous peoples of the Lesser Antilles and northern coastal South America, including the Kalinago and Kalina; the term came to be associated with 'cannibals'

Carijó: Indigenous people of Brazil from the Tupi-Guaraní region

cemanahuac: 'the place surrounded by water', Nahuatl term for the earth

Chibcha: language spoken by the Muisca peoples of present-day Colombia

cocoliztli: Nahuatl term for the 'great pestilence' that devastated sixteenth-century Mexico

criado: Spanish term for a dependant, applied to many unnamed travellers to Spain, from enslaved people to family members

Croatan: 'Talking Town', an Algonquian-speaking Indigenous group from what is now coastal North Carolina

Diné: 'the people', also known as Navajo; a tribe from what is now the southwestern United States

Eastern Woodlands: a cultural region of eastern North America including Algonquian, Iroquoian, Muskogean and Siouan-speaking peoples

encomienda: grant giving the holder (*encomendero*) the right to demand tribute and labour from Indigenous communities

esclavo: Spanish word for 'slave'

factor: Spanish royal treasury official

guaíza: small mask or sculpture of a face, a Taíno spiritual object

Guaraní: Indigenous peoples whose descendants currently live in Brazil, Paraguay, Bolivia and Argentina

guatiao: Taíno word for ritualised bonds of friendship or brotherhood

Haudenosaunee: 'peoples of the longhouse', a group of Indigenous nations commonly known as the Iroquois Confederacy

Hispaniola: La Española in Spanish, second largest island of the West Indies

indio/india: 'Indian', an anachronistic term for Indigenous peoples in colonial Spanish sources

Inka: often called 'Inca', the Indigenous nation that dominated much of modern-day Peru and the Andes from their capital at Cusco

Iroquois: Indigenous-language group, spoken by peoples including the Haudenosaunee and the Stadaconans of present-day Quebec

just war: 'justifiable' conflict (e.g. against rebels and cannibals) through which Indigenous enemy combatants could be enslaved

Kalina: mainland speakers of Carib languages

Kalinago: island speakers of Carib languages

K'iche': Maya language and cultural group, spoken principally in present-day Guatemala

ladino: Hispanised Indigenous person

Lenape: Indigenous people of Northeastern Woodlands

Māori: Indigenous peoples of New Zealand (Aotearoa)

maravedi: small unit of Spanish currency, worth 1/34th of a *real*

Maya: group of Indigenous peoples of Mesoamerica, today inhabiting Belize, El Salvador, Guatemala, Honduras and Mexico

Mesoamerica: historic cultural region of Mexico and Central America including societies such as Aztec-Mexica, Olmec, and Maya

mestizo/mestiza: mixed-heritage, a Spanish term for a person with one white European parent and one Indigenous parent

milpa: small, mixed-crop field in Mesoamerica

molinillo: whisk for chocolate drink

Muisca: Indigenous peoples living in the Altiplano of present-day Colombia

mulatto/mulatta: now a racial slur, at this time a Spanish term for someone of mixed Black and white heritage

Nahua: Nahuatl-speaker

Nahuatl: Indigenous language spoken by groups including the Aztec-Mexica and Tlaxcalans, in what is now Mexico

'Namgis: Indigenous nation from Vancouver Island

nepantla: Nahuatl for the 'in-between space', inhabited by *nepantleras* (people in the in-between, go-betweens)

ñusta: Inka 'princess'

Ossomocomuck: 'the land that we inhabit' or 'the dwelling house', an Algonquian-speaking region on the coast of what is now North Carolina

Powhatan: Algonquian-speaking peoples of Tsenacomoco from eastern Virginia, also the name of some of their leaders

Q'eqchi': Maya language and cultural group, spoken principally in present-day Guatemala and Belize

real: a Spanish unit of currency worth one-eighth of a peso

rescate (**Portuguese:** *resgate*): 'rescue' of people into slavery in the Spanish empire

Roanoke: Algonquian-speaking Indigenous people from what is now coastal North Carolina

Tabajara: Tupi-speaking tribe from north-eastern coastal Brazil

Taíno: name claimed by descendant communities for the diverse peoples of the Greater Antilles

Tamoio: 'forebear', a name adopted by descendants of the Tupinambá of southern Brazil

Tenochtitlan: capital city of the Aztec-Mexica

tlatoani: 'one who speaks', the Nahuatl term for ruler

Tlaxcala: long-standing enemy of the Aztec-Mexica, this confederacy of city-states was an important ally of the Spanish invaders

Tlaxcalans: people from Tlaxcala in Mexico, more properly Tlaxcalteca

Totonac: Indigenous peoples of eastern Mexico

Tupi: language and cultural group of what is now Brazil

Tupinambá: Tupi-speaking peoples of eastern Brazil

Turtle Island: term for the Americas used by many North American Indigenous peoples

visitador: literally 'visitor', a powerful royal inspector in the Spanish colonies

weroance: Algonquian word meaning leader or chief

Wyandot: Iroquoian Indigenous peoples of North America and Canada, also (offensively) called the Huron

Acknowledgements

When a book has been so long in the making, it is almost impossible to say enough about the people and communities who have helped me get to this point. I am bound to forget someone, and whoever they are I hope they will forgive me.

It is traditional in such thanks to leave family until last, but for me they come first. My husband James is why I do this, and why I can. He has supported me, and sacrificed for me, and he always comes up with the best titles! Without James this book would never have been written, and without him it would certainly never have been finished. This book is for him.

My parents, Catherine and Bill, are the reason I am a historian. Despite being of a scientific inclination themselves, they have been an unwavering practical and emotional support, as both parents and grandparents. My in-laws, Chris and Jim, are why any lockdown writing at all was possible and I cannot thank them enough for their willingness to help our family in ways both large and small. It truly does take a village to raise a child, especially the child of someone trying to finish a book. My daughter Rowan is the reason I write, and the reason I write so slowly. She would probably prefer the pages had purple edges, but her love means she can (mostly) overlook such minor failings in me.

Having worked in academia for a long time, I owe debts to people across the world, close friends and distant colleagues. So many people have been generous with their time, and offered advice and support. I must thank all my colleagues at Sheffield, which has been my home for more than a decade, especially Adrian Bingham for helping me find time to finish the book when Covid killed my research leave, and Andrew Heath, Tehyun Ma, Caoimhe Nic Dháibhéid, Colin Reid and Charles West, for friendship, support and snark.

I have been lucky in my career to have met and been advised by colleagues whose work has long inspired me. Dave Andress, Paul Cohen, Jennifer Raff and Coll Thrush read the whole manuscript and offered thought-provoking advice and friendly critique. I thank them all, as well as the many other colleagues and mentors who have also generously shared their support and expertise over the course of my career, including Philippe Buc, María Castañeda de la Paz, Nick Davidson, Rebecca Earle, Martial Staub and Jonathan Westaway. The community of Global Middle Ages scholars has always been a wonderful place to try out ideas and think capaciously and I found there friendship and collegiality, especially with Amanda Power and Naomi Standen, who are treasured correspondents. Camilla Townsend, who helped me with the descendants of Moctezuma, is an incredibly responsive and generous model of a senior scholar. Sara Gonzalez followed many exciting (and some very dull) trails in the Archive of the Indies – her support with research and transcription was invaluable at a time when I was unable to travel. Jack Hayes translated some fascinating French material that frustratingly ended up being dropped from the book and saved for another time. Paul Warde helped me untangle the maze of early modern wages and values.

This book has been built on, and with, the assistance of many scholars, both in person, and through their work. In a book like this, you're not allowed to gush as much about historiography as you might like, so I want to acknowledge here the multiple ways in which scholars such as Nancy van Deusen, Jack D. Forbes, Imtiaz Habib, Onyeka Nubia, Esteban Mira Caballos, David Olusoga, Olivette Otele, Johnny Pitts, José Carlos de la Puente Luna, Daniel Richter, Éric Taladoire, Alden T. Vaughan and Jace Weaver have transformed my understanding of the Atlantic world.

The history and wider communities on Twitter have been an incredible resource, as well as a source of support and cheer, the value of virtual friendship becoming all too acute in recent pandemic years. Sara Barker gave enthusiastic help with the Capuchins and Parisian geography. David Bowles generously translated Nahuatl *cantares*. Scott Cave shared his expertise in wrangling the demon of the PARES database. Taylor Green checked my contracts and offered invaluable legal advice. Matt Lodder and I talked tattoos. Sophie Pitman advised on Elizabethan taffeta. Mike Jones brought the transcription of the damaged 'Annals of Bristol' to my attention and led me down a rabbit warren about the Inuit. Mike Webb checked into a Bodleian reference, sadly unproductively. Juan José Ponce Vázquez, Magnus Pharao, François Soyer and others gave help with impossible palaeography. Catherine Fletcher and Amanda Madden shared their expertise on Italian sources. David Wengrow pointed me to some Indigenous intellectual histories. Christophe Maneuvrier shared French sources. Suzannah Lipscomb and others helped with French translation. I could not be more grateful to them and everyone who has helped, as well as those who have offered other kinds of support and friendship, including Bodie Ashton, Charlie Connelly, Amy Fuller, Greg Jenner, Sylvia de Mar, and Caroline Sharples.

Through Twitter, I was also fortunate enough to meet Adam Rutherford, who has become an unfailingly supportive and funny friend. He has not only helped with the book itself, but is a big part of the reason I met my lovely agent Will Francis, who has been a determined advocate and constant supporter, patiently tolerating my questions and calming my periodic panics. I am hugely grateful to Will and all the team at Janklow and Nesbit, who have shepherded me, and the book, through every step of the unfamiliar process of trade publishing. My thanks are also due to my 'other agent' Mel Flashman who made sure that the book will have an American audience and supported me from afar.

My appreciation is unbounded for my editors Maddy Price and Erroll McDonald, who shared and shaped my vision for this project and whose passionate, patient and critical guidance has infinitely improved the book. My enormous gratitude also goes to everyone else at Weidenfeld & Nicolson, Knopf, Orion and Penguin who believed in this idea, helped to transform my scrawl into this beautiful book, and got it fully formed into your hands, including Jenny Lord, Lucinda McNeile, Virginia Woolstencroft, Natalie Dawkins, and so many others (some of whom I never met or encountered too late in the process to credit by name here – thank you all so much!).

My special thanks go to Miss E. Margaret Wade (1946–2021), an inspirational teacher, voracious reader and history lover, who is warmly remembered and much missed by her family, friends and former students.

Above all, I owe infinite thanks to the Indigenous people whose scholarship, wisdom and knowledge have informed my work, in person, in print, and in the virtual world, especially Kai Minosh Pyle, Ruben Arellano Tlakatekatl, Robbie Richardson and the *Beyond the Spectacle* community. Most especially, my unending gratitude and friendship go to Leila Blackbird, whose meticulous comments on every single part of the manuscript, and patient tolerance of all my follow-up questions, have made this an immeasurably better book than it would ever have been without her.

(México, 1892), p. 77; *Colección de documentos inéditos relativos al descubrimiento, conquista y organización de las antiguas posesiones españolas de América y Oceanía, sacados de los archivos del reino y muy especialmente del de Indias*, 42 vols. (Madrid, 1864–84), Vol. 41, p. 91.

31   AGI, Mexico, l. 1, ff. 38r-40r; R. Jovita Baber, 'Empire, Indians, and the Negotiation for the Status of City in Tlaxcala, 1521–1550', in Ethelia Ruiz Medrano, Susan Kellogg and Russ Davidson (eds), *Negotiation within Domination: New Spain's Pueblo Indians Confront the Spanish State* (Boulder, 2010), pp. 37–8; Caroline Dodds Pennock, 'Aztecs Abroad: Uncovering the Early Indigenous Atlantic', *American Historical Review*, 125.3 (2020), pp. 787–814.

32   Gonzalo Fernández de Oviedo y Valdés, *Historia general y natural de las Indias, Part 2.2* (1853), Book XXXIII, Chapter XLIX; Díaz del Castillo, *The True History of the Conquest of New Spain*, Vol. 5, pp. 152–3.

33   Christoph Weiditz, *Trachtenbuch*, c.1530–40, Germanisches Nationalmuseum, Nürnberg, Hs, 22474, plates 1–13, https://tinyurl.com/ysh9c9ne.

34   Elizabeth Hill Boone, 'Seeking Indianness: Christoph Weiditz, the Aztecs, and feathered Amerindians', *Colonial Latin American Review*, 26.1 (2017), pp. 39–61.

35   AGI, Indiferente, 420, l. 8, ff. 185r-185v.

36   Giménez Fernández, 'El alzamiento de Fernando Cortés', pp. 41–3; Hugh Thomas, *The Conquest of Mexico* (London, 1994), p. 351.

37   For an excellent (if now slightly dated) starting point to the vast wealth of research on the *cantares* see John Bierhorst (trans. and ed.), *Cantares mexicanos: Songs of the Aztecs* (Stanford, 1985), pp. 537–52.

38   'Flowers rain gently down' is perhaps a metaphor for drizzle or spray. An alternative reading would be something like 'rain falls gently like petals'.

39   Literally 'makes us visible', with the same verb used for 'dawning'.

40   Or 'final'.

41   I am indebted to David Bowles, who is working on a new translation of the *Cantares mexicanos*, for sharing with me his rendering of these excerpts from Canto LXVIII, stanzas F and I, and for his permission to reproduce them.

42   James Lockhart, *We People Here: Nahuatl Accounts of the Conquest of Mexico* (Eugene, Ore., 2004), pp. 154–5. In fact, although this transatlantic voyage is widely reported, it seems that he may rather have accidentally accompanied Cortés on his 1524 expedition to Honduras. Nonetheless, Martín certainly seems to have undertaken an extended sea passage, which was remembered in Indigenous accounts. For an introduction to the various Martíns see Camilla Townsend's excellent new history of the Mexica, *Fifth Sun: A New History of the Aztecs* (Oxford, 2019), pp. 155–63,

which shows the Aztecs as a force before and after the Spanish invasion.

43   *Florentine Codex*, 11: 12: 247.

Chapter 1: Slavery

1   'Thursday 11 October', *Diary of Christopher Columbus*, King's Digital Lab, http://www.ems.kcl.ac.uk/content/etext/e020.html#doe434.

2   See, for example, Leila K. Blackbird, 'A Gendered Frontier: Métissage and Indigenous Enslavement in Eighteenth-Century Basse-Louisiane', *Journal for Eighteenth-Century Studies* 45.3 (forthcoming 2022); 'Monday 12 November', *Diary of Christopher Columbus*, https://tinyurl.com/bde78udb; Las Casas, *Historia de Las Indias*, Vol. 1, pp. 346–9; Gonzalo Fernández de Oviedo y Valdés, *Historia general y natural de las Indias: Part 1* (1535), Book II, Chapter VI, https://tinyurl.com/m25xu9bv.

3   Letter from Eugenio de Salazar to Miranda de Ron, in John H. Parry and Robert G. Keith (eds), *New Iberian World: A Documentary History of the Discovery and Settlement of Latin America to the early 17th century* (New York, 1984), pp. 431–40.

4   Las Casas, *Historia de Las Indias*, Vol. 1, p. 348; Fernández de Oviedo y Valdés, *Historia general*, Book II, Chapter VI. There is some debate about the location of the baptism, but the majority of the evidence points to Barcelona, which is the 'official' location of the baptisms, recorded in 1643 by an archivist compiling a catalogue of notable events in the city: Juan B. Olaechea Labayen, 'De Cómo, Dónde y Cuándo fueron bautizados los primeros indios', *Hispania Sacra*, 50.102 (1998), p. 624.

5   Angus A. A. Mol, *Costly Giving, Giving Guaízas: Towards an organic model of the exchange of social valuables in the Late Ceramic Age Caribbean* (Leiden, 2007); Claudia Jane Rogers, '"The People from Heaven?" Reading Indigenous responses to Europeans during moments of early encounter in the Caribbean and Mesoamerica, 1492–c.1585' (PhD thesis, University of Leeds, 2018), pp. 79–82; Oliver, *Caciques and Cemí Idols*.

6   'Letter from Columbus to Luis de Santangel', in Julius E. Olson and Edward Gaylord Bourne (eds), *The Northmen, Columbus and Cabot, 985–1503* (New York, 1906), pp. 266–7; Martyr d'Anghera, *De Orbe Novo*, Vol. 2, p. 38; Luis Joseph Peguero, *Historia de la conquista de la isla Española de S.to Domingo . . .* (1762), p. 49; 'Saturday 22 December', *Diary of Christopher Columbus*, https://tinyurl.com/2p93x6cr.

7   We do not have conclusive proof that this is the occasion when Diego was baptised, but it seems almost certain to be the case. Esteban Mira Caballos, 'Caciques guatiaos en los inicios de la colonización: el caso del indio Diego Colón', *Iberoamericana (2001–)*, 4.16 (2004), p. 10.

8   Laura Briggs, *Taking Children: A History of American Terror* (Berkeley, 2020); Andrés Reséndez, *The Other Slavery: The Uncovered Story of Indian Enslavement in America* (Boston, 2016), p. 142; Tanya Talaga, *All Our Relations: Indigenous trauma in the shadow of colonialism* (London, 2020).

9   Trevisan, 'Libretto', in Symcox et al. (eds), *Italian Reports on America*, Vol. 12, p. 88; Anna Brickhouse, 'Mistranslation, Unsettlement, La Navidad', *PMLA*, 128.4 (2013), p. 942.

10   Las Casas, *Historia de Las Indias*, pp. 346–9.

11   Lawrence Clayton, 'Bartolomé de Las Casas and the African Slave Trade', *History Compass*, 7.6 (2009), pp. 1526–41.

12   'Letter from Columbus to Luis de Santangel', in Julius E. Olson and Edward Gaylord Bourne (eds), *The Northmen, Columbus and Cabot, 985–1503* (New York, 1906), p. 270; Reséndez, *Other Slavery*, pp. 24–5; Forbes, *Africans and Native Americans*, p. 28; Bartolomé de Las Casas, *Historia de Las Indias* (Madrid, 1875), Vol. II, p. 323.

13   Samuel M. Wilson, *Hispaniola: Caribbean Chiefdoms in the Age of Columbus* (Tuscaloosa, 1990), p. 114; Reséndez, *Other Slavery*, p. 28; José R. Oliver, *Caciques and Cemí Idols: The Web Spun by Taíno Rulers between Hispaniola and Puerto Rico* (Alabama, 2009), p. 36; Erin Stone, 'Chasing "Caribs": Defining Zones of Legal Indigenous Enslavement in the Circum-Caribbean, 1493–1542', in Jeff Fynn-Paul and Damian Alan Pargas (eds), *Slaving Zones: Cultural Identities, Ideologies and Institutions in the evolution of global slavery* (Leiden, 2018), p. 130.

14   Pope Alexander VI, 'Inter Caetera: Division of the Undiscovered World Between Spain and Portugal' (1493), https://tinyurl.com/y6ezttd5.

15   AGI, Justicia, 1007, n. 1, r. 1.

16   AGI, Justicia, 741, n. 3; Esteban Mira Caballos, *Indios y mestizos americanos en la España del siglo xvi* (Madrid, 2000), pp. 62–6.

17   Reséndez, *Other Slavery*, p. 324; Franco Silva, 'El Indigena Americano en el Mercado de Esclavos', pp. 25–36. Leila Blackbird's ongoing research suggests an even higher figure in practice: Leila K. Blackbird, 'Entwined Threads of Red and Black: The Hidden History of Indigenous Enslavement in Louisiana, 1699–1824' (MA thesis, University of New Orleans, 2018), pp. 70–72.

18   Van Deusen, *Global Indios*, p. 2. Jace Weaver estimates that approximately 600,000 Indigenous enslaved people experienced 'blue water transshipment' (including to the Caribbean) but I have been unable to verify so high a figure: Jace Weaver, *The Red Atlantic: American Indigenes and the Making of the Modern World, 1000–1927* (Chapel Hill, 2014), pp. 17–18.

19   Though this is doubtless a significant underestimate, 1501–1600 shows

277,605 embarked enslaved people in *The Trans-Atlantic Slave Trade Database*, https://tinyurl.com/2p85eewj.

20 The Spanish Crown presented consistent opposition to the enslavement of Indigenous Americans from as early as 1500 when Queen Isabel (having already suspended the sale of imported Indigenous slaves in 1495) prohibited the enslavement of the Crown's American and Canarian subjects and vassals: Esteban Mira Caballos, 'Indios Americanos en el Reino de Castilla, 1492–1550', *Temas Americanistas* 14 (1998), pp. 2–3; Van Deusen, *Global Indios*, esp. pp. 114–18. Despite a genuine desire to free 'illegal' *indios* who were enslaved (demonstrated by the Crown's record of inspections, which resulted in the freeing of hundreds of *indios* in Spain)' Spanish prohibitions of slavery were patchy, often contradictory and difficult to enforce. Work on *indio* bondage in the Iberian peninsula includes: Franco Silva, 'El Indigena Americano en el Mercado de Esclavos', pp. 25–36; Esteban Mira Caballos, 'De Esclavos a Siervos: Amerindios en España tras las Leyes Nuevas de 1542', *Revista de Historia de América*, 140 (2009), pp. 95–109.

21 Forbes, *Africans and Native Americans*, p. 28; Las Casas, *Historia de Las Indias*, Vol. II, p. 46; Mira Caballos, *Indios y mestizos*, passim.

22 Reséndez, *The Other Slavery*, pp. 24–5; Anderson-Córdova, *Surviving Spanish Conquest*, p. 31.

23 Clements R. Markham (trans. and ed.), *The Letters of Amerigo Vespucci and Other Documents Illustrative of His Career* (New York, 1894), pp. 33–4. There is some disagreement about whether the number of enslaved people is 232 or 222, so I have followed the majority. Martin Dugard, *The Last Voyage of Columbus* (New York, 2005), p. 85.

24 Antonio de Herrera y Tordesillas, *Historia general de los hechos de los castellanos en las islas i tierra firme del mar oceano* (Madrid, 1730), decade 1, book IV, ch. II, p. 101 and ch. VI, p. 107; Archivo General de Simancas, CCA,CED,5,161,3.

25 For a remarkable chronology of the legal contortions of the Crown on the Indigenous slave trade 1495–1547 see Anderson-Córdova, *Surviving Spanish Conquest*, pp. 171–84.

26 Van Deusen, *Global Indios*, p. 3; Jose Antonio Saco, *Historia de la Esclavitud*, ed. Eduardo Torres-Cuevas (Havana, 2006), Vol. VI, p. 70; Erin Woodruff Stone, *Captives of Conquest: Slavery in the Early Modern Spanish Caribbean* (Philadelphia, 2021), pp. 34–9.

27 Alida C. Metcalf, 'The Entradas of Bahia of the Sixteenth Century', *The Americas*, 61.3 (2005), p. 375, n. 9; John Hemming, *Red Gold: the conquest of the Brazilian Indians* (Cambridge, Mass., 1970), pp. 530–31.

28 Damiáo de Goes, *Chronica Do Senhor Rey D. Manoel* . . . [post 1558], f.

35v, Arquivo Nacional Torre Do Tombo, PT/TT/CRN/20, https://tinyurl.com/2p89vr85.

29   Hélio A. Cristóforo, '"A Nova Gazeta da Terra do Brasil". Estudio Crítico', *Revista de História*, 17.36 (1958), p. 421; Diego García, *Primer Descubridor del Rio de la Plata, por Manuel Ricardo Trelles* (Buenos Aires, 1879), p. 35.

30   Alida C. Metcalf, *Go-betweens and the Colonization of Brazil: 1500–1600* (Austin, 2013), p. 62. This calculation (p. 35), along with information about many other early slaving voyages, can be found in Forbes, *Africans and Native Americans*, pp. 28–64; Afonso Arinos de Melo Franco, *O índio Brasileiro e a Revolução Francesa* (Brasília, 1976), pp. 36–7; Francisco Adolfo de Varnhagen, *História geral do Brazil antes da sua Separaçao e independencia de Portugal* (Rio de Janeiro, 1877), Vol. 1, p. 105.

31   Hemming, *Red Gold*, pp. 10, 530; Arinos de Melo Franco, *O índio Brasileiro*, pp. 41–2; Juliana Barr, 'From Captives to Slaves: Commodifying Indian Women in the Borderlands', *Journal of American History*, 92.1 (2005), pp. 19–46.

32   Michele da Cuneo, 'Letter to Gerolamo Annari, 15 October 1495', in Geoffrey Symcox and Luciano Formisano (eds), *Italian Reports on America 1493–1522: Accounts By Contemporary Observers* (Turnhout, 2002), p. 52.

32   William D. Phillips, Jr., *Slavery in Medieval and Early Modern Iberia* (Philadelphia, 2014), pp. 68–9.

33   Stefan Halikowski Smith, 'Lisbon in the sixteenth century: decoding the *Chafariz d'el Rei*', *Race & Class*, 60.2 (2018), pp. 63–81.

34   'Letter from Pietro Pasqualigo to his Brothers' (1501), in Clements R. Markham (trans. and ed.), *The Journal of Christopher Columbus (During His First Voyage, 1492–93) and Documents Relating to the Voyages of John Cabot and Gaspar Corte Real* (Farnham, 2010), p. 237; A. C. de C. M. Saunders, *A Social History of Black Slaves and Freedmen in Portugal 1441–1555* (Cambridge, 1982), pp. 20–23; Annette Kolodny, *In Search of First Contact: The Vikings of Vinland, the Peoples of the Dawnland, and the Anglo-American Anxiety of Discovery* (Durham, 2012), p. 278.

35   On English and French enslavement of Indigenous peoples see: Brett Rushforth, *Bonds of Alliance: Indigenous and Atlantic Slaveries in New France* (Chapel Hill, N.C., 2012); and Alan Gallay, *The Indian Slave Trade: The Rise of the English Empire in the American South, 1670–1717* (New Haven, Conn., 2002).

36   'Las Casas on the Alleged First Voyage of Amerigo Vespucci', in Markham, *The Letters of Amerigo Vespucci*, p. 95.

37   On the inspection see AGI, Justicia, 741, n. 3. For examples of appeals see Justicia, 908, n. 1; Justicia, 1178, n. 4; Justicia, 1162, n. 6, r. 2. For

many more cases and a wonderfully detailed analysis of individuals and structures involved in Indigenous petitions for freedom see van Deusen, *Global Indios, passim*. For the ways in which the notarial record constructs narratives see Kathryn Burns, *Into the Archive: Writing and Power in Colonial Peru* (Durham, 2010).

38 AGI, Justicia, 1037, n. 6, r. 3; Indiferente, 1964, l. 11, ff. 260r-260v. For more on Francisco and Juana see Van Deusen, *Global Indios*, pp. 132–3. Van Deusen states that they had two children, but the records I have seen only reference a daughter.

39 David S. Jones, 'Virgin Soils Revisited', *WMQ*, 60.4 (2003), pp. 703–42; Paul Kelton, *Epidemics and Enslavement: Biological Catastrophe in the Native Southeast, 1492–1715* (Lincoln, 2007); Donald A. Grinde Jr., 'Teaching American Indian History: A Native American Voice', *Perspectives*, 32 (September 1994), https://tinyurl.com/28cz4mmu.

40 Esteban Mira Caballos, 'Indios y mestizos en la España moderna', pp. 179–98.

41 Manuel Lucena Salmoral, 'El carimbo de los indios esclavos', *EHSEA*, 14 (1997), p. 125; Van Deusen, *Global Indios*, pp. 134–5.

42 Van Deusen, *Global Indios*, pp. 139–40. The case of Barbola and her mother is covered in detail throughout the book.

43 When Martín testified in another case in 1542, he said he was 28, which means he would have been born in 1514: Van Deusen, *Global Indios*, p. 268, n. 60. Unless specified, all references to Martín's case below are from AGI, Justicia, 1007, n. 1, r. 1.

44 Rosemary A. Joyce, 'Girling the Girl and Boying the Boy: The Production of Adulthood in Ancient Mesoamerica', *World Archaeology*, 31.3 (2000), pp. 477–8; *Florentine Codex*, 2: 37: 159–66.

45 Juan Manuel Pérez Zevallas, 'The Ethnohistory of the Huasteca', in Alan R. Sandstrom and E. Hugo García Valencía (eds), *Native Peoples of the Gulf Coast of Mexico* (Tucson, 2005), pp. 66–72.

46 AGI, Justicia, 716, n. 4. I have removed repeated references to 'the aforementioned' for ease of reading. On Juan de Cárdenas, in footnote, see: AGI, Indiferente, 420, l. 8, ff. 253v-255r.

47 Camilla Townsend, 'Slavery in Precontact America', in Craig Perry et al. (eds), *The Cambridge World History of Slavery*, Vol. 2 (Cambridge, 2021), pp. 553–70; Reséndez, *The Other Slavery*, p. 9.

48 Jack Forbes, *Africans and Native Americans: The Language of Race and the Evolution of Red-Black Peoples* (Urbana, 1993), pp. 26–35.

49 AGI, Justicia, 1013, n. 2, r. 4. Nancy Van Deusen, 'Seeing *Indios* in Sixteenth-Century Castile', *WMQ*, 69.2 (2012), pp. 205–34.

50 Van Deusen, *Global Indios, passim*, but especially pp. 41–7.

51 AGI, Justicia, 1024, n.1.

Chapter 2: Go-Betweens

1   Stephen Greenblatt, *Learning to Curse: Essays in Early Modern Culture* (New York, 1990), pp. 37–8.

2   Richard Eden's 1555 translation of Peter Martyr's *Decades*, intended to promote English exploration in the Americas, also sees translation as a priority. The book not only includes a glossary of 'The Indian language' (including '*canoa*, a boat of bark', which quickly slipped into European languages) but also describes how Columbus took with him to Spain ten Taíno people 'to lerne the Spanish tongue, to the intent to vse them afterward for interpretours'. Peter Martyr of Angleria, *The decades of the new worlde or west India* . . . trans. Richard Eden (London, 1555), p. 4.

3   Edward Augustus Kendall, *Travels through the Northern Parts of the United States in the Years 1807 to 1808* (New York, 1809), Vol. II, p. 230. According to William S. Simmons this refers to the Taunton River: *Spirit of the New England Tribes: Indian History and Folklore* (Hanover, 1986), p. 70.

4   Angelo Trevisan, 'Libretto about All of the Spanish Sovereigns' Navigations to the Newly Discovered Islands and Lands' (1504), in Symcox et al. (eds), *Italian Reports on America*, Vol. 12, p. 92.

5   Silke Jansen, 'Spanish Anthroponomy from an Ecological Linguistic Perspective: the Antillean Society in the Early Sixteenth Century', in Ralph Ludwig, Peter Mühllhäuser and Steve Pagel (eds), *Linguistic Ecology and Language Contact* (Cambridge, 2018), p. 156.

6   Martyr d'Anghera, *De Orbe Novo*, Vol. 2, pp. 95, 106; István Szászdi León-Borja, 'Las élites de los cristianos nuevos: Alianzo y vasallaje en la expansion atlántica (1485–1520)', *Jahrbuch für Geschichte Lateinamerikas*, 30 (1999), p. 30.

7   AGI, Indiferente, 418, l. 1, ff. 171v–172r.

8   It is not certain that the Diego Colón who granted these rights was the same Diego who travelled with Columbus, but I agree with Mira Caballos and others that the evidence is compelling: Mira Caballos, 'Caciques guatiaos', pp. 7–16. See also León-Borja, 'Las élites de los cristianos nuevos', p. 30.

9   Columbus's account of his second voyage says that he 'put ashore one of the four Indians that I had taken from there last year, who had not died as the others from smallpox on the departure from Cádiz'. This suggests that smallpox was the cause of death of several of the earliest travellers, and was potentially present in the Caribbean before 1518. Noble David

Cook, 'Sickness, Starvation, and Death in Early Hispaniola', *Journal of Interdisciplinary History*, 32.3 (2002), pp. 363–5.

10   The precise identity of *cocozliztli* has caused many squabbles between historians and epidemiologists about the causes of the sixteenth-century epidemics. The first time the word is used it relates to the 1518 outbreak, which was almost certainly smallpox, but later it seems to refer to general 'pestilence'. Many scholars have favoured some form of haemorrhagic fever as the epidemic cause, but some compelling recent research suggests the devastating *cocoliztli* pandemic of 1545 may have been a form of enteric fever caused by a rare strain of salmonella. See Åshild J. Vågene et al., '*Salmonella enterica* genomes from victims of a major sixteenth-century epidemic in Mexico', *Nature: Ecology and Evolution*, 2 (2018), pp. 520–28. On haemorrhagic fever see Rodolfo Acuna-Soto, Leticia Calderon Romero and James H. Maguire, 'Large epidemics of hemorrhagic fevers in Mexico 1545–1815', *American Journal of Tropical Medicine and Hygiene*, 1 (2000), pp. 733–9.

11   Research into genetics is revolutionising the way we understand Indigenous populations and historic epidemics, allowing us to trace movements of people and detect descendants of communities long claimed to be 'extinct'. See, for example, Maria A. Nieves-Colón et al., 'Ancient DNA Reconstructs the Genetic Legacies of Precontact Puerto Rico Communities', *Molecular Biology and Evolution*, 37.3 (2020), pp. 611–26; and Hannes Schroeder et al., 'Origins and genetic legacies of the Caribbean Taino', *PNAS*, 115.10 (2019), pp. 2341–6. For a sensitive discussion of the ways in which genetics and archaeology can (and cannot) help us to understand the deep history of the Indigenous peoples of the Americas see Jennifer Raff, *Origin: A Genetic History of the Americas* (New York, 2022).

12   *The Voyages of Jacques Cartier*, ed. Ramsay Cook (Toronto, 1993), p. 96.

13   *The Voyages of Jacques Cartier*, pp. 27, 50, 52–4, 70, 82–7, 96, 98, 125, 134, xxxix; *Ordonnances des intendants et arrêts portant reglements du conseil superieur de Québec . . .* (Quebec, 1806), Vol. II, p. 2.

14   AGI, Indiferente, 419, l. 6, ff. 493v-494r. Esteban Mira Caballos, 'La educación de indios y mestizos antillanos en la primera mitad del siglo XVI', *Revista Complutense de Historia de América*, 25 (1999), p. 61.

15   AGI, Indiferente, 419, l. 4, f. 70v; Vasco de Puga, *Prouisiónes cédulas Instruciones de su Magestad: ordenáças y difútos y uenacia, pa la uena expedició de los negocios y administració d justicia: y gouernació dsta nueva España: y pa el vué tratamiéto y conseruación de los yndios, dende el año de 1525. Hasta este presente de. 63* (Mexico City, 1563), f. 21.

16   Convento de Santo Domingo: AGI, Indiferente, 421, l. 12, ff. 211r-211v; Indiferente, 1952, l. 1, ff. 27v-28r; Indiferente, 1961, l. 2, ff. 15v-16.

Monasterio de Santa María de Duenas: Indiferente, 1961, l. 2, f. 47;
Indiferente, 1961, l. 2, f. 83. Monasterio de Las Cuevas: Indiferente, 421,
l. 12, f. 211v(3). Convento de San Francisco: Indiferente, 421, l. 12, ff.
211r–211v; Indiferente, 422, l. 15, f. 213r; AGI, Indiferente, 1961, l. 2, f. 16;
Indiferente, 1961, l. 2, f. 49.

17 AGI, Indiferente, 1961, l. 2, ff. 182v-184; Fernão Cardim, *Tratados da Terra
de Gente do Brasil*, ed. Rodolpho Garcia (Rio de Janeiro, 1925), p. 292.

18 Boris Jeanne, 'México-Madrid-Roma, un eje desconocido del siglo XVI
para un studio de las relaciones directas entre Roma y Nueva España
en la época de la contrarreforma (1568-1594)', in Magdalena Garrido
Caballero and Gabriela Vallejo Cervantes (eds), *De la monarquía
hispánica de la Unión Europea: relaciones internacionales, comercio e
imaginarios colectivos* (Murcia, 2013), pp. 19–39; Sabine Hyland, *The Jesuit
and the Incas: The Extraordinary Life of Blas Valera* (Michigan, 2003).

19 AGI, Indiferente, 1952, l. 1, ff. 26v-27v, 89v-91r; Indiferente, 1961, l. 2, ff.
16v-17.

20 From Spain's official tourism website: https://tinyurl.com/yyn5f6zp.

21 The 'two worlds' framework has been fairly critiqued as imposing a false
binary that assumes Indigenous identity is opposed to Europeanness
and to concepts such as 'modernity' and 'civility', rather than recognising
the existence of shared, and also more multiple, worlds: James Joseph
Buss and C. Joseph Genetin-Pilawa (eds), *Beyond Two Worlds: Critical
Conversations on Language and Power in Native North America* (Albany,
2014). Natalie Rothman has also made a convincing case that 'trans-
imperial' brokers operated in multiple and shifting worlds rather than
'positioned "in-between" a priori distinct societies': *Brokering Empire:
Trans-Imperial Subjects between Venice and Istanbul* (Ithaca, 2012), pp.
6–7. Nonetheless, while overly simplistic as a trope, such binaries had real
power in the colonial world, and profoundly affected the way in which
Native people, especially women, who were doubly 'Othered', experienced
liminal spaces.

22 Claudia Jane Rogers, '"The People from Heaven?" Reading Indigenous
responses to Europeans during moments of early encounter in the
Caribbean and Mesoamerica, c.1492–c.1585' (PhD thesis, University of
Leeds, 2018), especially p. 26. The concept of 'beachcombers' originates
with anthropologist Greg Dening: *Islands and Beaches: Discourse on a
Silent Land: Marquesas, 1774–1880* (Melbourne, 1980).

23 There is (rightly) a whole academic field dedicated to the study of
'go-betweens', intermediaries, cultural brokers and *nepantleras*, which
has produced rich work so vast that I cannot possibly do it justice in an
endnote.

24   Olive Patricia Dickason, *The Myth of the Savage and the Beginnings of French Colonialism in the Americas* (Edmonton, 1984), p. 211.

25   Scott Cave, 'Madalena: The Entangled History of One Indigenous Floridian Woman in the Atlantic World', *The Americas*, 74.2 (2017), pp. 171–200, quote from p. 175.

26   Felipe Fernández-Armesto, *Columbus on Himself* (Indianapolis, 2010), p. 106.

27   Sarmiento (1572), quoted in Olivia Harris, '"The Coming of the White People": Reflections on the Mythologisation of History in Latin America', *Bulletin of Latin American Research*, 14.1 (1995), p. 13. The claim of Cook's divinity was most famously made by Marshall Sahlins, and hotly contested by Gananath Obeyesekere. For the progress of their infamous, and at times rather personal, argument see: Marshall Sahlins, *Islands of History* (Chicago, 1985); Gananath Obeyesekere, *The Apotheosis of Captain Cook: European Mythmaking in the Pacific* (Princeton, 1992); and Marshall Sahlins, *What 'Natives' Think: About Captain Cook, For Example* (Chicago, 1995).

28   Camilla Townsend, 'Burying the White Gods: New Perspectives on the Conquest of Mexico', *American Historical Review*, 108.1 (2003), pp. 659–86.

29   D. Hernando Alvarado Tezozomoc, *Crónica Mexicana* (Mexico City, 1987), pp. 684–5. An almost identical account appears in Fray Diego Durán, *The History of the Indies of New Spain*, trans. and ed. Doris Heyden (Norman, 1994), pp. 495–6. Both Durán and Tezozomoc share much common material and are often believed to have relied heavily on the now lost *Crónica X*. Whatever their source, they share some confusion between the arrivals of Grijalva and Cortés. On feeding blood see *Florentine Codex*, 12: 8: 21.

30   For one account of Guerrero's remarkable life see Robert Calder, *A Hero for the Americas: The Legend of Gonzalo Guerrero* (Regina, Saskatchewan, 2017).

31   Díaz del Castillo, *The True History of the Conquest of New Spain*, Vol. 1, p. 152.

32   Camilla Townsend, *Malintzin's Choices: An Indian Woman in the Conquest of Mexico* (Albuquerque, 2006), pp. 171, 263–4 n. 40.

33   Díaz claimed 'Malinche' meant 'Marina's captain', but it is almost certainly a Hispanisation of 'Malintzin', which would have been hard for the Spanish to pronounce. Díaz del Castillo, *The True History of the Conquest of New Spain*, Vol. 1, p. 273.

34   Victoria Ríos Castaño, 'Fictionalising interpreters: traitors, lovers and liars in the conquest of America', *Linguistica Anteverpiensa*, 4 (2005), pp. 47–60.

35 Walter D. Mignolo wrote of a 'massive colonization of language' which began in the sixteenth century: 'On the Colonization of Amerindian Languages and Memories: Renaissance Theories of Writing and the Discontinuity of the Classical Tradition', *Comparative Studies in Society and History*, 34.2 (1992), pp. 301–33.

36 The *Oxford DNB*, which prides itself on providing biographies for the figures who shaped British history, dedicates an entire article to Hariot while relegating Manteo and Wanchese to one paragraph of a collective biography: J. J. Roche, 'Harriot, Thomas', *Oxford Dictionary of National Biography* (2004), https://doi.org/10.1093/ref:odnb/12379; Alden T. Vaughan, 'American Indians in Britain', *Oxford Dictionary of National Biography* (2004), https://doi.org/10.1093/ref:odnb/71116.

37 R. Holinshed, *Chronicles*, III (1587), p. 1369, from David Beers Quinn, *The Roanoke Voyages, 1584–1590: Documents to illustrate the English Voyages to North America under the Patent granted to Walter Raleigh in 1584*, Vol. 1 (London, 1952) p. 91; Richard Hakluyt, *The principal navigations, voyages traffiques & discoveries of the English nation*, III (1600), p. 251, in Quinn, *The Roanoke Voyages, 1584–1590*, Vol. 1, p. 116. Hakluyt's note was added to the printed text in 1600, so we do not know if it is original to the manuscript.

38 I have tracked back through the sources and find it difficult to verify specific claims about the status of Manteo and Wanchese. Scholars often claim that Manteo was a *wiroans* or *weroance*, an Algonquian word that literally means 'he is rich', but refers to a regional chief. See, for example, Alden Vaughan, 'Sir Walter Ralegh's Indian Interpreters, 1584–1618', *WMQ*, 59.2 (2002), p. 346. Michael Leroy Oberg makes what seems the most likely claim: that Manteo's mother may have been the *weroansqua* (leader) of the Croatans. Wanchese certainly seems to have been close to the Roanoke *weroance* Wingina: Michael Leroy Oberg, 'Between "Savage Man" and "Most Faithful Englishman": Manteo and the Early Anglo-Indian Exchange, 1584–1590', *Itinerario*, 24.2 (2000), pp. 146–69. The idea that both were 'high status' is commonplace, e.g. Michael Leroy Oberg, *The Head in Edward Nugent's Hand: Roanoke's Forgotten Indians* (Philadelphia, 2008), p. 50.

39 On the *weroance*'s brother Granganimeo's efforts to trade and establish friendly links with the English see 'Arthur Barlowe's Discourse of the First Voyage' (1584–5), in Quinn, *The Roanoke Voyages, 1584–1590*, pp. 98–105. For more on Indigenous ways of understanding the outsiders see Daniel Richter, *Facing east from Indian country: a Native history of early America* (Cambridge, Mass., 2003), esp. pp. 14–16.

40 Thomas Hariot, *A Briefe and True Report of the New Found Land of Virginia* (1588), ed. Paul Royster, *Electronic Texts in American Studies*, 20 (2007), p. 39, https://tinyurl.com/56nnb7fc.

41 V. von Klarwill (ed.), *Queen Elizabeth and some foreigners* (1928), p. 323, in Quinn, *The Roanoke Voyages, 1584–1590*, Vol. 1, p. 116.

42 On Carolinian Algonquin dress see Hariot, *A briefe and true report*, p. 34; and Christian F. Feest, 'North Carolina Algonquians', in *Handbook of North American Indians* (1978), Vol. 15, pp. 271–81.

43 During her reign, Elizabeth issued twelve detailed proclamations about what people could wear (more than twice as many as her father, Henry VIII): Susan J. Vincent, '"When I am in Good Habitt": Clothes in English Culture c.1550–c.1670' (PhD thesis, University of York, 2002), p. 159; 'Enforcing Statutes of Apparel', issued by Elizabeth I, Greenwich, 15 June 1574, from *Elizabethan Sumptuary Statutes*, https://tinyurl.com/2p96s3cn.

44 'Bill to Confirm Raleigh's Patent, as passed by the House of Commons' (December 1584) and 'The Case of the Cape Merchant, Thomas Harvey' (20 February 1591), in Quinn, *The Roanoke Voyages, 1584–1590*, Vol. 2, pp. 127, 232–3. Spelling modernised.

45 *Purchas His Pilgrimes. In Five Bookes . . .* Vol. 4 (London, 1625), p. 4283.

46 Frances F. Berdan, *Aztec Archaeology and Ethnohistory* (Cambridge, 2014), pp. 57–61.

47 *Purchas His Pilgrimes. In Five Bookes . . .* Vol. 4 (London, 1625), p. 4283.

48 Thrush, *Indigenous London*, p. 36.

49 'The letters patents, granted by the Queens Maiestie to M. Walter Ralegh now Knight, for the difcouering and planting of new lands and Countries', in Hakluyt, *The principal nauigations*, p. 243; 'Bill to Confirm Raleigh's Patent, as passed by the House of Commons', in Quinn, *The Roanoke Voyages, 1584–1590*, pp. 127–8. Language modernised.

50 Quinn, *The Roanoke Voyages, 1584–1590*, Vol. 1, pp. 178–9, n. 6; 'The Relation of Hernando de Altamirano' (June 1585), and 'Diego Hernández de Quiñones to Philip II' (12/22 June 1585), in Quinn, *The Roanoke Voyages, 1584–1590*, Vol. 2, pp. 741, 735.

51 The word 'Wococon' probably originally came from an Algonquian word meaning 'enclosed place' or 'fort', which suggests that there was a stockaded Indigenous village in the area. Quinn, *The Roanoke Voyages, 1584–1590*, Vol. 2, p. 867, n. 61; 'The Tiger Journal of the 1585 Voyage', in Quinn, *The Roanoke Voyages, 1584–1590*, Vol. 1, p. 189. Spelling modernised.

52 'Ralph Lane to Sir Francis Walsingham, 12 August 1585' and 'The Tiger Journal of the 1585 Voyage', in Quinn, *The Roanoke Voyages, 1584–1590*, Vol. 1, pp. 201, 189. Spelling in the former modernised.

53 Hariot, *A brief and true report*, p. 38; 'A Relation of the Indian War by
    Mr Easton, of Rhode Island, 1675', ed. Paul Royster, *Electronic Texts in
    American Studies*, 33 (2006), p. 10, https://tinyurl.com/je3cctcj; Karen
    Ordahl Kupperman, *Indians and English: Facing Off in Early America*
    (New York, 2000), p. 3.

54 'Ralph Lane's Discourse on the First Colony' (17 August 1585–18 June
    1586), in Quinn, *The Roanoke Voyages, 1584–1590*, Vol. 1, p. 280. Indig-
    enous authority structures are extremely difficult to ascertain. Here I
    follow Oberg, *The Head in Edward Nugent's Hand*, pp. 2–8.

55 'John White's narrative of the 1590 voyage to Virginia', in Quinn, *The
    Roanoke Voyages, 1584–1590*, Vol. 1, p. 602.

56 'Ralph Lane's Discourse on the First Colony', and 'John White's Narrative',
    in Quinn, *The Roanoke Voyages, 1584–1590*, Vol. 1 (London, 1952), pp. 271,
    530.

57 Brandon Fullam, *Manteo and the Algonquians of the Roanoke Voyages*
    (Jefferson, NC, 2020), p. 43.

58 'John White's Narrative', in Quinn, *The Roanoke Voyages, 1584–1590*, Vol.
    1, p. 531.

59 Quinn, *The Roanoke Voyages, 1584–1590*, Vol. 1, p. 543.

60 'The Relation of Pedro Diaz', in Quinn, *The Roanoke Voyages, 1584–1590*,
    Vol. 1, p. 790.

61 'Entries in the Bideford Parish Register', in Quinn, *The Roanoke Voyages,
    1584–1590*, Vol. 1, p. 495. Spelling lightly modernised.

62 Alden T. Vaughan, *Transatlantic Encounters: American Indians in Britain,
    1500–1776* (Cambridge, 2006), pp. 30–33; Walter Ralegh, *Discoverie of the
    Large, Rich and Bevvtifvl Empire of Gviana . . .* (London, 1596), pp. 7, 52,
    62, 74, 80; Lawrence Kemys, *A Relation of the Second Voyage to Guiana*
    (London, 1596), B2r, C3r; Thomas Masham, 'The third voyage set forth
    by Sir Walter Ralegh to Guiana, with a pinesse called *The Watte*, in the
    yeere 1596', in Hakluyt, *The principal nauigations*, p. 694. Masham also
    mentions a 'Leonard of Cawe', who is likely Leonard Ragapo. Vaughan,
    Transatlantic Encounters, pp. 32–3; 'Lady Ralegh to Secretary Sir R.
    Cecil' (July 1596), in Edward Edwards, *The Life of Sir Walter Ralegh . . .*
    (London, 1868), Vol II, p. 402.

63 'Captain Charles Leigh his voyage to Guiana and plantation there', in
    Purchas His Pilgrimes. In Five Bookes . . . Vol. 4 (London, 1625), pp.
    1250–51; 'Captaine Charles Leighs Letter to Sir Olave Leigh his Brother',
    in *Purchas His Pilgrimes. In Five Bookes . . .* Vol. 4 (London, 1625), pp.
    1253–5.

64 Unless otherwise stated, all references in this section are from Robert
    Harcourt, *The Relation of a Voyage to Gviana, Defscribing the Climate,*

Situation, Fertilitie, & Commodities of that Country: Together with the Manner and Cuftomes of the People (London, [1619] 1626), pp. 7, 9–12, 15–16, 18–20, 25–7, 33, 53, 59–60. Spelling lightly modernised.

65   'Cecil Papers: August 1604, 1–10', in *Calendar of the Cecil Papers in Hatfield House: Volume 16, 1604*, ed. M. S. Giuseppi (London, 1933), pp. 195–221, *British History Online*, https://tinyurl.com/bdcvta3s.

66   John Stowe, *Annales, or a generall chronicle of England* (London, 1632), p. 815.

67   *Orders thought meete by his Maiestie and his Priuie Counsell, to be executed throughout the Counties of this Realme, in Such Townes, Villages, and other places, as are, or may be hereafter infected with the Plague, for the stay of further increase of the same . . .* (London, 1603).

68   'Sir Walter Ralegh's Journal of his Second Voyage to Guiana', in W. Ralegh, *The Discovery of the Large, Rich, and Beautiful Empire of Guiana . . .* ed. Robert H. Schomburgk (New York, 1848), pp. 197–200. The phrasing offers a slim possibility that 'Harry' and 'the *cacique*' are two different people, and that Ralegh therefore had three Indigenous acquaintances in the region, but it is very unlikely. Ralegh to Winwood, 21 March 1618, quoted in Vaughan, *Transatlantic Encounters*, p. 37.

69   Anna Brickhouse, *The Unsettlement of America: Translation, Interpretation, and the Story of Don Luis de Velasco, 1560–1945* (Oxford, 2015), p. 28.

70   James Lockhart, *The Men of Cajamarca: A Social and Biographical Study of the First Conquerors of Peru* (Austin, 1972), pp. 448–55.

Chapter 3: Kith and Kin

1   Barbara Anne Ganson, *The Guaraní Under Spanish Rule in the Río de la Plata* (Stanford, 2003), p. 18.

2   For the primary source and fascinating details and commentary on Essomericq see: Leyla Perrone-Moisés, *Le Voyage de Gonneville (1503–1505) & la découverte de la Normandie par les Indiens du Brésil*, trans. Ariane Witkowski (Paris, 1995), pp. 22–31.

3   Jean Leblond, 'L'abbé Paulmier descendant d'un étranger des *Terres australes*? Notes sur la généalogie de l'abbé, la taxation des étrangers et la datation de la relation de voyage de Gonneville de 1505', *Australian Journal of French Studies*, 50.1 (2013), pp. 35–49.

4   See Jacques Lévêque de Pontharouart, *Paulmier de Gonneville: son voyage imaginaire* (Beauval en Caux, 2000). Though the book has many flaws, it nonetheless left important doubts. For an introduction to the debates

see the *AJFS* special edition, especially Margaret Sankey, 'The Abbé Jean Paulmier and French Missions in the *Terres australes*: Myth and History', *Australian Journal of French Studies*, 50.1 (2013), pp. 3–15. I tend, however, to follow Christophe Maneuvrier's line: 'Paulmier de Gonneville et le Portugal: un navigateur normand dans la première mondialisation', *Revista de História da Sociedade e da Cultura*, 16 (2016), pp. 95–109.

5   Dorothée de Linares, *Sur les traces d'Essomericq*, https://essomericq.com/; Leia Também, 'Em livro, descendente de índio alçado à burguesia na França refaz passos do parente', *Bem Paraná*, 27 October 2018, https://tinyurl.com/29fzzw7z; 'Essoméric: Un Prince Indien à Courtonne', *Courtonne-La-Meurdrac: Au Coeur de Pays d'Auge*, https://tinyurl.com/2p9cmnka.

6   *Le Discours de la Navigation de Jean et Raoul Parmentier de Dieppe: Voyage à Sumatra en 1529. Description de l'isle de Sainct-Domingo* (Paris, 1883), pp. 3, 50; *André Thevet's North America: A Sixteenth-Century View*, ed. and trans. Roger Schlesinger and Arthur P. Stabler (Kingston, 1986), p. 9; *The Voyages of Jacques Cartier*, pp. 27, 50, 52–4, 70, 82–7, 96, 98, 125, 134, xxxix.

7   Arinos de Melo Franco, *O índio Brasileiro*, p. 49; Jean de Léry, *History of a Voyage to the Land of Brazil, Otherwise Called America . . .* (Berkeley, 1992), trans. Janet Whatley, pp. 130–31.

8   Simão de Vasconcelos, *Crônica de la Companhia de Jesus*, quote and other details from Lisa Voight, who has kindly granted permission to reproduce her translation: *Writing Captivity in the Early Modern Atlantic: Circulations of Knowledge and Authority in the Iberial and English Imperial Worlds* (Chapel Hill, 2009), pp. 224–5.

9   Two dates appear in the scholarship, with many prominent histories claiming her voyage was in the late 1540s. Given the baptismal certificate, and the fact Pero Fernandes Sardinha (who studied in Paris in the 1520s and was in India and Portugal for most of the 1540s) is supposed to have seen the couple in France, I can only think this originates from a misreading of Salvador, who mentions the voyage as part of a backstory to some events involving Caramuru as occurring 'in the same year [1549]'. Frei Vincente do Salvador, *Historia do Brasil* (S. Paulo, 1918), p. 149.

10   Voight, *Writing Captivity in the Early Modern Atlantic*, p. 243, n. 39; Pedro Calmon, *História da fundacão da Bahia* (Bahia, 1949), p. 50, n. 5.

11   David Treece, 'Caramuru the Myth: Conquest and Conciliation', *Ibero-amerikanisches Archiv* (1984), 10.2, pp. 154–5; The baptismal record, approached from a purely French point of view, has been incorrectly used to argue that the dates of Cartier's first voyages were mistaken, or

that he travelled to Brazil before his better-known expedition to Canada, returning with a young girl. Olga Obry, *Catherine du Brésil: Filleule de Saint-Malo* (Paris, 1953), pp. 164–5; James P. Baxter, *A memoir of Jacques Cartier* (New York, 1906), p. 14, n. 1.

12   Vincente do Salvador, *Historia do Brasil*, pp. 149–50.

13   For this, and a rare summary in English of Paraguaçu's life see Joan Meznar, 'Catarina Álvares Paraguaçu (1510s–1582): Indian Visionary in Brazil and France', in Karen Racine and Beatriz G. Mamigonian (eds), *The Human Tradition in the Atlantic World, 1500–1850* (Lanham, 2010), pp. 1–12.

14   Santa Rita Durão, *Caramuru: Poema Épico do Descubrimiento da Bahia* (Lisbon, 1781), *Library of Congress Global Gateway*, https://tinyurl.com/2p9efu3u.

15   Benito Cao, 'White Hegemony in the Land of Carnival: The Apparent Paradox of Racism and Hybridity in Brazil' (PhD thesis, University of Adelaide, 2008), pp. 66–74.

16   Christovão de Avila, *Brasões de Armas: Armorial Histórico da Casa de Garcia d'Ávila* (Rio de Janeiro, 2014), pp. 24–8; Maria Aparecida Schumaher, *Dicionário mulheres do Brasil: De 1500 até a actualidade* (Rio de Janeiro, 2000), no page numbers online.

17   'Missa lembra valor histórico da índia Catarina Paraguaçu', *Correio da Bahia*, 27 January 1999, https://tinyurl.com/mryscvkc; Karla Mendes, 'In Rio de Janeiro, Indigenous people fight to undo centuries of erasure', *Mongabay*, 31 June 2021, https://tinyurl.com/mr3adbs3. Guaibimpará's will is held in the archives of the Mosteiro de São Bento de Bahia in Salvador. The records of the monastery reference her repeatedly – usually under the name 'Catherina Álvares' or 'Catherina Alvarez Caramurú'. Here petitioning for the completion of a bequest of some lands to her: Célia Marques Telles (ed.), *Coleçâo Livros Do Tombo Do Mosteiro de São Bento da Bahia: Editando 430 anos de história, Livro III do Tombo: Ediçâo semidiplomática* (2012), ff. 12v–14r, http://saobento.org/livrosdotombo/. On the bequest of her lands and other matters see also: ff. 25v–32v, 35r, 38r–43r.

18   Covadonga Lamar Prieto, 'El Mestizo', in Rebecca M. Seaman, *Conflict in the Early Americas: An Encyclopaedia of the Spanish Empire's Aztec, Incan and Mayan Conquests* (Santa Barbara, 2013), p. 131.

19   Anna Lanyon, *The New World of Martín Cortés* (Crow's Nest, New South Wales, 2003), p. 65. Lanyon's engrossing book is the best history of Martín's life in English, though some of the details have been superseded by María del Carmen Martínez Martínez, *Martín Cortés: Pasos recuperados (1532–1562)* (León, 2018).

20 Archivo Histórico Nacional, Madrid, OM-CABALLEROS_SANTIAGO, EXP. 2167; 'Expediente de Martín Cortés, niño de siete años, hijo de Hernán Cortés y de la india Doña Marina. Toledo, 19 Julio, 1529', *Boletín de la Real Academia de la Historia*, 21 (1892), pp. 199–202.

21 Lanyon, *The New World of Martín Cortés*, pp. 45–6; Letter to Francisco Nuñez, 20 June 1533, quoted in Townsend, *Fifth Sun*, p. 157.

22 Scholars (including Lanyon) assumed that Martín remained in Spain until 1562, until María del Carmen Martínez Martínez discovered an earlier visit: Townsend, *Fifth Sun*, p. 272, n. 6. Although only the younger Martín is recorded, the scholarly consensus is that it is highly unlikely the younger brother would have travelled without the elder: Lanyon, *The New World of Martín Cortés*, p. 65; *The Chronicle of Queen Jane, and of Two Years of Queen Mary, and especially of the Rebellion of Sir Thomas Wyat. Written by a resident in the Tower of London*, ed. John Gough Nichols (London 1850), p. 81. Spelling modernised.

23 José Carlos de la Puente Luna, *Andean Cosmopolitans: Seeking Justice and Reward at the Spanish Royal Court* (Austin, 2018), p. 132.

24 Heather Dalton, *Merchants and Explorers: Roger Barlow, Sebastian Cabot, and Networks of Atlantic Exchange 1500–1800* (Oxford, 2016), pp. 115–16; Arinos de Melo Franco, *O Índio brasileiro*, p. 43; João Batista de Castro Júnior, 'Língua Portuguesa, Língua Tupi e Língua Geral: Jesuítas, Colonos e Índios em São Paulo de Piratininga: O Que Entendiam, o Que Practicavam, o Que Conversavam' (PhD thesis, Universidade Federal da Bahia, Salvador, 2011), pp. 83–4, inc. n. 190. Quote by Antonio Ponce.

25 Richard Godbeer, *Sexual Revolution in Early America* (Baltimore, 2002), pp. 158–66.

26 In a survey of marriages in the Mexican province of Puebla in 1534, 20 out of 65 married Spanish men were married to 'Indian women': Pedro Carrasco, 'Indian-Spanish Marriages in the First Century of the Colony', in Susan Schroeder, Stephanie Wood, Robert Stephen Haskett (eds), *Indian Women of Early Mexico* (Norman, 1999), p. 88.

27 Royal women were a notable exception: the daughters of Moctezuma were extremely desirable marriage partners, legitimising Spanish authority by blending their heritage with that of the invaders.

28 This compelling story was uncovered by Nancy van Deusen: 'Passing in sixteenth-century Castile', *Colonial Latin American Review*, 26.1 (2017), pp. 85–103.

29 Archivo de la Real Chancellería, Valladolid, Registro de Ejecutorias, caja 1192, 44; Van Deusen, *Global Indios*, pp. 95–6; Nancy van Deusen, 'The Intimacies of Bondage: Female Indigenous Servants and Slaves and Their Spanish Masters, 1492–1555', *Journal of Women's History*, 24.1 (2012), pp. 17–18.

30   AGI, Indiferente, 1963, l. 7, ff. 217v-218r. Such relationships were not
     uncommon. For example, in 1536, another *india*, Juana, brought a young
     Spanish girl to her family in Spain: AGI, Indiferente, 1962, l. 5, ff. 44r-44v.
     For cases of abuse see, for example, Indiferente, 1963, l. 4, f. 27; Justicia,
     1162, n. 6, r. 2.

31   Van Deusen, 'The Intimacies of Bondage', pp. 22, 24–7; *Recopilación de las
     Leyes de las Indias* (Madrid, 1680), Book 6, Title 1, Ley 8. At least fifteen
     licences were also granted to bring *mestizo* children to the peninsula
     in the period 1515–24. Esteban Mira Caballos, *Las Antillas Mayores,
     1492–1550: ensayos y documentos* (Madrid, 2000), p. 292. See also Juan
     Gil, 'Los primeros mestizos indios en España: Una voz ausente', in Berta
     Ares Queija and Serge Gruzinski (eds), *Entre dos mundos: Fronteras
     Culturales y Agentes Mediadores* (Seville, 1997), pp. 15–36.

32   Mira Caballos, *Indios y mestizos*, p. 93.

33   AGI, Justicia, 741, n. 3, im. 18, 30–35.

34   Esteban Mira Caballos, 'Dos Bautizas de Indias en Carmona (1504)',
     El Descubrimiento de los Otros, https://tinyurl.com/u4w9rkmm; AGI,
     Justicia, 908, n. 1; van Deusen, *Global Indios*, pp. 34–60.

35   Lanyon, *The New World of Martín Cortés*, pp. 213–14, 238.

36   Anastasia Kalyuta, 'Isabel de Moctezuma: the emperor's favourite
     daughter?', *Mexicolore*, https://tinyurl.com/5n95secv.

Chapter 4: The Stuff of Life

1   Christopher Columbus, *Santangel letter*, King's Digital Lab, https://
     tinyurl.com/y8tezyvx. I am indebted to Barry Ife for his permission to
     reproduce this quotation, which can also be found in B. W. Ife, *Letters
     from America: Columbus's First Accounts of the 1492 Voyage* (London,
     1992), pp. 49–51.

2   Clarissa Hyman, *Tomato: A Global History* (London, 2019); Heather
     Arndt Anderson, *Chillies: A Global History* (London, 2016); Kaori
     O'Connor, *Pineapple: A Global History* (London, 2013); Stephen L. Harp,
     A World History of Rubber: Empire, Industry, and the Everyday (Oxford,
     2015); Larry Zuckerman, *The Potato: How The Humble Spud Rescued
     the Western World* (New York, 1999); Iain Gately, *Tobacco: A Cultural
     History of How an Exotic Plant Seduced Civilization* (New York, 2003);
     Marc Aronson and Marina Budhos, *Sugar Changed the World: A Story of
     Magic, Spice, Slavery, Freedom, and Science* (New York, 2010); Carmella
     Padilla and Barbara Anderson (eds), *A Red Like No Other: How Cochi-
     neal Coloured the World* (New York, 2015); Arturo Warman, *Corn and
     Capitalism: How a Botanical Bastard Grew to Global Dominance* (Chapel

Hill, 2003); Thomas Felling, *Cocaine Nation: How the White Trade Took Over the World* (Cambridge, 2012).

3   Sidney Mintz, *Sweetness and Power: The Place of Sugar in Modern History* (New York, 1985).

4   Christopher Columbus, 'Thursday 11 October' and 'Saturday 13 October', *Diary*, King's Digital Lab, https://tinyurl.com/57j4a6vs; López de Gómara, *Historia General*, Vol. II, p. 48. Works which (implicitly or explicitly) assume globalisation to be synonymous with a 'world economy' include: Jan de Vries, 'The limits of globalization in the early modern world', *Economic History Review*, 63.3 (2010), pp. 710–33 and articles by Dennis O'Flynn and Arturo Giráldez, beginning with their 'Born with a "Silver Spoon": The Origin of World Trade in 1571', *Journal of World History*, 6.2 (1995), pp. 201–21.

5   Leanne Betasamosake Simpson, 'Indigenous Resurgence and Co-resistance', *Critical Ethnic Studies*, 2.2. (2016), especially pp. 21–3. David Wengrow and David Graeber have argued that archaeological and ethnographic evidence suggests many cultures historically practised self-conscious egalitarianism: *The Dawn of Everything: A New History of Humanity* (Dublin, 2021).

6   Georges E. Sioui, *For an Amerindian Autohistory*, trans. Sheila Fischman (Montreal and Kingston, 2001), p. 8; *Popol Vuh: The Mayan Book of the Dawn of Life*, trans. Dennis Tedlock (New York, 1996), p. 146; Caroline Dodds Pennock, *Bonds of Blood: Gender, Lifecycle and Sacrifice in Aztec Culture* (Basingstoke, 2008), pp. 109–10; Klara Kelley and Harris Francis, *A Diné History of Navajoland* (2019), p. 6.

7   Armando de Melo, 'De América a Abya Yala – Semiótica da descolonização', *Revista de Educação Pública*, 23.53/2 (2014), pp. 501–31.

8   *The First Letter of Christopher Columbus to the Noble Lord Rafael Sanchez, announcing the Discovery of America*, trans. R.H. Major (Boston, 1890), p. 26; Gabriel Archer 'Description of the River and Country . . .' in P. L. Barbour, *The Jamestown Voyages Under the First Charter, 1601–1609* (Cambridge, 1969), p. 101; Francisco de Vitoria, 'On the American Indians', in his *Political Writings*, ed. Anthony Pagden and Jeremy Lawrence (Cambridge, 1991), pp. 231–92; John Smith, *A map of Virginia With a description of the countrey, the commodities, people, government and religion . . .* (Oxford, 1612), p. 63.

9   Linda Tuhiwai Smith, *Decolonizing Methodologies: Research and Indigenous Peoples* (London, 2012), p. 13; Robin Wall Kimmerer, *Braiding Sweetgrass: Indigenous Wisdom, Scientific Knowledge and the Teachings of Plants* (London, 2020), pp. 381–3; Jessica Hernandez, *Fresh Banana Leaves: Healing Indigenous Landscapes through Indigenous Science*

(Huichin, unceded Ohlone land, AKA Berkeley, 2002).

10 *Florentine Codex*, 9: 10: 45–9; Sara Florence Davidson and Robert Davidson, *Potlach as Pedagogy: Learning Through Ceremony* (Winnipeg, 2018), pp. 4–5; 'Audio clips: Potlach means to give – Chief Bill Cramer', *Living Tradition: The Kwakwaka'wakw Potlach on the Northwest Coast*, https://tinyurl.com/5ha6x536.

11 Sioui, *For an Amerindian Autohistory*, pp. 72–3; Graeber and Wengrow, *The Dawn of Everything*, pp. 48–59.

12 Norton, *Sacred Gifts, Profane Pleasures*, p. 105.

13 Sean M. Rafferty and Rob Mann, *Smoking and Culture: The Archaeology of Tobacco Pipes in Eastern North America* (Knoxville, 2004), pp. 62–5; Shannon Tushingham et al., 'Molecular archaeology reveals ancient origins of Indigenous tobacco smoking in North American Plateau', *PNAS*, 115.46 (2018), pp. 11742–7.

14 Fernández de Oviedo y Valdés, *Historia general y natural de las Indias*, Book XVII, Chapter XV.

15 Anthony R. Rowley, 'How England Learned to Smoke: The Introduction, Spread and Establishment of Tobacco Pipe Smoking in England before 1640' (PhD thesis, University of York, 2003), pp. 31–2; Nicolás Monardes, *Segunda parte del libro, de las cosas que se traen de nuestras Indias Occidentales . . .* (Seville, 1571), ff. 5, 22.

16 Norton, *Sacred Gifts, Profane Pleasures*, pp. 182, 257; Zachary C. Rich and Shuiyuan Xiao, 'Tobacco as a Social Currency: Cigarette Gifting and Sharing in China', *Nicotine & Tobacco Research*, 14.3 (2012), pp. 258–63.

17 Norton, *Sacred Gifts, Profane Pleasures*, p. 112; Monardes, *Segunda parte del libro*, f. 22; Fernández de Oviedo y Valdés, *Historia general*, Book V, Chapter II.

18 *Florentine Codex*, 8: 13: 39–40.

19 Rocío Cortés, 'The Colegio Imperial de Santa Cruz de Tlatelolco and Its Aftermath: Nahua Intellectuals and the Spiritual Conquest of Mexico', in Sara Castro-Klaren (ed.), *A Companion to Latin American Literature and Culture* (Oxford, 2008), pp. 86–105; Villella, *Indigenous Elites and Creole Identity in Colonial Mexico*, pp. 72–9 81–5; Millie Gimmel, 'Reading Medicine in the Codex de la Cruz Badiano', *Journal of the History of Ideas* 69.2 (2008), pp. 169–92.

20 David M. Carballo, *Collision of Worlds: A Deep History of the Fall of Aztec Mexico and the Forging of New Spain* (Oxford, 2020), p. 113.

21 Terry G. Powis et al., 'Oldest chocolate in the New World', *Antiquity: A Review of World Archaeology*, 314.81 (2007); 'The Utah Chocolate Story', *Natural History Museum of Utah*, https://nhmu.utah.edu/chocolate; Patricia Crown et al., 'Ritual drinks in the pre-Hispanic US Southwest

and Mexican Northwest', *PNAS*, 112.37 (2015), pp. 11436–42; *Florentine Codex*, 6: 41: 256.

22 *Florentine Codex*, 6: 23: 129.

23 Gabrielle Vail, 'Cacao Use in Yucatán Among the Pre-Hispanic Maya', in Louis E. Grivetti and Howard-Yana Shapiro (eds), *Chocolate: History, Culture, and Heritage* (Hoboken, 2009), no page numbers online. On renaming codices see: See Marten Jansen and Gabina Aurora Pérez Jiménez, 'Renaming the Mexican Codices', *Ancient Mesoamerica* (2004), 15.2, pp. 267–71.

24 Norton, *Sacred Gifts, Profane Pleasures*, p. 30; Sophie D. Coe and Michael D. Coe, *The True History of Chocolate* (London, 1996), p. 63; Douglas E. Brintnall, *Revolt Against The Dead: The Modernization of a Mayan Community in the Highlands of Guatemala* (New York, 1979), p. 82. Although Brintnall's anthropological work was conducted in the 1970s, this still seems to be the case in traditional marriage ceremonies.

25 Agustín Estrada Monroy, *El mundo k'ekchi' de la Vera-Paz* (Guatemala City, 1979), pp. 194–5. This is the first recorded date, but chocolate almost certainly appeared in Europe earlier. Columbus and Cortés both encountered it, many Native travellers precede this date, and a lawsuit alleges that the *encomendero* Gonzalo de Salazaar forced his Indigenous tributaries to provide him with 'a thousand pounds "of ground cacao ready to drink"' for his journey to Spain in 1531. Nonetheless, Native people were clearly essential to these networks of exchange. Norton, *Sacred Gifts, Profane Pleasures*, p. 103.

26 He is also known as don Juan Matalbatz. Juan seems to have been his baptismal name, and the latter was likely a Spanish garbling of the original. After important community work recovering their histories, his name was changed on municipal monuments to the Maya original. The mural dubs him 'chief of chiefs': Sarah Ashley Kistler, 'Writing about Aj Pop B'atz': Bruce Grindal and the Transformation of Ethnographic Writing', *Anthropology & Humanism*, 40.2 (2015), p. 173, n. 2.

27 S. Ashley Kistler, 'The Original Ancestor: Aj Pop B'atz' as a Model of Q'eqchi' Kinship', *Journal of Family History*, 38.3 (2013), p. 289.

28 Estrada Monroy, *El mundo k'ekchi'*, pp. 179–83, 194. On the oral tradition regarding the journey see: Kistler, 'Writing about Aj Pop B'atz'', p. 173, n. 3. For more on the Q'eqchi' manuscript, now held by the *cofradia* of San Luis see: S. Ashley Kistler, 'The House in the Market: Kinship, Status, and Memory Among Q'Eqchi' Market Women in San Juan Chamelco, Guatemala' (PhD thesis, Florida State University, 2007), pp. 104–6.

29 Oswaldo Chinchilla Mazariegos, 'Tecum: the Fallen Sun: Mesoamerican Cosmogony and the Spanish Conquest of Guatemala', *Ethnohistory*, 60.4

(2013), pp. 693–719. On the appropriation of Tecún Umán see Sarah Ashley Kistler, 'Writing about Aj Pop B'atz': Bruce Grindal and the Transformation of Ethnographic Writing', *Anthropology & Humanism*, 40.2 (2015), pp. 162–3.

30 Estrada Monroy, *El mundo k'ekchi'*, p. 201.

31 Estrada Monroy, *El mundo k'ekchi'*, p. 196; Kistler, 'Writing about Aj Pop B'atz", p. 167.

32 S. Ashley Kistler, 'The Aj Pop B'atz' Project', *Mesoweb* (2012), https://tinyurl.com/urp85s4p; Kistler, 'Writing about Aj Pop B'atz", pp. 157–76; Kistler, 'The House in the Market'.

33 Estrada Monroy, *El mundo k'ekchi'*, pp. 203–5, 209, 212–13, 215–18.

34 Kistler, 'Writing about Aj Pop B'atz", p. 168.

35 Fernández de Oviedo y Valdés, *Historia general*, Book VIII, Chapter XXX.

36 Rebecca Earle, *Feeding the People: The Politics of the Potato* (Cambridge, 2020), pp. 30, 46; J.G. Hawkes and J. Francisco-Ortega, 'The early history of the potato in Europe', *Euphytica*, 70.1 (1993), pp. 86–97; Roger Schlesinger, *In the Wake of Columbus: The Impact of the New World on Europe, 1492–1650* (Wheeling, 2007), pp. 94–6; Ken Albala, *Eating Right in the Renaissance* (Berkeley 2002), pp. 237–8.

37 David Gentilcore, *Pomodoro! A History of the Tomato in Italy* (New York, 2010), pp. 1–2, 10, 11, 25.

38 Caroline Dodds Pennock, '"A Remarkably Patterned Life": Domestic and Public in the Aztec Household City', *Gender & History*, 23.3 (2011), pp. 528–46; *Florentine Codex*, 6: 31: 172; 8: 16: 49.

39 Despite acknowledging the 'ample mention of stirrers', Sophie and Michael Coe conclude that the *molinillo* 'must have been introduced from Spain during the 16th century': *The True History of Chocolate*, p. 88. Paul Chrystal, without citing any evidence, claims that after the visit of the Q'eqchi', 'Charles' people added cane sugar to make it sweet and invented the *molinillo* to froth it up with': *The History of Sweets* (Barnsley, 2021), p. 93. Miguel León-Portilla, 'Otro testimonio de aculturación hispano-indígena: Los nahuatlismos en el castellano de España', *Revista Española de Antropología*, XI (1981), p. 235; Marcy Norton, 'Tasting Empire: Chocolate and the Internalization of Mesoamerican Aesthetics', *American Historical Review*, 11.3 (2006), p. 683.

40 Karen Dakin and Søren Wichmann, 'Cacao and Chocolate: An Uto-Aztecan Perspective', *Ancient Mesoamerica*, 11.1 (2000), pp. 55–75.

41 Tuhiwai Smith, *Decolonizing Methodologies*, p. 190.

42 Leanne Simpson, *Dancing on Our Turtle's Back: Stories of Nishnaabeg Re-creation, Resurgence and a New Emergence* (Winnipeg, 2011), pp. 49–63.

43   *Viajes por España de Jorge de Einghen del Baron Leon de Rosmithal de Blatna, de Francisco Guicciardini y de Andrés Navajero*, ed. D. Antonio María Fabié (Madrid, 1889), pp. 272–4; Tuhiwai Smith, *Decolonizing Methodologies*, p. 92.

44   Cortés, *Letters From Mexico*, p. 86.

45   Lewis Hyde, *The Gift: How the Creative Spirit Transforms the World* (Edinburgh, 2006), pp. 3–4.

46   Léry, *History of a voyage to the land of Brazil*, pp. 102–3, quoted with the kind permission of Janet Whatley; Raoni Metuktire, 'We, the peoples of the Amazon, are full of fear. Soon you will be too', *Guardian*, 2 September 2019, https://tinyurl.com/3zbb557y.

Chapter 5: Diplomacy

1   Some aspects of Tenamaztle's story are disputed, including his claim to *cacique* status, but this was his stated identity and the Crown seems to treat him with the respect and grants commensurate with noble status: José-Juan López-Portilla, 'Another Jerusalem': Political Legitimacy and Courtly Government in the Kingdom of New Spain (1535–1568) (Leiden, 2018), p. 214; AGI, Indiferente, 425, l. 23, f. 215v; Indiferente, 425, l. 23, f. 227v(1); Indiferente, 425, l. 23, f. 239r.

2   Brickhouse, *The Unsettlement of America*; Camilla Townsend, 'Mutual Appraisals: The Shifting Paradigms of the English, Spanish, and Powhatans in Tsenacomoco, 1560–1622', in Douglas Bradburn and John C. Coombs (eds), *Early Modern Virginia: Reconsidering the Old Dominion* (Charlottesville, 2011), pp. 57–89; 'Don Luís de Velasco / Paquiquineo (fl. 1561–1571)', *Encyclopedia Virginia*, https://tinyurl.com/zdw6e97h; Puente Luna, *Andean Cosmopolitans*, especially pp. 124–33, 141–7, 152; Archivo Histórico Nacional, OM-EXPEDIENTILLOS, n. 140.

3   AGI, Indiferente, 425, l. 23, f. 215v; Indiferente, 425, l. 23, f. 227v(1); Indiferente, 425, l. 23, f. 239r; Contaduría, 1050, f. 420; 'Documento 19. Tenamaztle: La voz de los chichimecas sobre la ética de la guerra (1555)', in Alberto Carrillo Cázares, *El debate sobre la Guerra Chichimeca, 1531–1585* (Zamora, 2000), vol. 2, pp. 513–35; Lawrence A. Clayton, *Bartolomé de Las Casas: A Biography* (Cambridge, 2012), pp. 438–40; Miguel León-Portilla, *Francisco Tenamaztle: Primer guerrillero de América, Defensor de los derechos humanos* (Mexico City, 2005), pp. 175–6.

4   Quoted in León-Portilla, *Francisco de Tenamaztle*, pp. 175–6.

5   AGI, Indiferente, 425, l. 23, f. 249r(2); Indiferente, 425, l. 23, f. 253v.

6   Lewis Hanke, *The Spanish Struggle for Justice in the Conquest of America* (Philadelphia, 1949), p. 89. I cannot access the original source, but have

taken the liberty of changing the word 'negroes' to '*negros*', which is the likely Spanish term.

7   Rafael Varón Gabai, *Francisco Pizarro and His Brothers: The Illusion of Power in Sixteenth-Century Peru* (Norman, 1997), pp. 102–3.

8   María Rostworowski de Diez Canseco, *Doña Francisca Pizarro: Una ilustre mestiza 1534–1598* (Lima, 1992), pp. 38, 44, 62, 128–37; Rafael Varón, 'The Pizarro Family Enterprise in Sixteenth-Century Peru' (UCL, PhD thesis, 1994), p. 155; Karen Vieira Powers, *Women in the Crucible of Conquest* (Albuquerque, 2005), pp. 80–81.

9   Varón Gabai, *Francisco Pizarro and His Brothers*, p. 293; Rostworowski de Diez Canseco, *Doña Francisca Pizarro*, pp. 51–3, 73–4.

10   María Castañeda de la Paz and Miguel Luque-Talaván, 'Privileges of the "Others": The Coats of Arms Granted to Indigenous Conquistadors', in Simon McKeown (ed.), *The International Emblem: From Incunabula to the Internet: Selected Proceedings of the Eighth International Conference of the Society for Emblem Studies, 25th July – 1st August, 2008, Winchester College* (Cambridge, 2010), pp. 283–316. Castañeda de la Paz and Luque-Talaván claim that Pedro's arms were not granted until the day of his death in 1570, but in fact they were approved on 15 October 1539 but only sent from Spain on 11 September 1570. Donald Chipman, *Moctezuma's Children: Aztec Royalty under Spanish Rule, 1520–1700* (Austin, 2005), pp. 85, 162, n. 39.

11   AGI, Mexico, l. 1, ff. 38r-40r; Baber, 'Empire, Indians, and the Negotiation for the Status of City in Tlaxcala, 1521–1550', pp. 34, 37–8, 42–3; Bartolomé de Las Casas, *Historiadores de Indias: Tomo I – Apologética Historia de las Indias* (Madrid, 1909), p. 589; Charles Gibson, *Tlaxcala in the Sixteenth Century* (Stanford, 1952), p. 165; Camilla Townsend, *Here in this year: Seventeenth-century Nahua Annals of the Tlaxcala-Puebla Valley* (Stanford, 2009), no page numbers online.

12   AGI, Indiferente, 422, l. 16, f. 201r; Patronato, 275, r. 41; *Actas de Cabildo de Tlaxcala, 1547–1567*, ed. Eustaquio Celestino Solis, Armando Valencia R. and Constantino Medina Lima (Tlaxcala, 1984), pp. 125, 128, 194, 196; Gibson, *Tlaxcala in the Sixteenth Century*, pp. 164–9, 229–34; Éric Taladoire, *De América a Europa: Cuando los indígenas descubrieron el Viejo Mundo (1493–1892)* (Paris, 2014), pp. 54–6; Luis Fernando Herrera Valdez, 'Origen y significado del escudo de Tlaxcala', *Potestas*, 8 (2015), pp. 83–104; 'Fragmento de la visita hecha á don Antonio de Mendoza', in Joaquin García Icazbalceta (ed), *Colección de documentos para la historia de México* (México, 1866), vol. 2, p. 87.

13   Gibson, *Tlaxcala in the Sixteenth Century*, p. 165; AGI, Patronato, 275, r. 41; *Actas de cabildo de Tlaxcala, 1547–1567*, p. 289; Las Casas,

Historiadores de Indias, p. 590.

14 *Actas de cabildo de Tlaxcala*, p. 433; For an interactive reconstruction of the *lienzo* along with detailed context see: 'Lienzo de Tlaxcala', *Mesolore*, https://tinyurl.com/2rtf5s8k.

15 *Actas de cabildo de Tlaxcala, 1547–1567*, pp. 125/321, 128/324, 150/347, 162–3/360.

16 Gibson, *Tlaxcala in the Sixteenth Century*, pp. 163–9; Charles Gibson, 'The Identity of Diego Muñoz Camargo', *Hispanic American Historical Review* 30.2 (1950), pp. 195–208; 'Historia de Tlaxcala', Glasgow University Special Collections (January 2003), https://tinyurl.com/ysuendd4.

17 Sean F. McEnroe, *A Troubled Marriage: Indigenous Elites of the Colonial Americas* (Albuquerque, 2020), pp. 165–73. For an explanation of the significance of the Spanish Crown's dual role as both administrator and moderator of law see John Lynch, 'The Institutional Framework of Colonial Spanish America', *Journal of Latin American Studies*, 24, Supplement S1 (1992), pp. 69–81.

18 Pedro Carrasco, 'Don Juan Cortés, Cacique de Santa Cruz Quiché', *Estudios de Cultura Maya*, VI (1967), pp. 253–4; Stephanie Wood, 'The Social vs Legal Context of Nahuatl *Títulos*', in Elizabeth Hill Boone and Tom Cummins (eds), *Native Traditions in the Postconquest World* (Washington, DC, 1998), pp. 201–31; Allan Greer, *Property and Dispossession: Natives, Empires and Land in Early Modern North America* (Cambridge, 2018), pp. 138–41.

19 Allen J. Christenson, *The Burden of the Ancients: Maya Ceremonies of World Renewal from the Pre-Columbian Period to the Present* (Austin, 2016), pp. 84–5; *Popol Vuh*, pp. 195, 315, n. 179.

20 Juan Rodríguez Freyle, *Conquista y descrubimiento del nuevo Reino de Granada . . .* (Bogota, 1890), pp. 8–9.

21 Luis Fernando Restrepo, 'Narrating Colonial Interventions: Don Diego de Torres, *Cacique* of Turmequé in the New Kingdom of Granada', in Alvaro Félix Bolaños and Gustavo Verdesio (eds), *Colonialism Past and Present: Reading and Writing about Colonial Latin America Today*, p. 99. See also, for the details of don Diego's life: Joanna Rappaport, 'Buena sangre y hábitos españoles: repensando a Alonso de Silva y Diego de Torres', trans. Mercedes López, *Anuario Colombiano de Historia Social y de la Cultura*, 39.1 (2012), pp. 20–48; Luis Fernando Restrepo, 'El cacique de Turmequé o los agravios de la memoria', *Cuadernos de Literatura*, 14.28 (2010), pp. 14–33; Hernán Alejandro Olano García, 'La defensoría del pueblo: ¿Una institución escandinava o chibcha?', *Díkaion*, 6 (1997), pp. 51–83.

22 See, for example, Gloria Helena Rey, 'COLOMBIA: The Chibcha Culture – Forgotten, But Still Alive', *Inter Press Service*, 30 November 2007,

https://tinyurl.com/mup69xzj.

23   Restrepo, 'El cacique de Turmequé', p. 23.

24   The details of this lawsuit are outlined by María Paula Corredor Acosta, 'Entre el laberinto jurídico de la monarquía hispánica: El caso de un cacique del Nuevo Reino de Granada (1571–1578)', Universidad del Rosario repository (2017), https://tinyurl.com/ewjn72u8.

25   'El *Memorial de Agravios* de don Diego de Torres, cacique de Turmequé, 1584', ed. Jorge Orlando Mejo, https://tinyurl.com/3euhy8nm; AGI, MP-PANAMA, 8. See also MP-PANAMA, 7. Restrepo, 'El cacique de Turmequé', p. 23.

26   AGI, Indiferente, 741, n. 16. See also Indiferente, 1952, l. 2, f. 73; Indiferente, 527, l. 1, f. 83v; Indiferente, 426, l. 29, f. 54r; Indiferente, l. 28, f. 6v; Indiferente, 426, l. 27, f. 158r(1); Indiferente, 426, l. 27, f. 171r; Indiferente, 426, l. 27, ff. 134v-135r; Indiferente, 426, l. 27, f. 139r; Indiferente, 426, l. 27, ff. 164v-165r; Indiferente, 426, l. 27, f. 152r; Indiferente, 426, l. 28, ff. 25r-25v.

27   AGI, Indiferente, 741, n. 197. In 1633, Diego's widow Juana de Oropesa was granted three hundred pesos a year in place of the tributes she should have been receiving from the *indios* of Soracá, in the New Kingdom of Granada, an *encomienda* confirmed by the courts in 1628: AGI, Santa Fe, 168, n. 44; Contratación, 959, n. 19.

28   Eufrasio Bernal Duffo, 'Diego de Torres y Moyachoque, cacique de Turmequé', *Geografía Cultura de Boyacá*, https://tinyurl.com/mttcm8pk.

29   AGI, Quito, 211, l. 2, ff. 111r, 112v, 113r; Indiferente, 426, l. 26, f. 63v(2); Lauri Uusitalo, 'An Indigenous lord in the Spanish royal court: The transatlantic voyage of Don Pedro de Henao, Cacique of Ipiales', in Jenni Kuuliala and Jussi Rantala (eds), *Travel, Pilgrimage and Social Interaction from Antiquity to the Middle Ages* (Manchester, 2019), pp. 297–8.

30   Carla Rahn Phillips, 'Visualizing Imperium: The Virgin of the Seafarers and Spain's Self-Image in the Early Sixteenth Century', *Renaissance Quarterly*, 58 (2005), p. 826.

31   Uusitalo, 'An Indigenous lord in the Spanish royal court', p. 305.

32   AGI, Indiferente, 1952, l. 2, ff. 171r-171v; Quito, 211, l. 2, f. 130v; Quito, 211, l. 2, ff. 131r-131v; Quito, 211, l. 2, f. 133r; Quito, 211, l. 2, ff. 132r-132v; Quito, 1, n. 16; Uusitalo, 'An Indigenous lord in the Spanish royal court', pp. 300–301; José Carlos Pérez Morales, 'Un encargo escultórico de malograda fortuna: Pedro de Henao y el ornato de la iglesia de Ipiales (Colombia) a fines del siglo XVI', *Revista digital del Seminario de Escultura* (2008), pp. 26–39.

33   AGI, Quito, 211, l. 2, ff. 156r-156v; Indiferente, 426, l. 27, f. 128r; Quito, 211, l. 2, f. 162r. Uusitalo puts his passage home in January, but the *merced*

granting passage and expenses on the fleet is dated 15 February 1586, a
month after the grant for costs travelling to Seville: Indiferente, 1957, l. 4,
ff. 126v-127r; Uusitalo, 'An Indigenous lord in the Spanish royal court', p.
301.

34   Pérez Morales, 'Un encargo escultórico de malograda fortuna', pp. 26–39.
35   Puente Luna, *Andean Cosmopolitans*, pp. 176–7, 87.
36   Uusitalo, 'An Indigenous lord in the Spanish royal court', pp. 305–6.
37   Pedro de Cieza de Leon, *The Discovery and Conquest of Peru: Chronicles
     of the New World Encounter*, ed. and trans. Alexandra Parma Cook and
     Noble David Cook (Durham, 1998), p. 223; John TePaske, *A New World of
     Gold and Silver* (Leiden, 2010), p. 142.
38   AGI, Indiferente, 741, n. 133; Puente Luna, *Andean Cosmopolitans*, pp. 139,
     153; Uusitalo, 'An Indigenous lord in the Spanish royal court', p. 306.
39   Basil Morgan, 'Hawkins, William', *Oxford Dictionary of National Biog-
     raphy* (2004); 'A voyage to Brasill, made by the worshipfull *M. William
     Haukins of Plimmouth, father to* sir Iohn Haukins, Knight, now liuing,
     in the yeere 1530', in Clements R. Markham (ed.), *The Hawkins Voyages
     during the Reigns of Henry VIII, Queen Elizabeth, and James I* (London,
     1878), pp. 3–4. Spelling lightly modernised.
40   'The Old War Office Building: A History' (Ministry of Defence), p. 27,
     https://tinyurl.com/48efv7p5; *Hansard*, HL Deb. vol. 160, cols. 853–4, 15
     February 1949, https://tinyurl.com/4fmcmstj.
41   Olive Patricia Dickason, 'The Sixteenth-Century French Vision of the
     Empire: The Other Side of Self-Determination', in Germaine Warkentin
     and Carolyn Podruchny (eds), *Decentring the Renaissance: Canada and
     Europe in multidisciplinary perspective, 1500–1700* (Toronto, 2001), pp.
     87–109. 'A voyage to Brasill', in Markham (ed.), *The Hawkins Voyages*, p.
     4. Spelling lightly modernised.
42   'A voyage to Brasill', in Markham (ed.), *The Hawkins Voyages*, p. 4.
     Spelling lightly modernised.

Chapter 6: Spectacle and Curiosity

1   *C'est la deduction du sumptueux ordre plaisantz spectacles et magniques
     théâtres dresses et exhibés par les citoiens de Rouen, ville métropolitaine du
     pays de Normandie, A la Sacrée Majeseté du Treschristian Roy de France,
     Henry second leur souverain Seigneur, Et à Tres illustre dame, ma Dame
     Katherine de Medicis, La Royne son éspouse . . .* (Rouen, 1551), image 81.
2   'Naturelz sauvages', real, original, natural or true 'savages'. *Ibid.* I have
     retained the French in order better to evoke the original intent while
     avoiding the racial slur.

3   There is also a third account and depiction of the village from 1557, but the image is almost identical to *C'est la deduction*. See *Les Pourtres et Figures du sumpteux Ordre Plaisantz spectacles, et magnifiques Theatres, dresses et exhibés par les citoiens de Rouen* . . . (1557), https://tinyurl.com/2twyjkyx.

4   *C'est la deduction*, images 81–2. Michael Wintroub, 'Civilizing the Savage and Making a King: The Royal Entry Festival of Henri II (Rouen 1550)', *Sixteenth Century Journal*, XXIX.2 (1998), esp. p. 469; Ferdinand Denis, *Une Fête Brésilienne célèbrée à Rouen en 1550* (Paris, 1851), p. 10.

5   *C'est la deduction*, image 81. It is also possible that this is a reference to the *homo sylvestris* (wild man) of European myth, who was hairy and bestial, and often conflated with early Americans in travel writing, but I find this unlikely given the way in which the Tupinambá were framed as allies and trading partners to the French. It may be that the 'spikiness' was, in fact, a reference to the feathers erect in the hair and on the heads of the 'Brazillian' villagers, but I find it more humanising to imagine them shivering in the unfamiliar cold – something which very likely happened, whether it was in the text or not. Many thanks to Francois Soyer, Martial Staub and Charles West for a lively discussion about this, helpful references and expert advice.

6   John M. Monteiro, *Blacks of the Land: Indian Slavery, Settler Society, and the Portuguese Colonial Enterprise in South America*, ed. and trans. James Woodard and Barbara Weinstein (Cambridge, 2018), pp. 7–39.

7   *Eusebii Cesariesis Episcopi Chronicon . . . Ad quem & prosper & Matthęs Palmerius/& Matthias Palmerius* . . . (Henricvs Stephan, 1512), f. 174; Daniel J. Weeks, *Gateways to Empire: Quebec and New Amsterdam to 1664* (Lanham, 2019), pp. 21–2; Jack D. Forbes, *The American Discovery of Europe* (Urbana, 2011), pp. 75–6; Vincent Masse, 'Les "sept hommes sauvages" de 1509: fortune éditoriale de la première séquelle imprimée des contacts franco-amérindiens', in Andreas Motsch and Grégoire Holtz (eds), *Éditer la Nouvelle-France* (Québec, 2011), p. 90.

8   Olive Patricia Dickason, 'The Brazilian Connection: A Look at the Origin of French Techniques for Trading with Amerindians', *Revue française d'histoire d'outre-mer*, 71.264–265 (1984), pp. 133–4; Th. Pompeu Sobrinho, 'Línguas Tapuias desconhecidas de nordeste', *Boletim de Antropologia*, 2.1 (1958), pp. 12, 18; Cameron J.G. Dodge, 'A Forgotten Century of Brazilwood: The Brazilwood Trade from the Mid-Sixteenth to Mid-Seventeenth Centuries', *e-journal of Portuguese History*, 16.1 (2018); Beatriz Perrone-Moisés, 'L'alliance normando-tupi au XVIe siècle: la celebration de Rouen', *Journal de la société des américanistes*, 94.1 (2008), p. 48; Olive Patricia Dickason, 'Dyewood to Furs: The Brazilian Origins

of French-Amerindian Trade', *Yearbook (Conference of Latin Americanist Geographers)*, 10 (1984), p. 24.

9   Hans Staden, *Hans Staden's True History: An Account of Cannibal Captivity in Brazil*, ed. and trans. Neil L. Whitehead and Michael Harbsmeier (Durham, 2008), p. 119; *C'est la deduction*, image 82.

10   Surekha Davies, *Renaissance Ethnography and the Invention of the Human: New Worlds, Maps and Monsters* (Cambridge, 2016), pp. 133–4.

11   Amy J. Buono, 'Representing the Tupinambá and the Brazilwood Trade in Sixteenth-Century Rouen', in Regina R. Félix and Scott D. Juall, *Cultural Exchanges between Brazil and France* (West Lafayette, 2016), pp. 22–6; E.-T. Hamy, 'Le Bas Relief de l'Hotel du Brésil au Musée Départemental d'Antiquités de Rouen: Notes et figures réunies', *Journal de la Société des américanistes*, Nouvelle Série, 4 (1907), pp. 1–6.

12   Denis, *Une Fête Brésilienne célèbrée à Rouen*, pp. 25–7. Many scholars follow Denis on the details of the festival, but I can see no particular reason to credit this nineteenth-century chronicler with any privileged evidence not presented in his work. Michael Wintroub, *The Voyage of Thought: Navigating Knowledge across the Sixteenth-Century World* (Cambridge, 2017), pp. 8–62; Davies, *Renaissance Ethnography and the Invention of the Human* pp. 112–13; Michael Wintroub, *A Savage Mirror: Power, Identity, and Knowledge in Early Modern France* (Stanford, 2006), p. 38; *L'entrée du Roy à Bordeaux, avecques les carmes latins qui luy on esté presentez & au Chancelier* (Paris, 1565), p. 5; Philippe Desan, 'Le simulacre du Nouveau Monde: à propos de la rencontre de Montaigne avec des Cannibales', *Montaigne Studies*, XXII (2010), p. 108.

13   'The Great Chronicle of London', in R. A. Skelton and James A. Williamson, *The Cabot Voyages and Bristol Delivery under Henry VII* (Cambridge, 1962), p. 220. Spelling modernised; original capitalisation preserved. For a discussion of the various versions of this early source see Vaughan, *Transatlantic Encounters*, pp. 263–4, n. 31.

14   For unexplained reasons, Quinn says these people were 'not identifiable, clearly Indians not Eskimo, probably from as far south as New England', but I concur with Thrush: David B. Quinn, *Sources for the ethnography of northeastern North America to 1611* (Ottawa, 1981), p. 12; Thrush, *Indigenous London*, p. 2.

15   'From an Inquisition at Bristol, 3 September 1481 . . .', in Skelton and Williamson, *The Cabot Voyages and Bristol Delivery*, p. 189; and Skelton and Williamson, *The Cabot Voyages and Bristol Delivery*, p. 15.

16   William Shakespeare, *The Tempest*, Act 2, Scene 2; Thrush, *Indigenous London*, p. 80.

17   Jacqueline Fear-Segal, 'Buffalo Bill's Lakota "Indians" in 1887', *Beyond the*

Spectacle blog, https://tinyurl.com/bdf3nm3c; Linda Scarangella McNenly, 'Foe, Friend, or Critic: Native Performers with Buffalo Bill's Wild West Show and Discourses of Conquest and Friendship in Newspaper Reports', *American Indian Quarterly*, 38.2 (2014), pp. 160, 162.

18 José Alexandrino de Sousa Filho and Philippe Desan have argued that Montaigne could not have met the 'cannibals' in Rouen in 1562, but must have met them in Bordeaux at the entrance of Charles IX on 9 April 1565. It is certainly possible that Montaigne altered the chronology for effect, or placed his own arguments in the mouths of the Brazilians, but it does not alter the power of the account, or the fact that these were exactly the kinds of reactions which would have been likely, and which we see from other Indigenous travellers. It also seems unlikely that the (then fifteen-year-old) king would have been seen as a 'child' at that time. See José Alexandrino de Sousa Filho, 'Le <<Conte Cannibale>> de Montaigne: Réalité Historique et Represéntation Littéraire', in *La France et le Monde Luso-Brésilien: Échanges et Représentations (XVIᵉ-XVIIIᵉ Siècles – Études réunies et présentées par Saulo Neiva* (Clermont-Ferrand, 2005), pp. 111–40; Philippe Desan, 'Le simulacre du Nouveau Monde: à propos de la rencontre de Montaigne avec des Cannibales', *Montaigne Studies*, XXII (2010), pp. 101–18. Another sceptical voice is Alphone Grün, *La Vie publique de Michel de Montaigne – Étude biographique* (Paris, 1855), pp. 144–5.

19 For an accessible, recent translation of this famous work see Michel de Montaigne, 'On the Cannibals', trans. Ian Johnston, from *Les Essais* (1595), https://tinyurl.com/2p8mcvt2.

20 *Catlin's Notes of Eight Years Travels and Residence in Europe with his North American Collection with Anecdotes and Incidents of the Travels and Adventures of Three Different Parties of American Indians whom he introduced to the Courts of England, France and Belgium* (New York, 1848), Volume II, p. 143.

21 Denys Delâge, *Bitter Feast: Amerindians and Europeans in Northeastern North America, 1600–64*, trans. Jane Brierley (Vancouver, 1993), p. 126.

22 Maungwudaus, *Account of the Chippewa Indians, who have been travelling among the whites, in the United States, England, Ireland, Scotland, France and Belgium . . .* (Boston, 1848).

23 Montaigne, 'On the Cannibals'.

24 Arinos de Melo Franco, *O Índio brasileiro*, p. 51; Léry, *History of a Voyage to the Land of Brazil*, p. 42.

25 Claude Haton, *Mémoires de Claude Haton contenant le récit des événements accomplish de 1553 a 1582 principalement dans la Champagne et la Brie* (Paris, 1857), Vol. 1, p. 40.

26 Martyr d'Anghera, *De Orbe Novo*, Vol. II, Fifth Decade, pp. 191, 195–8, 202–4.

27 Kurly Tlapoyawa, *We Will Rise: Rebuilding the Mexikah Nation* (Indiana, 2000), pp. 147–53; Caroline Dodds Pennock, 'Mass Murder or Religious Homicide: Rethinking Human Sacrifice and Interpersonal Violence in Aztec Society', *Historical Social Research*, 27.3 (2012), pp. 276–302.

28 Mary W. Helms, 'Essay on objects: Interpretations of distance made tangible', in Stuart B. Schwartz (ed.), *Implicit Understandings: Observing, Reporting, and Reflecting on the Encounters between Europeans and Other Peoples in the Early Modern Era* (Cambridge, 1994), p. 373.

29 *Thomas Platter's Travels in England 1599*, ed. and trans. Clare Williams (London, 1937), pp. 171–3; Detlef Heikamp, *Mexico and the Medici* (Florence, 1972), quoted in Mary W. Helms, 'Essay on objects: Interpretations of distance made tangible', in Stuart B. Schwartz (ed.), *Implicit Understandings: Observing, Reporting, and Reflecting on the Encounters between Europeans and Other Peoples in the Early Modern Era* (Cambridge, 1994), p. 371.

30 Dan Hicks, *The Brutish Museums: The Benin Bronzes, Colonial Violence and Cultural Restitution* (London, 2020), quote on p. 185; Blackbird and Dodds Pennock, 'How making space for Indigenous peoples changes history', p. 249.

31 Lia Markey, *Imagining the Americas in Medici Florence* (University Park, Penn., 2016), quote on p. 161. The term 'invention of America' was coined by Edmundo O'Gorman, *The Invention of America: An Inquiry into the Historical Nature of the New World and the Meaning of its History* (Bloomington, 1961); see also José Rabasa, *Inventing America: Spanish Historiography and the Formation of Eurocentrism* (Norman, 1993).

32 Stuart Campbell et al., 'The mirror, the magus and more: reflections on John Dee's obsidian mirror', *Antiquity* (2021), pp. 1–18. On the 'Inca mirror' in Paris see Thomas Calligaro, Pierre-Jacques Chiappero, François Gendron and Gérard Poupeau, 'New Clues on the Origin of the "Inca Mirror" at the *Museum National d'Histoire Naturelle* in Paris', *Latin American Antiquity*, 30.2 (2019), pp. 422–8.

33 Lia Markey, *Imagining the Americas in Medici Florence* (University Park, Penn., 2016), pp. 13, 38, 52; Marten Jansen and Gabina Aurora Pérez Jiménez, 'Renaming the Mexican Codices', *Ancient Mesoamerica*, 15.2 (2004), p. 270.

34 Alan Riding, 'A Stolen Relic is a Problem for Mexicans', *New York Times*, 29 August 1982, https://tinyurl.com/4k8crvux; Ian Mursell, 'The extraordinary story of the *Tonalamatl de Aubin* (3)', *Mexicolore*, https://tinyurl.com/yv7ee472.

35 'Request for repatriation of human remains to New Zealand: Minutes of meeting of the Trustees – April 2008', *The British Museum*, https://tinyurl.com/fx3up7tr; second quote from '2.2 Summary of meeting with representatives from Te Papa Tongarewa 17.11.04 (pdf)', linked from page. 'Request for repatriation of human remains to the Torres Strait Islands, Australia', *The British Museum*, https://tinyurl.com/4mn3793h; info from '2.4 The briefing note on the skulls provided for the meeting on 30 June 2011 by N McKinney including two Bioarchaeological Reports by D Antoine (BM)'. Tuhiwai Smith, *Decolonizing Methodologies*, p. 30.

36 Sadiah Qureshi, *Peoples on Parade: Exhibitions, Empire, and Anthropology in Nineteenth-Century Britain* (Chicago, 2011); P. Blanchard et al. (eds), *Human Zoos: Science and Spectacle in the Age of Colonial Empires* (Liverpool, 2008); Nina Jablonski, *Living Color: The Biological and Social Meaning of Skin Color* (Berkeley, 2012).

37 Simão de Vasconcellos, *Chronica da Companhia de Jesv do Estado do Brasil . . .* (Lisbon, 1663), p. 11; Arinos de Melo Franco, *O Índio brasileiro*, p. 38; Masse, 'Les "sept hommes sauvages" de 1509', pp. 86–8.

38 W.C. Sturtevant, Mattheus Francker and Hans Wolf Glaserr, 'The first Inuit depiction by Europeans', *Études/Inuit/Studies*, 4.1/2 (1980), pp. 47–9.

39 Michael Lok, 'East India by the Northwestw[ard]', in Richard Collinson (ed.), *The Three Voyages of Martin Frobisher, in search of a Passage to Cathaia and India by the North-West, A.D. 1576–8* (London, 1867), p. 87. English modernised. George Best, *A true discourse of the late voyages of discouerie, for the finding of a passage to Cathaya, by the Northwest, vnder the conduct of Martin Frobisher . . .* (London, 1578), p. 50; Sturtevant and Quinn, 'This New Prey', p. 73; Dorothy Harley Eber, *Encounters on the Passage: The Inuit Meet the Explorers* (Toronto, 2008), p. 4.

40 Neil Cheshire, Tony Waldron, Alison Quinn and David Quinn, 'Frobisher's Eskimos in England', *Archivaria*, 10 (1980), p. 24. Sturtevant and Quinn, 'This New Prey', p. 72. English modernised. The accounts are transcribed in full in William Brenchley Rye, *England as Seen by Foreigners in the Days of Elizabeth and James I . . .* (London, 1865), pp. 205–6, n. 40.

41 Best, *A trued discourse*, pp. 11, 19–21, 23, 25; Eber, *Encounters on the Passage*, p. 6; Dionyse Settle, 'A True Reporte of Martin Frobisher's Voyage, 1577' (London, 1577), pp. 33–5; Vaughan, *Transatlantic Encounters*, p. 262, n. 14.

42 Differences in the Inuits' clothing, depicted by John White, suggest they were from different Inuit groups. Cheshire et al., 'Frobisher's Eskimos in England', p. 24. Best, *A true discourse*, pp. 23–6, 30.

43   Edward Dodding, 'Reporte of the Sicknesse and Death of the Man at
      Bristoll *which* Capt. Furbisher brought from the North-west' (8 Novem-
      ber 1577), in Cheshire et al., 'Frobisher's Eskimos in England', p. 42.
44   Dodding, 'Reporte of the Sicknesse and Death', in Cheshire et al.,
      'Frobisher's Eskimos in England', p. 42; Sturtevant and Quinn, 'This New
      Prey', pp. 115–16. See also Vihjalmur Stefansson (ed.), *The Three Voyages
      of Martin Frobisher in search of a passage to Cathay and India by the
      north-west, A.D. 1576–8* (London, 1938), Vol. II, pp. 235–6; translation of
      the Dutch text accompanying Adrian Coenen's pictures, in Sturtevant
      and Quinn, 'This New Prey', p. 137; Cheshire et al., 'Frobisher's Eskimos
      in England', p. 30; *Adams's Chronicle of Bristol* (Bristol, 1910), p. 115; Evan
      T. Jones (ed.), 'Bristol Annal: Bristol Archives 09594/1' (version 30 Sept.
      2019), https://tinyurl.com/2p9xuvky; 'Annals of Bristol', in W. Tyson (ed.),
      The Bristol Memorialist (Bristol, 1823), pp. 117–18. The latter two items
      appear to be the source(s) used by Samuel Seyer, *Memoirs Historical
      and Topographical of Bristol and It's [sic] Neighbourhood from the earliest
      period down to the present time* (Bristol, 1823), p. 247.
45   Sturtevant and Quinn, 'This New Prey', pp. 80, 88–9; Jennifer L. Morgan,
      '"Some Could Suckle over Their Shoulder": Male Travelers, Female
      Bodies, and the Gendering of Racial Ideology, 1500–1770', *WMQ*, 54.1
      (1997), pp. 167–92; Vaughan, *Transatlantic Encounters*, pp. 6–8.
46   Edward Dodding, 'Reporte of the Sicknesse and Death', in Cheshire et al.,
      'Frobisher's Eskimos in England', pp. 40–42.
47   Cheshire et al., 'Frobisher's Eskimos in England', p. 30. Several people
      have checked the parish records, including for the possibility that the two
      Inuit might have been buried under Christian names, and – although the
      records are complete – their names are missing.

Afterword

1   James Welch, *The Heartsong of Charging Elk* (New York, 2000), pp. 97–8.
2   Ben Knight, 'German "Wild West" museum to repatriate Native Amer-
     ican scalp', *DW*, 24 November 2020, https://tinyurl.com/2a5u2bwf;
     Brenda Haas, 'Karl May Museum returns Native American human scalp',
     DW, 13 April 2021, https://tinyurl.com/ycy3dtbc.
3   David Stirrup, 'From 1736 to 2006: Cycles of Native Presence in
     London', *Beyond the Spectacle blog* (25 October 2017), https://tinyurl.
     com/2p87cn63; 'Burying A Chief, 270 Years Later', *CBS News*, 22 Novem-
     ber 2006, https://tinyurl.com/4uy6ey9w; 'Our Vision', *Mohegan Tribe*,
     https://tinyurl.com/4kymcn83.
4   'Shrunken heads', *Pitt Rivers Museum*, https://tinyurl.com/22mbv3dy.

5   Alison K. Brown and Laura Peers, 'The Blackfoot Shirts Project: "*Our Ancestors Have Come to Visit*", in Sharon Macdonald and Helen Leahy (eds), *The International Handbooks of Museum Studies* (Oxford, 2014), pp. 1–21.
6   Blackbird and Dodds Pennock, 'How making space for Indigenous peoples changes history', p. 247

Picture Credits

Figure 1. Museum of the Americas – Auch

Figure 2. Alamy/Heritage Image Partnership Ltd

Figure 3. http://dlib.gnm.de/item/Hs22474 (Public Domain Creative Commons)

Figure 4. http://dlib.gnm.de/item/Hs22474 (Public Domain Creative Commons)

Figure 5. http://dlib.gnm.de/item/Hs22474 (Public Domain Creative Commons)

Figure 6. http://dlib.gnm.de/item/Hs22474 (Public Domain Creative Commons)

Figure 7. Alamy/The Picture Art Collection

Figure 8. From the Lienzo de Tlaxcala fragment in the Nettie Lee Benson Collection, University of Texas Library. Photograph by Stephanie Wood (30 May 2014), reproduced with her permission

Figure 9. Alamy/GRANGER – Historical Picture Archive

Figure 10. The Algonquian orthography created by Manteo and Harriot, 1585. Reproduced from Jacqueline Stedall, 'Symbolism, combinations, and visual imagery in the mathematics of Thomas Harriot', Historia Mathematica, 34.4 (2007), pp. 380-401. Courtesy of Westminster School

Figure 11. Alamy/Gainew Gallery

Figure 12. Shutterstock/Alexandre Meneghini/AP

Figure 13. Antonio Ponce, *A still life of peaches, fish, chestnuts, a tin plate, sweet box, chocolate grinder and Mexican lacquer cups and shawl* (Valladolid, 1608 – Madrid, 1677). From Galería Caylus, Madrid, Spain

Figure 14. David Maawad (Mexicolore)

Figure 15. Alamy/Art Collection 4

Index